# MICROFINANCE FOR MACRO CHANGE EMERGING CHALLENGES

# MICROFINANCE FOR MACRO CHANGE EMERGING CHALLENGES

Deepali Pant Joshi

GYAN

Microfinance For Macro Change Emerging Challenges

Rs.750



ISBN: 978-81-212-1048-5



Published in 2010 in India by
Gyan Publishing House
23, Main Ansari Road, Darya Ganj
New Delhi-110002
Phones : 23282060, 23261060
Fax : 011-23285914
E-mail: books@gyanbooks.com
Website: www.gyanbooks.com

*Lasser Type Setting by*: Rudra Computer Graphics, Delhi
*Printed at* : Gian Ridhi Offset Printers, Delhi

**DEDICATION**

*For the sacred memory of my revered father Shri Jagdish Mohan Pant Administrator General and Official Trustee High Court of Judicature at Allahabad 1917-1998*

*"Whose blessings are ever with me and make all things possible."*

"Long years ago we made a tryst with destiny, and now the time comes when we shall redeem our pledge, not wholly or in full measure, but very substantially the past is over and it is the future that beckons to us now.

That future is not one of ease or resting but of incessant striving so that we might fulfill the pledges we have so often taken and the one we shall take today. The service of India means the service of the millions who suffer. It means the ending of poverty and ignorance and disease and inequality of opportunity. The ambition of the greatest man of our generation has been to wipe every tear from every eye. That may be beyond us but so long as there are tears and suffering, so long our work will not be over.

And so we have to labour and to work, and work hard, to give reality to our dreams. Those dreams are for India, but they are also for the world, for all the nations and peoples are too closely knit together today for any one of them to imagines that it can live apart. Peace has been said to be indivisible, so is freedom, so is prosperity now, and so also is disaster in this one world that can no longer be split into isolated fragments."

**Jawaharlal Nehru**

**“You must be the change you wish to see in the world”**

**Mahatma Gandhi**

**"Jo Sab tab Pratap Raghurai,**
**Nath na Kachu Mor Prabhutai"**

Hanuman extract from the Sundarkand.
This work has been achieved through the benevolence and Grace of the almighty; to him alone I attribute the successful achievement of this task.

**Ramayana**

# *Contents*

# *Foreword*

I am happy to write the Foreword for the book "Microfinance for Macro Change Emerging Challenges" by Dr. Deepali Pant Joshi. The author has produced an extremely useful book on microfinance. She has looked at every dimension of microfinance and has made useful recommendations for toning up the delivery system.

The access to finance by the poor and vulnerable groups is a pre-requisite for poverty reduction and social cohesion. Financial inclusion denotes delivery of financial services at an affordable cost to the vast sections of the disadvantaged and low income groups. The objective of financial inclusion is to extend the scope of activities of the organized financial system so as to include within its ambit people with low incomes. Through graduated credit, an attempt must be made to lift the poor from one level to another so that they can come out of poverty. Thus microfinance becomes an important instrument for achieving financial inclusion.

The SHG-bank linkage programme can be regarded as an important initiative to deliver the financial services to the poor in a sustained manner. The programme has been growing rapidly and the number of SHGs finance have exceeded 30 lakh. The author has examined at length the strengths and weaknesses of the programme. One of the distinctive features of the SHG-bank linkage programme has been the high recovery rate. The financial inclusion achieved through SHG is sustainable and scalable on account of its various positive features. SHGs need to graduate from mere providers of credit for non-productive purposes to promoters of micro enterprises. There is also the question of the rate of interest that is charged by SHGs to members. lt is important to ensure that the earning capacity of the borrowers is sufficiently enhanced enabling them to bear the cost of borrowing.

I recommend the book of Dr. Deepali Pant Joshi to all those interested in the area of microfinance. This is a useful addition to the literature on the subject.

**C. Rangarajan**

# *Acknowledgements*

This book is possible due to the blessings of my late father, elders and the beneficence and grace of the good Lord Hanuman who showers his blessings upon me.

As far is this work goes I humbly acknowledge the debt of perennial gratitude to my mother Professor Dr Chandra Pant, Dr C Rangarajan one of the greatest Indian Economists, who has also very kindly written the foreword to the book and countless others who have been a source of inspiration through the years.

I could not have devoted time to this work but for the guidance and constant support of my husband Shri Rajeev Joshi and my affectionate encouraging sons Paritosh and Kunal.

The views expressed are personal and do not reflect the views of the institution with which I am associated. I also thank the publishers Gyan Publishing House and convey anticipatory thanks to the prospective readers.

**Deepali Pant Joshi**
Reserve Bank of India

# Introduction

In the past few years the enormous promise of access to capital as an effective instrument enabling the poor to work their way out of poverty has challenged established paradigms and erupted into the world's consciousness.

Promoting development from the bottom up, in ways that enable the poor to create income and wealth for themselves, is now a widely shared global ideal and is not restricted to the developing countries. Microfinance consists of accumulating financial capital and spreading it around among the poor. Microfinance is a valid tool for improving the productivity of the poor in the developing countries and poverty reduction can result from co-creating a market around the needs of the poor. New and creative approaches are needed to convert poverty into an opportunity for all the players be it the Government, NGO's, Development institutions, private institutions and most importantly the poor themselves.

Today, the Indian economy shows high promise of growth, economist's scholars and international leaders across the globe are united in the thinking that India's growth can be sustained, India in its march to the new millennium as a major world economic player needs to ensure growth with equity to address the issue of poverty. For the last five decades poverty has been at the core of our Planning processes. Despite the phenomenal increase in the physical presence and capacity of outreach of the mainstream financial institutions, the rural poor continue to rely on informal sources of finance to meet their emergent credit and consumption needs. Nationalization resulted in widening geographical spread and functional reach of banks and led to the creation of a mainframe rural financial architecture which is quantitatively impressive (with penetrative outreach of one bank branch per 16000 population) but is qualitatively deficient; inhibited and unable to offer the full suite of savings/ credit/ retail financial products to the poorest of the poor who remained marginalized. On one side, formal financial institutions possess extensive infrastructure and systems; they are highly leveraged institutions with access to funds and opportunities for portfolio diversification enabling them to offer a wider range of services. However, they may be further removed from clients, particularly remote rural clients, which make obtaining adequate information and contract enforcement difficult. Informal institutions, on the other hand, usually operate close to rural clients, possess better information, are better able to screen borrowers, have effective enforcement mechanisms and are typically more flexible and innovative. However, they can be constrained in the type of services they offer since informal institutions lack resources and infrastructure to serve clients beyond a small geographic area microfinance attempts to bridge the Access Gap. Formal financial institutions are inhibited in their ability to deal with borrowers at the bottom of the pyramid, whose credit needs are small, frequent, pressing and paramount, who are unable to offer conventional collateral. Cumbersome procedures, paperwork constrain the borrowers and risk perceptions of the mainstream financial institutions have led to the creation of access gap. This grim scenario led to the search for alternative policies savings and loan products other complementary services new delivery mechanisms to meet this access gap and led to the emergence of microfinance. Microfinance is the provision of a broad range of financial services credit and insurance to low income households and their micro enterprises. Through the provision of credit it enables consumption smoothing, livelihood opportunities. It enables the poor to set up income generating projects, expand micro enterprises and work their own way out of poverty. In India the SHG Bank linkage program is the dominant paradigm. It is unique as it assigns a central role to Banks, the SHG Bank linkage program attempts to bridge this gap through financial linkages between the SHGs and the Banks. The specific efficiency gain for Banks through the SHG Bank linkage program is externalization of part of the credit cycle ; screening of borrowers, assessment of credit needs/appraisal/disbursal and enforcement of contracts are taken care of. The groups are also assured of finance streams and do not have to be dependent on relatively small corpus of own funds or uncertain donor grants. Hence in the long run this model which is the dominant model in India carries with it the promise of inherent sustainability which is part of the program design.

Microfinance enables and demonstrates viable models and ways to transform India's primarily rural population into a gainfully employed modern sector, methods to achieve sustainability and consolidation, how to deal with infrastructural inhibitors especially in terms of finite financial resources and the competing claims on the fiscal resources and suggests ways to meet the emerging challenges to translate the promise of microfinance into an ever present reality. The goal of microfinance is to build effective rural financial institutions that are accessible to all segments of the rural population through a financial systems approach; it aims to expand the frontier of institutional sustainability and outreach to the poor.

The gigantic size of the Indian economy and markets means that what happens in India over the coming days will have long-term implications for global growth inequality and poverty. This is a book meant for anyone interested in these larger global and macroeconomic issues as well as in understanding the complex interplay between macro and micro economic policies, politics and development. This book sets out a systematic framework of challenges, opportunities and options for the planning of interventions. The policy actions to be taken for responding to these and newer emerging challenges are detailed in the book.

The following key challenges characterize rural finance:

- Ensuring the participation of stakeholders principally the poor in the development of rural finance.
- Building a differentiated rural financial infrastructure that are diversified according to local conditions.
- Enhancing institutional sustainability and outreach to the rural poor.
- Promoting a conducive policy and regulatory environment.

This book offers a broad and dispassionate survey of Microfinance in India and its continuing challenges. It answers key questions, will India fulfill its manifest destiny. What do we need to get there. This book promises answers.

Chapter one provides a comprehensive and synoptic overview it furnishes the necessary background of how microfinance has come to occupy center stage and is now a dominant paradigm a way of thinking amongst the planners grappling with issues of poverty alleviation. Eradication of poverty and bridging the access gap is paramount concern for, India to realize its full potential. Chapter two discusses the various delivery models that are being used to promote microfinance as per the Indian experience and analyses their successes and limitations. Chapter three delves into the NABARD sponsored SHG-Bank Linkage program and the emerging policy concerns. Chapter Four, discusses the success/ failure of the Regional Rural Banks (RRB's) and District Central Cooperative Banks (DCCB)'s vis-à-vis delivery of micro credit to the poor. Chapter Five is devoted to the empowering role of Microfinance and centers round the theme of the many ways in which microfinance has changed the lives of women through the study of the Self Employed Women's Association, SEWA, and examples from other countries. Chapter Six deals with the issue of how microfinance has empowered the poor with concrete examples from a host of developing countries. Chapter Seven discusses how the frontiers of conventional finance are being pushed outward. How technology is helping ramp up access to the poor and again concrete examples show how this has been done. Chapter Eight sets out the emerging challenges, Issues and Concerns. While Commercial microfinance is also discussed there is conceptual clarity that mission drift must not take place and the focus must remain on the poor. There are a lot of concerns for planners, the government and regulatory authorities, as to how microfinance can effectively and efficiently achieve the goal of alleviating poverty. These are extensively analyzed and set out in great depth and though there are many concerns it identifies the hidden weaknesses that if unaddressed may cramp and hinder the sectors growth, if addressed may unleash tremendous growth and show the way forward which is the theme of the final chapter which brings together all the strands of the earlier discussion and presents a clear comprehensive action plan for the future.

The policy planners have through their policies and strategies supported solutions to these emerging concerns through a diversity of challenges. Among them, the challenge of up scaling and of replicability of successful experiments, the issue of networking among microfinance institutions, the utility of federations, upgrading and mainstreaming informal finance, linking banks with local financial institutions and self help groups. The growth of outreach for sustainable poverty reduction is contingent upon the dynamic growth of self reliant institutions. Banks must demonstrate their products and services thereby opening up access to increasingly poor and geographically diversified clients. Our policy planners have confirmed their commitment to continually seeking more effective ways of enabling and empowering the rural poor to combat poverty and create sustainable means of livelihood for themselves and for the generations to come.

Today, the Indian economy shows high promise of growth, economist's scholars and international leaders across the globe are united in the thinking that India's growth can be sustained, India in its march to the new millennium as a major world economic player needs to ensure growth with equity to address the issue of poverty

Though essentially the book is India centric it also takes into account the International experience and presents a comprehensive look at microfinance which is analytical incisive and informative. The work shows how incentives and efficiency take account of local power structures, human dignity and reciprocity. In the process it sheds light on a host of important and contentious issues in microfinance (Credit or credit plus Banks or Donors Interest rate caps or cost covering rates to regulate or not to regulate microfinance) and the outcome is the work which will enormously enrich the debates it is bound to engender. The message is unequivocal. Microfinance which provides participatory governance structures and sustainable economic infrastructure is both empowering and transformational.

**Dr Deepali Pant Joshi**

Flat No 12, Bank House
156, Backbay Reclamation
Mumbai 400020

# 1

# *"The Microfinance Approach and its Role as a Poverty Intervention Effort"*

Since independence poverty eradication has been an overriding concern of economic policy. The Banking System was envisaged as central to the effort. The Nationalisation of Banks in 1969 marked a significant watershed as post nationalisation there was an increased impetus to mass banking which led to great branch expansion and exponential growth in the number of rural bank branches. There have been concerted efforts to ensure access of the rural poor to the financial system. An impressive rural financial Infrastructure was built up, which adopted a pluralistic and a multidimensional approach to the problem of bringing the poor from the margin to the mainstream and providing access to financial services to them. Thus the cooperative banks, the agricultural land development banks, the Commercial banks, the regional rural banks and the Local Area Banks are all engaged in the endeavour of increasing, facilitating, enabling access to credit and financial services to the vast majority of our people.

**Bank Branch Building.** The main emphasis lay in the spread of bank network and the introduction of new networks and on poverty focussed subsidy linked credit programs is to make the financial system more responsive to the needs of the poor and of the weaker sections of society, the small and marginal farmers, rural artisans landless agricultural and non agricultural labourers and other small borrowers falling below the poverty line.

| *Year* | *No. of rural branches* | *No. of semi urban branches* | *Total* |
|---|---|---|---|
| 1969 (June) | 1833 | 3342 | 5175 |
| 1991 (March) | 35206 | 11344 | 46550 |
| 2001 (March) | 32562 | 14597 | 47159 |
| 2005 (March) | 32082 | 15403 | 47485 |
| 2007 (March) | 30551 | 16361 | 46912 |

(*Source* BSR:RBI).

The exponential growth of branch building activity led to the great spread of the branch network of Banks Burgess and Pande (2003) have argued that the policy of forcing banks to open more branches in the rural areas using the 1:3 rule (banks get a licence to open one branch in a location that already has a branch of another bank only if they open branches in three other unbanked locations) was instrumental in making significant impacts on poverty. This rule was abandoned in 1990 and, since then, we can see stagnation in the expansion of rural branches.

## Reaping the Rewards

The population per branch in the country has declined from 63 thousand to 16 thousand and in the rural and semi urban areas from 82 thousand to 17 thousand during the period

June 1969 to March 2007. Credit to agriculture, SSI and other priority sectors has increased from 14 per cent to 37 per cent of bank credit and represent an annual growth of 21 per cent. Rural and semi urban credit growth clocked an annual growth rate of 19 per cent per annum between 1993 and 2007. The number of savings bank accounts per 100 adult population increased from 7.1 in 1971 to 48.9 in 2007 and the number of loan accounts from 1.3 to 12.4. These are the significant positive effects of the policy of Branch building.

**The Lead Bank Scheme**

The Lead Bank Scheme (LBS) has largely achieved its original objective of bringing about overall improvements in branch expansion, mobilisation of deposits and lending to the priority sectors, especially in rural/semi urban areas. The LBS has been able to mould itself to meet the emerging needs as perceived by the concerned State Governments and banks in each State. As a forum where the top officials of banks and government meet at the State/district level to the utility of SLBC/ DCC as a forum of communication and coordination is its biggest achievement. In the initial years of the LBS, branch expansion in unbanked/ underbanked areas and credit planning was pursued vigorously but over the years there was a significant slowdown in the process with the result that the total number of rural and semi urban branches in the country has remained almost stagnant since 2001.

**Financial Repression**

At the level of policy credit to priority sectors was mandated at 40%, concessional interest rates were prescribed for loans to the weaker sections. The strategies adopted undoubtedly built a broad based institutional infrastructure for the delivery and deployment of credit to widen the base of the pyramid. The achievements have not been insignificant; access in terms of rural branches increased from1,8333 in 1969 to around 32,200, the population per rural branch declined from 2,01,854 in 1969 to 16000 at present. The proportion of borrowings of rural households from institutions increased from 7% in 1951 to 60%. The remaining 40% needs of the poorer sections continued to be met by the informal sector where money lenders, and indigenous sui generis models of lending as Bishis, Chit funds and affinity group lending was and remains quite firmly entrenched. The recent data available from various sources shows that large sections of rural population and urban poor still do not have access to banking facilities. Out of nearly 6 lakh inhabited villages in the country, 2.3 lakh villages have a population of over 1000. There are around 47,000 branches of scheduled commercial banks at rural and semi-urban centres. Penetration of banking in several parts of the country continues to be limited. The need for **greater banking and credit penetration of the rural areas by the formal financial institutions therefore still remains valid.**

## Financial Development

Post Nationalisation commercial banks were actively engaged in purveying credit to the weaker sections. In 1975 Regional Rural Banks combining the local feel and familiarity of the cooperatives with the managerial expertise and professionalism of the commercial banks were established specifically to meet the credit needs of the weaker sections. The policy focussed on capital subsidies and very low rates of interest on loans, target oriented poverty programs, credit guarantee for small loans, sectoral guarantees for disbursement of credit, long loan maturities, grace periods, frequent resort to loan waivers, increasing reliance of the rural credit system on concessional finance from higher financial sources and target orientation in all government programs. This led to improper selection of borrowers and frequent defaults, mounting nonperforming assets further constrained the ability of Banks to make fresh loans. The transaction costs of administering several small loans to poor borrowers were high for Banks and the rural credit portfolio was unattractive for them yet they carried it through due to cross subsidisation of the mandated borrowing program of the priority sectors and due to deployment of the transfer pricing mechanism. That the rural branches might incur losses was almost accepted by the Banks and did serve to considerably dampen their enthusiasm for such loaning. However Banks ensured that the mandated targets were fulfilled.

Prior to the 1970s financial restrictions were often favoured in developing countries which were capital scarce, on the grounds that usury could be prevented money supply better controlled and higher Invest met savings target met than if the financial markets were liberalised. The public policy response was extending protection to the most vulnerable sectors of the population through Interest Rate policies which were calibrated to hold the line.

## FINANCIAL REPRESSION

During this phase the rates of interest were at administered levels. The RBI decided the rates of interest the Banks could charge on priority sector loans and these rates were kept low. This policy was followed by several developing countries to spur development and economic prosperity and was famously to be described as "financial repression" by Mc Kinnon and Shaw. What comprises Financial Repression? The analytical framework for this approach drew heavily on the argument that

1. Governments must intervene in financial markets,
2. Ration credit and
3. Administer sectoral credit schemes
4. Through imposition of regulations.
5. Mc Kinnon and Shaw held that these objectives were seldom sub served. They held that to create an environment that is conducive to financial intermediation financial repression is best avoided.

**What is Micro Finance?**

Microfinance emerged in the 1980s in response to disappointment with existing paradigms of delivery of targeted subsidized agricultural credit. The earlier emphasis on achievement of set targets through rapid disbursement of subsidized loans shifted to encouragement of sustainable participatory grassroots initiatives to serve the poor.

Micro finance is the delivery of small, collateral free, loans to the poor on the basis of social or group collateral where repayments are adjusted to the borrower's income stream and loans are guaranteed by group collateral.

The new paradigm of credit delivery rested on the following broad premises.

**PARADIGM SHIFT FROM CREDIT DELIVERY TO SUSTAINABLE FINANCE**

1. Subsidized credit is cold money which undermines development of a credit culture.
2. Poor people can pay interest rates high enough to cover transaction costs and the consequences of the imperfect information markets in which the lenders operate.
3. The goal of sustainability cost recovery and eventual profit is the key to institutional permanence in lending and in making the lending institution more efficient and focused.
4. As loan sizes to poor people are small MFIs must achieve sufficient scale if they are to become sustainable.
5. Poor people need secure savings facilities as much as consumption and production credit.
6. To evaluate the success of microfinance programs, measurable enterprise growth as well as impacts on poverty cannot be demonstrated easily or accurately.
9. Outreach and repayment rates can serve as proxies for impact.

**THE PROMISE OF MICROFINANCE**

1. Microfinance holds out the promise of reaching even the poorest of the poor also known as the "hardcore" and "asset

less" poor, as, it is lending without the backing of formal collateral thus it makes possible extension of support for income generation projects of very low income households.

2. Microfinance holds the promise of financial sustainability. Microfinance activities can build financially self sufficient subsidy free often locally managed institutions.
3. Microfinance services are attractive to clients as they mimic traditional systems which the poor are familiar with as they often use those systems, like the Rotating Savings and Credit Institutions and provide the same services in even more flexible ways at more affordable prices and on a more sustainable basis.
4. Microfinance contributes to strengthening and expanding existing formal financial systems by expanding the markets for both savings and credit products and thereby beefing up the profitability of Commercial Banks, Regional Rural Banks Cooperatives Private Banks who offer savings services.
5. SUSTAINABILITY and TENABILITY of Microfinance Institutions make this far more attractive than subsidised lending. In sharp contrast to tales of woe of state run institutions with contaminated balance sheets and high defaults due to poor loaning there are well documented success stories with microfinance recording repayment rates of 90%.
6. Microfinance offers INNOVATIVE SOLUTIONS to problems which have always plagued formal administered credit programs as the problem of targeting the right recipients of credit The problem of SCREENING of borrowers has been resolved as groups self select their members.

Lack of COLLATERAL has been resolved through the acceptance of COLLATERAL SUBSTITUTES group based and character based lending High DEFAULTS have been addressed through JOINT LIABILITY group lending which ensures that the next member of the group does not get a loan if any member of the group has not repaid his loan.

REPAYMENT DISCIPLINE has also been instituted and reinforced through the high frequency of repayment collection, the use of social and peer pressure and the promise of higher repeat loans.

The issue of high costs of administration of small loans, HIGH TRANSACTION COSTS has been solved by moving some of these costs down to the group level and by increasing outreach: designing staff incentives to achieve greater outreach and high repayment. High transaction cost has been resolved by enabling groups to retail credit and to externalize part of the credit cycle.

## INTEGRATING INFRASTRUCTURE WITH MICRO CREDIT

Integrating Infrastructure with microcredit and self help groups is natural and necessary and has shown positive externalities in the realisation of the potential of watershed development, pro poor programs, horticulture and dairying etc. Success of these activities depend on Infrastructure transport, storage and markets and credit Institutional finance support systems as well as enabling policy environments which enable SHGs to come to full fruition.

## SUSTAINABLE RURAL LIVELIHOOD PROMOTION

Requires the integration of SHGs resources livelihoods, institutions and infrastructure the success of activities petty business and services hinge on the overall improvement in rural livelihoods

Thus an analytical framework is as under

PROVIDORS OF FINANCIAL SERVICES

**FORMAL SECTOR**

**BANKS**

Commercial Banks, Cooperative Banks, Regional Rural Banks, Local Area Banks.

Non Bank Finance Companies
**Semi Formal Sector**
SHGs
NGOs
MFIs
**INFORMAL**
**SECTOR**
Traders and Shopkeepers
Savings Associations
Friends
Neighbours
Relatives
Moneylenders

## OBJECTIVES OF MICROFINANCE

The objectives of microfinance are as under:

1. To attack poverty by creating employment and income opportunities through the setting up and expansion of income generating projects and micro enterprises.
2. To empower women and other disadvantaged population groups by increasing the incomes of vulnerable groups;
3. To address covariance risk, by encouraging the development of new businesses for e.g., dependence of rural families on drought prone crops is reduced through diversification of their income generating activities.

Within microfinance two schools of thought have emerged one which only focuses on credit and the other which favours credit plus approaches the division between them is referred to as the microfinance schism.

## MICROFINANCE SCHISM TWO SCHOOLS OF THOUGHT

The two schools of thought differ in their objectives, underlying philosophy and target clientele. There is the Credit approach, which favours microfinance being targeted to the poorer among the poor the destitute and disabled and the second credit plus approach which focuses on the entrepreneurial poor not the hardcore and asset less poor.

As the objective of many microfinance institutions is poverty reduction they often need to focus on those at the bottom of the pyramid. They measure Outreach in terms of scale or number of people reached and depth or the level of poverty of their clients. Many practitioners of microfinance feel that loans may just be an additional burden on the poorest of the poor who do not have the inherent ability to service the loans and that they should more appropriately be aided by "State Transfers" insistence on extension of credit to poor borrowers in extremis can lead to overextension and imperilment of the financial sustainability of microfinance programs.

Using data from research in several countries Hulme and Mosley in their book "Finance against Poverty", compared increases in borrower's income with those in a control **group.** Their findings suggest that successful institutions contributing to poverty reduction are particularly effective in improving the status of the middle and upper segments of the poor. However clients below the poverty line were worse off after borrowing than before. The impact on the client's income seemed to be directly related to the level of income which reinforced the tendency of those MFIs wishing to preserve their viability to concentrate on the less poor. A related consequence being that the development and refinements of microfinance products remain focused on the middle and upper segments of the poor leaving the poorest behind. Hulme and Mosley contend that recognizing the heterogeneity of the poor should lead to greater innovation and experimentation which would serve to deepen the downward reach of financial services. There is a need for reaching financial sustainability hence the trade off between minimizing costs and focusing on the poorest clients. The unmet demand for financial services among the bankable poor those with a capacity for debt presents an opportunity which can be met by mainstreaming the existing approaches. Thus the depth of outreach of an MFI will depend on its ability to design products and services suitable to the level of poverty it is targeting. Low income men and women face formidable barriers in gaining access to mainstream financial services from formal financial institutions. Ordinary financial intermediation alone cannot surmount the gaps created by poverty, illiteracy, gender and remoteness, poor men and women without tangible assets often live in geographically remote areas. Thus providing microfinance services to low income clients is a complex process a Systems approach enables a holistic view. Within the systems framework four broad categories of financial services are provided.

## SYSTEMS APPROACH TO THE PROVISION OF FINANCIAL SERVICES TO THE POOR

**Financial Intermediation** is the provision of financial products and services as savings, credit, insurance, credit card and payment systems.

**Social Intermediation** is the process of building the human and social capital required by sustainable intermediation for the poor. Social capital is explained as "Those features of social organisation as networks norms and trust that facilitate cooperation and coordination for mutual benefit." Social capital is an important tool to bridge the gaps between Banks and Poor people.

**Enterprise Development Services that Assist Microentrepreneurs** is the provision of services that include Business training, marketing and technology services, skill development and sub sector analysis.

**Social Services** is the provision of nonfinancial services that focus on improving the well being of micro entrepreneurs include health, nutrition, education and literacy training.

**Minimalist Approach** Minimalist approach offers only credit an integrated approach looks at much more than credit provision to create an enabling environment for empowerment of the poor and disadvantaged.

**One piece missing –Credit**
Financial Intermediation
Working capital
Fixed asset loans
Savings
Insurance
**Integrated Approach**
Financial and non financial services
**Social Intermediation**
Group Formation
Leadership Training
Cooperative learning
Enterprise Development services
Marketing
Business Training
Production Training
Subsector analysis
Social services
Education
Health and Nutrition
Literacy training

There are two key imperatives to be considered in designing financial services.

The Financial services which are offered should be able to respond quickly and effectively to demand and preferences of clients.

They should design products that are simple and can be easily understood by the clients and easily managed by the MFI.

### Financially viable lending to entrepreneurs adopt the following principles

They are short term loans compatible with enterprise outlay appropriate for meeting the day to day financial requirements of business.

Full repayment of one loan provides access to another through repeat lending this enables the borrowers to support financial management as a continuing and sustainable process rather than as an isolated event. This also enables relatively unrestricted use of funds as there is an assurance of more to come.

**Concerns of Public Policy**

The eradication of poverty has been an overriding concern of Public Policy for the last six decades since Independence; this is reflected in the steady increase in the expenditure on Agriculture and Rural development as a percentage of total plan outlay over the plans.

| *Plan Period* | *Expenditure on Agri and rural development (Rs in crores)* | *Percentage of total outlay* |
|---|---|---|
| I Plan(1951-56) | 291 | 15.0 |
| II Plan (1956-61) | 530 | 11.0 |
| III Plan (1961-66) | 1089 | 12.7 |
| Annual Plans (1966-69) | 1107 | 16.7 |
| IV Plan (1969-74) | 2320 | 14.7 |
| V Plan(1974-79) | 4865 | 12.3 |
| Annual Plan (1979-80) | 1996 | 16.4 |
| VI Plan (1980-85) | 12338 | 12.8 |
| VII Plan (1985-90) | 31509 | 14.4 |
| VIII Plan (1992-97) | 63642 | 14.7 |

*Source.* All India Rural Credit Survey Committee Report Volume II RBI Mumbai 1955.(2) Debt and Investment Survey, National Sample Survey Organisation, Ministry of Planning and Program Implementation, Government of India July 1998 pp. 22-27.

Informal sources of lending were the dominant paradigm for the extension of rural credit Informal contracts prevailed and the credit needs of small and marginal farmers ,the poorer sections, destitute and dispossessed were met by the village money lenders, the landlord, relatives and friends though the share of money lenders has declined they still retain a presence.

Informal lending was once the only form credit took in rural settings. Evidence suggests that as farm size increases, private credit sources, village moneylenders and PAWN brokers chit funds with an array of implicit interest rates, and friends or relatives grow less important than banks. With the implementation of development plans, official lending complements but clearly does not supersede informal sources.

Sample surveys supply the information on the extent of informal lending practices. They indicate that its volume is far greater than that of organized institutions. It is characterized by a much shorter processing time, better screening techniques and enforcement devices (noted in the lower default rate), and higher interest rates, with a median around 50 percent and a variance much higher than institutionalized credit rate.

The lower delinquency rates reported in informal credit sources are to a large extent due to better assessment of creditworthiness, ability to exert social pressure for repayment, and the frequent practice of tying (interlinking) credit contracts with other input or output contract. Documentation of the use and characteristics of the latter practice is quite extensive. Sharecropping contracts are quite often interlinked with credit contracts. Credit contracts between landlords and tenants are often in the form of production loans and tied to the purchase of fertilizer, seeds and other forms of capital with different tenants paying different interest rates on their loans. These interlinkage practices have been viewed as a way to address the adverse selection problem and the moral hazard problem indigenous to these markets. Until recently conventional wisdom held that imposing low ceilings on interest rates and allocating massive amounts of credit to rural financial markets would speed rural development and improve income distribution. But by and large policies directed along these lines have failed. Indeed, most often they have made matters worse. Low interest rate ceilings provide income transfers to loan recipients, distorting the real price ratio of investment opportunities by sectors. To the standard cost of distorted resource allocation, add the specific costs and consequences of implementing credit programs in poor impact. The record overwhelmingly shows credit programs' objectives have not been met. These credit policy failures can be attributed to basic flaws intrinsic to formal rural credit markets out of which arise persistent problems.

**TABLE A Characteristics of Rural Financial Markets**

Basic Flaws

- Weakness of competitive forces
- Weak legal enforcement of contracts
- Computation and lack of accountability in institutions, patronage and income transfer practices, which are partly due to poorly designed or non-existent incentive mechanisms to induce accountability on both sides of the market.
- Significant information problems and uncertainty regarding the ability of borrowers to meet future loan obligations.
- Inability to monitor the use of funds.
- Lack of collateral often due to land tenure arrangements or ill-defined property rights (e.g. parts of North East)
- Lack of coherent financial savings mobilization program.
- Higher opportunity cost of capital in other sectors because of interest rate ceilings.

Persistent Problems

- Credit loans to wealthy farmers, small farmers rationed out of the credit market.
- Loans for agricultural programs diverted to non-agricultural users.
- Credit policies that encourage consumption and discourage savings
- The term structure of agricultural loans contracts or fails to expand.
- Low adoption rates of cost-saving technologies in agriculture and in financial services.

- Low recovery rate.
- Significant distortions in the optional allocation of resources across markets.
- Extensive use of interlinking credit contracts with labour and contracts.

## MORAL HAZARD AND ADVERSE SELECTION

The modern theory of contractual equilibrium under imperfect information focuses on the moral hazard and adverse selection features commonly found in rural developing economies. High interest rates most often encourage those who are not going to repay the loans to come forward to avail of the loan at the higher cost as they know they will not repay that is the moral hazard but due to asymmetries of information the Bank Manager does not know this leading to wrong ie adverse selection of borrower. Assymetry of information lies in that the borrower knows he will not repay so he has more knowledge than the Branch manager who is advancing the loan to him in the good faith that he will repay as he has the ability to borrow at high rates of interest through his evaluation of the borrowers present and future Income stream.

## INTERLINKAGE OF CREDIT AND LABOR MARKETS

In rural credit markets there is a natural interlink age of credit and labor markets The "moral hazard" features as pertaining to the interlinking credit with labor and land contracts are : Individuals are not paid on the basis of observable work and they often do not rent land for a fixed sum since that imposes too much risk on them. Hence the contractual arrangements involve at least some form of sharecropping; as a result, tenants do not obtain the full marginal product of their efforts.

In particular, the landlord has an incentive to induce tenants to behave as he wishes. This is attempted through influencing the amount and terms of credit at which the tenant borrows and by the goods/food he can purchase with the amount of money he borrows.

Another rationale for interlinking is the "adverse selection" effect, where interlinking credit and tenancy contracts may screen the high-ability from the low-ability borrower. Braverman and Stiglitz have shown that there is no presumption that innovation results either in a reduction or in an increase in tenants' demand for credit. Whether the demand for credit itself is increased or decreased depends critically on both how the technical change affects the probability distribution of yields and on tenants' utility functions. The presence of interlink age between credit and land markets does not preclude either resistance to or encouragement of the adoption of technological innovations. Either is possible. In some cases, it might actually encourage the adoption of technologies which otherwise would not be adopted, even though the innovation itself reduces tenants' demand for credit. So it becomes clear that the impact of an innovation on a landlord-cum-lender may be quite different from the impact of the same innovation on a landlord who does not control the borrowing activities of his tenants.

Share of Debt by Different Asset Holding Classes

| *Household Assets(OOO)* | *Institutional Agency* | *Non Institutional A* | *All* |
|---|---|---|---|
| Less than 5 | 42 | 58 | 100 |
| 5-10 | 47 | 53 | 100 |
| 10-20 | 44 | 56 | 100 |
| 20-30 | 68 | 32 | 100 |
| 30-50 | 55 | 45 | 100 |
| 50-70 | 53 | 47 | 100 |
| 70-100 | 61 | 39 | 100 |
| 100-150 | 61 | 39 | 100 |
| 150-250 | 68 | 32 | 100 |
| 250 and above | 81 | 19 | 100 |
| All classes | 66 | 34 | 100 |

*Source*. Debt and Investment Survey GOI 1992.

## DEPENDENCE ON INFORMAL SOURCES OF CREDIT

Further the percentage share of the amount of debt contracted from institutional and non institutional credit agencies by each asset holding classes at All India level revealed that households in the lower asset groups were more dependent on the non-institutional credit agencies. The share of debt from the non institutional credit agencies was as high as 58% in the case of the lowest asset group of less than Rs 5000 as against a low of 19% in the highest asset group of Rs 2.5 lakh and above (as on 30$^{th}$ June 1991). Agricultural purposes constituted the bulk of the lending of the banks in the rural areas and it was the landless agricultural and non agricultural labourers, rural artisans and asset less poor who had not received adequate attention from banks.

**ALL INDIA DEBT AND INVESTMENT SURVEY**. At present, the decennially conducted AIDIS is the only nation-wide enquiry providing data on household assets, indebtedness and capital expenditure. This report presents the estimates pertaining to certain aspects of assets, borrowings, repayments and indebtedness of households belonging to scheduled tribe (ST), scheduled caste (SC), other backward classes (OBC) and residual other households not belonging to any of these three categories (described as 'Other'). For the rural and urban areas at the all-India level. About 27 per cent of the rural households were indebted while only 18 per cent of the urban households were indebted. The proportion of indebted households or incidence of indebtedness was highest for OBC households in both rural and urban areas, and was 29 per cent for rural and 21 per cent for urban households. For ST households, the incidence was 18 per cent in the rural areas and 12 per cent in the urban areas. For SC households, this was 27 per cent in the rural areas and 19 per cent in the urban areas.

About 59 per cent of the debt of rural ST households was incurred for farm related work and 25 per cent for household expenditure as high as 69 per cent of the debt was taken for household expenditure Among the ST households in the urban areas. Only 26 per cent of the debt of rural SC households was for farm related work, while as high as 51 per cent was for household expenditure. About 76 per cent of the debt of urban SC households was for household expenditure.

In the rural areas, about 11 to 13 per cent of the ST, SC and OBC households reported institutional agencies as the source of credit. This was 16 per cent for 'Other' households. In the urban areas, about 7 to 10 per cent of households reported institutional agencies as the source of credit.

In the rural areas, the share of institutional agencies in total amount of debt for ST, SC and OBC households was about 69 per cent, 45 per cent, and 51 per cent respectively. It was 68 per cent for 'Other' households while the overall institutional share in the amount of debt was 57 per cent. In the urban areas, the share of institutional debt varied from 65 per cent for OBC to 82 per cent for 'Other' group. The overall share of institutional debt was 75 per cent.

For rural areas, the debt to asset ratio, which represents the value of debt per 100 rupees of owned assets, was between 2.3 for ST households to 3.7 for SC households. In urban areas, the debt to asset ratio was between 2.4 for 'Other' households to 4.2 for SC households.

Among various types of securities against which loans are advanced, personal security was the most prominent one – about 18% of households in the rural areas and 12% of households in the urban areas reporting indebtedness against personal security.

In rural areas, for outstanding debt, the personal security accounted for as much as 64 per cent for SC households. It was 41 per cent for ST households, 51 per cent for OBC households and 38 per cent for 'Other' households. In case of urban areas, the figures 48 per cent for Scheduled Caste households, 35 per cent for Scheduled Tribe households, 44 per cent for Other Bakward Caste houlds and 37 per cent for 'Other' households.

The All India Debt and Investment Survey conducted by the National Sample Survey Organization has pointed out that between 1991 and 2002, the share of institutional finance in the outstanding cash dues of rural households decreased by 7 percentage points to 57 per cent, while share of non-institutional sources showed a corresponding increase. The survey also shows that the non-institutional agencies had advanced credit to 15.5 per cent of rural households, while the institutional agencies had financed 13.4 per cent households. Thus, on the whole, only about 29 per cent of the rural households obtained some form of financial assistance.

Occupational Category wise dependence of Indebted Rural Households on Non Institutional Agencies.

| *Year* | *Cultivators* | *Non Cultivators* | *All* |
|---|---|---|---|
| 1961 | 81.6 | 89.5 | 83.7 |
| 1971 | 68.3 | 89.2 | 70.8 |
| 1981 | 36.8 | 63.3 | 38.8 |
| 1991 | 33.7 | 44.7 | 36.0 |

**How Was the Credit Used**. Priority across different types of financial resources for the rural poor has been consumption credit, savings, production credit and Insurance .Consumption constituted two thirds of credit usage usually demanded for very short periods for meeting pressing personal needs as illness and household expenses during the lean season. While almost 75% of production credit is met by the formal sector, mainly banks and cooperatives the entire demand for consumption credit is met by informal sources at high to exploitive interest rates.

## THE POVERTY RATIOS ARE UNEVEN ACROSS STATES HENCE DIVESRE MEASURES ARE TO BE ADOPTED

Poverty levels continue to rule high and state wise poverty line and per capita incomes are uneven and are not uniform hence eradication strategies need to be Fine-tuned and policy responses calibrated to the divergent needs of different states.

**State-wise Per capita Income at Current Prices 2005-2006**

| *Sr. No.* | *Name of the State* | *Per capita Income at current Prices 2005-06* |
|---|---|---|
| 1. | Andhra Pradesh | 26,211 |
| 2. | Bihar | 7,875 |
| 3. | Chhattisgarh | 20,151 |
| 4. | Goa | 70,112 |
| 5. | Gujarat | 34,157 |
| 6. | Haryana | 38,832 |
| 7. | Himachal Pradesh | 33,805 |
| 8. | Jammu & Kashmir | 18,630 |
| 9. | Jharkhand | 19,066 |
| 10. | Karnataka | 27,291 |
| 11. | Kerala | 30,668 |
| 12. | Madhya Pradesh | 15,647 |
| 13. | Maharashtra | 37,081 |
| 14. | Assam | 1,859 |
| 15. | Arunachal Pradesh | 23,783 |
| 16. | Manipur | 20,323 |
| 17. | Meghalaya | 23,430 |
| 18. | Mizoram | 22,417 |
| 19. | Nagaland | 20,998 |
| 20. | Tripura | 24,706 |
| 21. | Orissa | 16,306 |
| 22. | Punjab | 36,759 |
| 23. | Rajasthan | 17,863 |
| 24. | Sikkim | 26,412 |
| 25. | Tamil Nadu | 29,958 |
| 26. | Uttarakhand | 24,585 |

*(Contd.)*

*(Contd. Table)*

| *Sr.No.* | *Name of the State* | *Per capita Income at current Prices 2005-06* |
|---|---|---|
| 27. | Uttar Pradesh | 13,262 |
| 28. | West Bengal | 25,233 |
| 29. | Delhi | 61,676 |
| 30. | Andaman & Nicobar | 34,853 |
| 31. | Chandigarh | 86,629 |
| 32. | Pudducheri | 48,477 |

| *Sr.No.* | *Name of the State* | *Per capita Income at current Prices 2005-06* |
|---|---|---|
| | **Central Region** | |
| 1. | Chhattisgarh | 20,151 |
| 2. | Madhya Pradesh | 15,647 |
| 3. | Uttar Pradesh | 13,262 |
| 4. | Uttaranchal | 24,585 |
| | **Eastern Region** | |
| 5. | Andaman & Nicobar | 34,853 |
| 6. | Bihar | 7,875 |
| 7. | Jharkhand | 19,066 |
| 8. | Orissa | 16,306 |
| 9. | West Bengal | 25,233 |
| | **North Eastern Region** | |
| 10. | Assam | 1,859 |
| 11. | Manipur | 20,326 |
| 12. | Meghalaya | 23,430 |
| 13. | Mizoram | 22,417 |
| 14. | Nagaland | 20,998 |
| 15. | Sikkim | 26,412 |
| 16. | Tripura | 24,706 |

*(Contd.)*

*(Contd. Table)*

| *Sr.No.* | *Name of the State* | *Per capita Income at current Prices 2005-06* |
|---|---|---|
| | **Northern Region** | |
| 17. | Haryana | 38,832 |
| 18. | Himachal Pradesh | 33,805 |
| 19. | Jammu & Kashmir | 18,630 |
| 20. | New Delhi | 61,676 |
| 21. | Punjab | 36,759 |
| 22. | Rajasthan | 17,863 |
| | **Southern Region** | |
| 23. | Andhra Pradesh | 26,211 |
| 24. | Karnataka | 27,291 |
| 25. | Kerala | 30,668 |
| 26. | Pondicherry | 48,477 |
| 27. | Tamil Nadu | 29,958 |
| | **Western Region** | |
| 28. | Goa | 70,112 |
| 29. | Gujarat | 34,157 |
| 30. | Maharashtra | 37,081 |

## WHY THE SEARCH FOR ALTERNATIVE SYSTEM OF CREDIT DELIVERY?

As a prerequisite for the financial liberalization programs, stabilization policies have been designed to ensure macroeconomic stability, low inflation and reduced budget deficits. The focus has been on liberalizing interest rates, deregulation of the financial sector, strengthening the banking system, introduction of new financial instruments, and development of securities markets, in particular the stock market. Stock market is viewed as a medium to encourage savings, help channel savings into productive investment, and improve the efficiency and productivity of investments. As

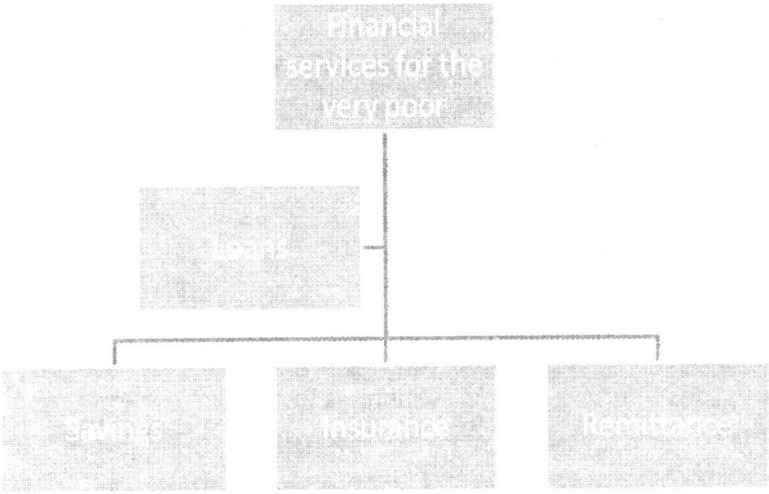


liberalization of financial markets was an approach of the free market a theology designed to lend to the poor on market principles was also required hence the adoption of the new paradigm.

## WHAT IS THE CAUSE OF THE STAGNATION IN RURAL LENDING

Underlying the stagnation in rural lending are two pernicious problems high transaction costs and poor recoveries which stem from poor targeting. The microfinance model especially the JLG Joint Liability Group Model where the groups self select their group members the issue of targeting is easily resolved via this simple expedient. Transaction costs of group transactions are lower than individual transaction cost for several small transactions and recoveries show significant improvements.

Despite an impressive financial architecture of commercial banks both public sector and private sector RRBs and cooperatives gaps in credit delivery remain. As per AIIDIS and NSO data a great portion is unreached by formal credit.

**Share of rural households by sources of credit All India -1951 - 91**

| *Year* | *Banks* | *Coop* | *Government* | *Total* | *Friends* | | *Others* |
|---|---|---|---|---|---|---|---|
| 1951 | 1.1 | 4.6 | 3.1 | 8.8 | 14.4 | 68.6 | 8.2 |
| 1961 | 0.3 | 10.4 | 6.6 | 17.3 | 5.8 | 60.9 | 16.0 |
| 1971 | 2.4 | 20.1 | 6.7 | 29.2 | 13.8 | 36.9 | 20.1 |
| 1981 | 28.6 | 28.6 | 0.4 | 61.2 | 9.0 | 16.9 | 12.9 |
| 1991 | 29.0 | 18.6 | 0.7 | 53.3 | 6.7 | 15.7 | 24.3 |

AIDIS Others include non-institutional sources.

Other than friends, relatives, moneylenders as traders, agriculturists, moneylenders, landlord etc. The share of money lenders has declined.

Commercial banks (both Public Sector Banks and Private Sector Banks) account for the larger share of credit from the formal sector they hold 51% of household deposit.

RRBs 34% and 31% credit. Other formal sources as post offices, cooperatives play a modest role in providing saving and credit services to rural households. The segments of the economy which need finance are widely dispersed and beyond the ken of banks thus new and innovative methods are required to extend the penetrative outreach of the Banking sector.

## HOW CAN MICROFINANCE BE MESHED IN THE POVERTY ERADICATION EFFORTS

The Microfinance program needs to be contextualised from the point of macroeconomic objectives it is essential to make all efforts to ensure broad based and decentralised growth of the economy, in this connection we have to pay serious attention to rethink the role of different financial institutions involved in the process and their competencies.

| Policy Level | RBI |
|---|---|
| Wholesalers of credit | NABARD/SIDBI/RMK/Banks |
| Retailers of credit | Banks/MFIs/SHGs |
| Banks as retailers | Commercial/Cooperative/RRBs |

Public sector/private sector banks

Microfinance emerged in the 1980s in response to disappointment with existing paradigms of delivery of targeted subsidized agricultural credit. The earlier emphasis on achievement of set targets through rapid disbursement of subsidized loans shifted to encouraging of sustainable participatory grassroots initiatives to serve the poor While on one hand, the goal of Union Government to double the flow of farm credit in three years was achieved in two years and micro-credit amounting to Rs. 39,042 million disbursed to 10,79,091 Self Help Groups (SHGs) in 2004 increased to Rs. 1,13,975.5 million covering 22,38,565 SHGs in 2006, on the other, the share of institutional credit declined to 57% in 2001 as compared to 64% in 1991.

Moreover, debt sourced from money lenders, the very informal agents the institutionalization of credit was designed to replace, increased in overall share of rural debt from nearly 18% in 1991 to nearly 30% in 2001.

According to a recent Survey, formal institutional credit provision in India now accounts for only 27% of total cultivator debt, and that this reduces to just 20%, if data for the five States reporting the highest proportion of formal rural debt are removed. Moreover, nearly 90% of households reporting no debt [either formal or informal] are headed by small and marginal farmers.

Andhra Pradesh, the State with the highest concentration of SHGs, Micro Financial Institutions (MFIs) and banks, reports the highest proportion of rural non-institutional debt [nearly 73%], according to All India Debt and Investment Survey, 1991 and 2001.

Advantages of the alternative model

Choice of intermediaries

While the NGOs/ MFIs and various other formal and informal organizations would be the automatic choice of banks for appointment as Business Facilitator/ Correspondents, other private agencies working in the rural sector can be used for the purpose. This could include the kiosks, e-choupals and the retail chains being established in rural areas by several corporate. The regulations also permit individuals to be appointed as 'Business Facilitators', who would provide support services without handling cash.

- Cost issues

This is the most important advantage of this model. The use of intermediaries in services delivery through the Business Facilitaror/ Correspondent models can help banks in reducing their cost. Studies have shown that the all-inclusive cost of delivery of small amounts of loans up to Rs 25,000 directly by banks comes to above 20 per cent of the loan amount and the cost would be proportionately higher in the case of smaller loan amounts. In one study reported by the Institute for Financial Management and Research (IFMR), Chennai, it is observed that the intermediary (here an MFI) has the cost advantage in delivery of small value loans – while the cost for banks for loans up to Rs 10,000 is reported as 33.1 per cent, that for the MFI is 22.7 per cent. A bank can, therefore, address the cost issue to certain extent if it provides the service through an intermediary in the form of Business Facilitator or Correspondent. Of course, the actual costs would depend on the nature of the intermediary, its efficiency of operations and the methodology adopted by it to reach out to the customers.

- Harnessing local knowledge

The banking sector, which has a problem in expanding its outreach beyond a certain point, now has the opportunity to take the advantage of the local knowledge of these persons/ agencies in providing financial services in hitherto unreached remote areas. They can support institutions and organisations that can deliver real services as also conceive and implement capacity building initiatives.

Technology in intermediation

Many of the NGOs/ other intermediaries are quite technology savvy and use various products to reduce cost of operations. Partnership with these organizations would provide the banks an opportunity to look at technology-based solutions and low cost delivery mechanisms that will reduce transaction cost of such services with the volumes required to make such a model sustainable. Use of IT-enabled products and services at the bank and the intermediary level (in the form of simputers, personal digital assistants etc.) have proved to be useful in providing low-cost intermediation, at the same time addressing the issues of speedy accounting of the transactions at the bank level.

**Other issues**

While the amount of compensation to be paid to the intermediaries by the banks would vary from case to case and also would depend on the nature of service provided, there is a need for uniformity in the method of application of compensations to avoid any problems in future as also to clearly address the issue of costs to the customer.

Most of the innovations in financial services have taken place as a response to customer perception of cost and margin factors and risk management. In catering to the poor, banks may have to look for composite products including both savings and loans components and having appropriate linkage with insurance so as to make it a package.

**Impact**

Any policy or programme for delivering financial support services to the poor aims at improving their standard of living and helping them to cross the poverty barrier. The impact of such programmes has to be judged with reference to its success in this regard, achieved through asset creation with credit combined with appropriate hand-holding and linkage facilities.

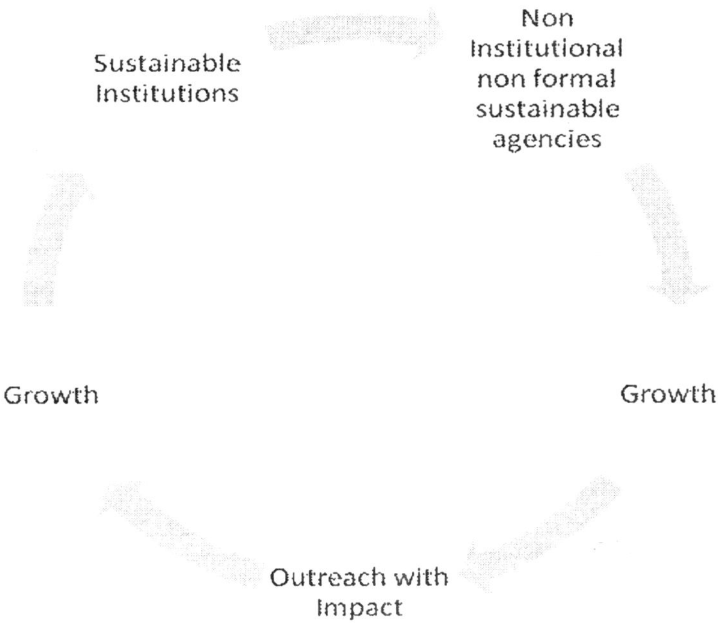


In this, the role of domain-specific knowledge providers such as extension agencies in the farm sector, technical training institutes in the non-farm sector and rural development and self employment training institutes set up by many banks, is important, as proper utilization of credit is possible only with a sound knowledge of viable practices and alternatives available at the ground level.

## Sustainability

Any economic activity undertaken with the help of credit has to be self-sustaining. Further, the institutions providing these credit facilities should also be able to sustain their activities. This needs appropriate designing and pricing of the products and appropriate delivery methods which should, inter alia, address the cost issues, as any outreach expansion and provision of financial services to the poor has cost implications for the institutions.

There is a need for banks to redesign their business strategies to incorporate specific plans to promote financial inclusion of the low-income groups treating it not only as a corporate social responsibility, but also as a business opportunity. The business opportunity lies in exploiting the low margins-high volumes situation at the 'bottom of the pyramid' and seen in this context, financial inclusion would not only be socially desirable, but also would make a lot of economic sense. To quote noted economist Prof. C.H. Hanumantha Rao, "Considering the prevailing socio-economic structure and the nature of our polity, the challenges for achieving more inclusive growth are much greater than for stepping up the GDP growth rate.

It has been found that SHGs often do not include the poorest of the poor for various reasons.

Firstly due to Social Factors the poorest are most often those who are socially marginalised due to caste as scheduled castes scheduled tribes, they are also used to being on the fringes of society and are the most sceptical of the benefits of collective association. Secondly economic factors tend to exclude rather than include them. The poorest lack basic steady financial resources to enable them to contribute to the savings of the group. They are also part of the shifting population they migrate in search of livelihood and work or they belong to nomadic tribes. Thirdly there are inherent biases operable against them in that all implementing organisations whether formal as Banks or informal as SHGs and NGOs accept that they are more difficult to reach and motivate thus they tend to be ignored and left to eke out bare survival Training and Capacity Building and some visionary individuals can still help and have succeeded in breaking through these barriers by imparting Training and capacity building. First basic skills building on what they know pottery, basket weaving, broom making etc and then entrepreneurial training in basic book keeping, accountancy,and business planning these enable even the socially marginalised and economically disadvantaged to be drawn into the economic mainstream.

## References


1. Stategic Issues in Microfinance (2002) edited Mwangi S Kimenyi Robert C Wieland and JD Von Piscke Ashgate Publishing House U.K.
2. Poverty and Sustainable Development Deepali Pant Joshi Gyan Publishing House 2005
3. Akerlof GA (1970) The market for lemons quality uncertainity and the market mechanism The Quarterly Journal of economics 84(3) pgs 488-500 3.StiglitzJ and A Weiss (1981) Credit Rationing in Markets with Imperfect Information American Economic Review 71(3) pp. 351-66.
4. Burgess and Pande (2003) Do rural banks matter evidence from the Indian Social banking Experience.
5. Mc Kinnon and Shaw model 1973 quoted in Financial Refgorm Gerard Caprio, Izak Atiyas and James A Hanson Cambridge University Press (2008).
6. Hulme and Mosley Finance Against Poverty Vol. I and II.
7. All India Rural Credit Survey Committee Report Volume II RBI Mumbai 1955. (2) Debt and Investment Survey, National Sample Survey Organisation, Ministry of Planning and Program Implementation, Government of India July 1998 pp. 22-27.

# 2

# *"Delivery Models Micro Credit Through Micro Finance Institutions (MFI)-scaling Up Pro Poor Interventions"*

Microcredit in microfinance-microfinance institutions (MFIs) are institutions enabling access to financial services by poor people and are now accepted as instruments for poverty reduction and for empowering the poor and dispossessed. Micro Finance institutions (MFIs) are defined by the RBI as those which provide thrift, credit and other financial services and products of very small amounts to the poor in rural, semi urban or urban areas for enabling them to raise their income levels and improve their living standards. The acceptance of Microfinance as a business proposition has led to a revision in the strategy of public policy in assignment of lead roles to banks in microfinance with a view to breaking the hold of the money lender as also in the provision of sharply targeted small value loans to the rural poor.

1. The MFIs are broadly classified as NGOs which are mainly, engaged in promoting self help groups (SHGs) and their

federations at a cluster level and in the Self Help group Bank Linkage model (SBLP ) promoted by NABARD. An SHG is an unregistered entity of between10-20 individuals, having own rules and regulations, office bearers and books of accounts.

2. They can also take the form of Societies registered under the Societies Registration Act of 1860.

| | |
|---|---|
| Not for Profit MFIs | Societies registered under Societies Regulation Act 1860 or similar State Acts.<br>Public Trusts registered under the Indian trusts Act 1882.<br>Non profit companies registered under Section 25 of the Companies Act 1956. |
| Mutual Benefit MFIs | State Credit Cooperatives<br>Multistate Cooperative Act or National Credit Cooperatives.<br>Mutually Aided Cooperative Societies (MACs Act Andhra Pradesh). |
| For Profit MFIs | Non Bank Financial Companies registered under Companies Act 1956. |

SHGs and federations

Societies and Trusts

Co-operative societies

Co-operative Banks

Regional Rural Banks

Local Area Banks

Public and private sector banks

Companies incorporated under Section 25 of the Companies Act

Companies registered with the RBI as NBFCs

Eligible organizations under BC/BF guidelines of RBI

Legal structure determines

Clarity of ownership

Initial capital requirement

Ability of the MFI to mobilize deposits
Ability to raise equity
Ability to raise grants
Ability to raise funds from banks and FIs
Regulatory requirements
Tax implications

(1) MFI -NGO – MFI NGO - MFIs can assume the form of Trusts or Societies. They cannot accept Public Deposits and are governed by their Society's Bye Laws and the rules as laid down by the Registrar of Cooperative Societies or registered under similar State Acts of the state where they are registered.

(2) Societies can be registered under the Societies Registration Act, 1860 or under respective state acts.

(3) A society can be registered by any seven persons associated for any literary, scientific or charitable purposes by subscribing their names to a memorandum of association and filing with the registrar.

(4) Registration does not require any minimum initial capital contribution.

(5) Difficulty to determine ownership makes banks uncomfortable in lending large sums.

(6) Cannot raise equity so scalability is an issue.

(7) Cannot accept public deposit.

(8) Exempt from Income Tax if registered under Section 12A of the Income Tax Act.

(9) Need registration under FCRA to be able to accept foreign grants.

They can also be Public Trusts registered under the Public Trusts Act 1882.

Public Trusts registered under the Indian Trust Act 1860 on any state enactment governing religious or charitable Public Trusts can be established under the respective state regulations. Trusts find it Difficult to attract commercial equity and loans.

(10) There is no minimum capital requirements.
They cannot accept public deposits however they are eexempt from Income Tax if registered under Section 12A of the Income Tax Act.

(11) Need registration under FCRA to be able to accept foreign grants.

(12) Micro Finance Institutions including Cooperative Societies may be registered under the Cooperative Societies Act of the respective state or the Central Multi Sate Cooperative Act 1984 as Mutual Benefit Trusts or as Nidhis under Sec 620 of the Companies Act 1956.

(13) Mutually Aided Cooperative Societies (MAC).
These acts have enabled the promotion of self reliant and vibrant. Cooperative Societies based on thrift and self help, under the MACS Act, in order to secure operational freedom, the Cooperative Societies have to forego Government sponsorship in the form of grants in aid/ external support. They can neither accept share capital contributions nor loans from State Governments. Mutual Benefit MFI.

(1) State Credit Cooperatives.
(2) Natural Credit.
(3) Mutually Aided Cooperative Societies (MACs).

Companies registered under Section 25 of the Companies Act are not for profit companies some Non Bank Finance Company Institutions which are registered as MFI's (not for profit). Section 25 NBFC - MFI under RBI Notification dated 13.1.2000 are exempt from the fulfilment of NBFC norms as they are not allowed to mobilize deposits.

(a) Such an MFI cannot pay any dividend or distribute profits to its members
(b) Relevant provisions of RBI Act 1934 are not applicable to such not for profit (NBFC)
(c) They have to be licensed under Section 25 of the Companies Act, 1956.

(d) They can provide credit only up to Rs. 50,000/- for a business enterprise and up to Rs. 1,25,000/- for meeting the cost of a dwelling unit of any poor person.

(1) For profit NBFC/MFIs

(a) Must be registered with the RBI,

(b) They must have net owned fund of Rs. 2 crore,

(c) They are considered companies registered under the Companies Act,

(d) They are regulated by RBI,

(e) They have to fulfil Capital Adequacy stipulations and adhere to prudential norms.

MFIs morphing to NBFCs must have a minimum entry capital of Rs. 2 crore, capital adequacy of 12% and maintain liquid assets of 15% of Public Deposits, under the Foreign Contribution Regulation Act (FCRA) contribution is permissible to US$ 5,00,000, they are prohibited from acceptance of deposits.

External Commercial Borrowing (ECB)

(1) Should be routed through normal banking channels

(2) ECB can be accessed from International Banks

(3) Multilateral Financial Institutions Export Credit Agencies

(4) Organisations (individuals which are Know Your Customer (KYC)/Anti Money Laundering (AML) compliant.

(5) Interest Rate deregulation for MFIs is a contentious issue MFIs are of the view that they should be allowed to charge cost covering interest rates, 'Cost + reasonable margin' approach, while there is a concern that the rates may be far higher than those which the poor borrowers are able to service.

In comparison with the 3-4% administrative/operating expenses incurred by banks servicing their average borrowers, efficient MFIs incur 10-14%. Compared to the average MFI client who takes loans of around Rs 5-6,000 with average outstanding of just over Rs 3,300, even a relatively small client of a bank has loans of Rs 35,000-50,000. Micro finance interest rates are perceived to be on the higher side.

**Table 3: Determinants of Interest Rate on Micro-Credit in India**

(on declining balance)

| *Description* | *Annual Percentage Rate (%)* |
|---|---|
| (a) Average Financial Cost of Funds assuming borrowing at 10-12% but around 70% of on-lending funds comes from borrowings while the rest is from grants or internal generation of surplus or a small amount from "compulsory savings" (or cash collateral) | 6-9 |
| (b) Operating Expenses | 10-14 |
| (c) Loan Losses | 1-2 |
| (d) Desired Capitalization Rate – assuming a 30% growth rate and a capital adequacy ratio of 15%, banks will lend to MFIs if they raise around 4.5% in the form of "own funds" – part internal resource generation (which is this amount) and part equity finance from SIDBI, NABARD and MF equity funds currently in existence and being established | 3-4 |
| Annual Effective Interest Rate | 22-26 |

The MFI answer to this argument is that they enable access to credit possible for the poorest and that the only alternative for the poor borrower is the money lender who charges extortionate rates of interest so it remains a contentious point.

(6) Banking Facilitator Model Properly identified Business Facilitator under 'contractual model' to be enabled to act as 'pass through' agents, MFIs as "business Facilitator" can provide value added services as :

(1) Disbursal of small value credit

(2) Recovery of Principal/collection of interest ma

(3) They provide only social and developments services and encourage people's participation with the ultimate

objective of setting up self help groups. A SHG is defined as a small economically homogenous and affinity group of rural poor who come together voluntarily to save small amounts regularly and mutually agree to contribute to a common fund to meet emergency needs. They operate through simple and flexible rules. They are generally responsive to members needs, they rely on collective decision making, and conflict resolution through mutual discussion they extend collateral free loans to members but charge market driven rates of interest. They develop thrift habits and enable safe keeping of small savings while providing access to funds. As grassroots level institutions the groups allow for social and economic intermediation for focussing on the poor.

In design the model especially the immensely popular and dominant paradigm of the NABARD SHG BANK LINKAGE program combines the collective wisdom of the poor the organisational capabilities of the NGOs and the financial strengths of Banks to access funds. To express it very simply. This is a flexible and responsive system best adapted to the needs of poorer people. Associations through groups rest on the base of reciprocity of trust confidence and obligation, small savings are pooled together in a common fund, to meet emerging credit needs both short-term lifecycle needs and long term working capital needs. Transaction costs are reasonable making it a cost effective system. It enables large numbers of poor to access formal financial services, as an alternative to the money lender and due to joint liability group efficiencies recovery is high and loan defaults an aberration rather than the norm as is the case in Government sponsored programs.

## SHG FEDERATIONS

The federated SHG approach allows the individual SHGs to federate together in a three tier structure which has shown

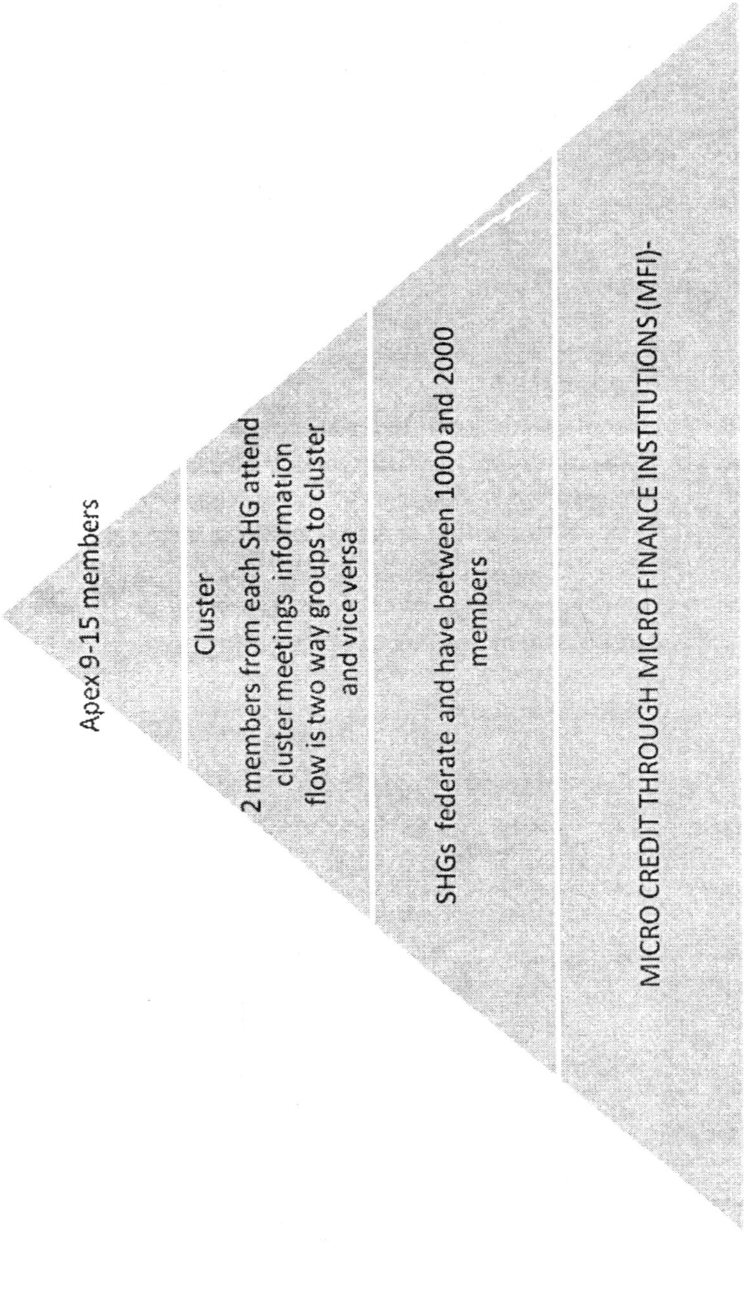
Apex 9-15 members
Cluster
2 members from each SHG attend cluster meetings information flow is two way groups to cluster and vice versa
SHGs federate and have between 1000 and 2000 members
MICRO CREDIT THROUGH MICRO FINANCE INSTITUTIONS (MFI)-

Apex body
SHG executive committee
SHG intermediate cluster
SHG Basic unit

itself to be highly effective for group monitoring and strengthening.

SHG federations by the virtue of their inherent strength and credibility are able to nurture some of the best practices in the process of their evolution.

- Facilitate bank linkage to SHGs
- Matured federations serve as a model for others.
- SHG federations effectively manage insurance, distribution of pensions
- SHG Federations are able to offer services to their members for a fee
- Help members respond to natural disasters
- SHG Federations are primarily concerned about sustainability
- Mobilize funds to meet their cost, at least partially
- Performing roles such as SHG monitoring, social audit

**WHAT IS THE UTILITY OF FEDERATIONS**

The question which is most frequently asked is what is the utility of Federations, are they not creating large structured bureaucratised structures which are losing the flexibility and responsiveness of Self Help Groups along the way?

These two the creation of bureaucratised structures and loss of spontaneity are real dangers but on balance the benefits of federations outweigh the costs.

1. In the absence of federations the entire costs of setting up SHGs have to be borne by the promoter organisations.
2. Federations not only ensure that the SHGs bear all their maintenance costs as also the costs of setting up new SHGs.
3. Though the number of SHGs is large the quality of SHGs varies from those who are highly organised to those who are merely living on the list.
4. Even if all SHGs become well organised they are many in number and far too dispersed to be reached by an external agency for the provision of inputs.

5 Quality inputs and grouping of SHGs into clusters is required.

Thus there seems to be utility in federations.

6. SHG federations also enable the SHGs to access and service a larger quantum of funds from banks.

7. Federation allows for greater sustainability and enables members to pool together and share their resources information and experiences.

TheNGO retreats and the leaders of the SHG federations come to the forefront and in this transition the SHG grows more responsive to the needs of its members and has a transformational effect. The federated SHGs approach builds upon the unique features of SHG based microfinance and contributes to factors that improve the sustainability of SHGs. Federations increase the economic opportunity offered by the SHGs, expand empowerment through leadership building and address the component of security through Insurance services. Federations come under the purview of the Societies Registration Act PRADAN and MYRADA are two examples among many of successfull SHG Federations

## THE GRAMEEN BANK REPLICATION MODELS

In the Grameen Bank model homogenous affinity groups of five are formed at village level. Facilitated by the field workers all the group members undergo a seven day compulsory training of one to two hours each day some groups undergo the group recognition test (GRT) a screening mechanism to distinguish between serious and non serious groups. Eight joint liability groups come together to form a centre, there are weekly meetings of the centre. Attendance in the meetings is treated as mandatory. Bank representative attends the meetings. Instalment collection and fresh loan application approval forms an important part of these meetings. Peer pressure is high and exercised through the weekly meeting forums. Collateral for loans is replaced by peer pressure and is often euphemistically referred to as 'Social Capital'. The group leader is entrusted with the task of collecting all the loan repayments and savings before the group meeting. These are to be handed over to the Centre head that in turn passes them on to the bank representative. They are deposited in the branch on the same day. The collected money is not used for fresh loans and as it has to be deposited on the same day leakages and malpractices are avoided. Similarly the field workers ensure that loans are utilised for the purposes for which they are advanced. The transaction costs remain low as the group self selects and screens its borrowers. Peer pressure works as group collateral. All kinds of loans productive and consumption are granted repayment is in small regular instalments and loan sanction is quick. The Grameen replicators predominate in South India, SHARE Microfin Ltd, Activists for Social Alternatives (ASA) and in Uttar Pradesh Mirzapur CASHPOR Financial and Technical Services have adopted the methodology with variations.

The Cooperative Model

Cooperative Societies can be registered under

Co-operative Societies Act, 1912, or

Relevant state Co-operative Societies acts, or

Relevant state Mutually Aided Co-operative Societies Act, or

Multi-state Co-operative Societies Act, 1995

They are primarily regulated by registrar of co-operative societies.

Can access equity as well as deposits from their members and can lend to their members.

Their membership is generally restricted to individuals, other co-operatives and government (including government corporations).

Mobilization of equity is restricted as co-operative societies can raise equity only from their members. It is sometimes felt that the principle of 'one person one vote' acts as disincentive to equity mobilization from the members.

Banks are reluctant to lend to co-operative societies because of non-equity based ownership and their tendency to get political.

Cooperatives can be Primary co-operative bank (urban co-operative banks).

State co-operative bank

Central co-operative bank

They are registered under Multi state cooperative acts. Regulated by Registrar atives for registration, management and audit.

Regulated under the Banking Regulation Act, 1949 by the Reserve Bank of India for licensing, area of operations and interest rates.

Can undertake most of the banking activities

Face difficulty in raising equity and have a tendency to get politicized.

Respective state governments have close control over central co-operative banks and state cooperative banks. Many of these cooperative banks are not well-managed.

Series of irregularities have been noted by RBI. In many primary co-operative banks and it has taken action against several existing banks.

The organisation that has been the most successful in using the cooperative form in rural microfinance in India has been the Cooperative Development forum (CDF). Hyderabad. CDF's approach has relied on a credit union model involving a 'savings first' strategy. It has built up a network of financial cooperatives based upon women's and men's thrift groups. After lobbying successfully for an enabling legislation in the state of Andhra Pradesh for the flexible functioning of cooperatives (which resulted in the Andhra Pradesh Mutually-Aided Cooperative Societies Act), it has registered the associations of thrift groups promoted by it under this Act.

The MACS Act has become landmark legislation which has been used by other organisations as well to register associations based on other approaches such as SHGs and Grameen joint liability groups (JLGs) as MACS.

The main features of the CDF system are as under:

The primary entities in CDF's mF (cooperative) system are the women's/men's thrift cooperative (WTCs and MTCs) which consist of 300 members, usually from the same village. The size of a group is often dictated by the capability of its leader, who is nominated by the members of the group. A leader continues as long as he enjoys the confidence of the group.

CDF had started off by promoting much smaller units, but over time it encouraged these small units to merge into larger units as it felt that smaller units would not be viable.

This is based on CDF's past experience in working with multipurpose cooperatives, wherein it was found that economies of scale were essential to run a successful cooperative venture, justify resources (staff) and also meet statutory/administrative requirements, such as audits.

However, even today, the W (M) TCs are divided into smaller groups (10 to 50 members) to facilitate better monitoring of thrift and loan payments. Each group is headed by a leader, who convenes the group meetings, collects savings, and monitors the repayment of loans.

Though groups serve some administrative purposes, CDF has encouraged members to identify more strongly with their W(M)TCs rather than with the groups, as they are the primary legal entities and viable units of operation.

Initially, the W(M)TCs promoted by CDF were not formally registered, as they preferred to work outside the earlier Cooperative Act which was extremely restrictive in its functioning. However, due to the persistent efforts of CDF and sister organisations a progressive Cooperative Act, which allows for greater flexibility and autonomy in operations, was promulgated in 1995. Following this, most of the WTCs/MTCs decided to register themselves under this new (MACS) Act.

MFIs which are specifically organised as cooperatives such as SEWA Bank and various Mutually Aided Cooperative Thrift and Credit Societies (MACTS) in Andhra Pradesh and MFIS which are organised as Non Banking Finance Companies such as BASIX,CFTS Mirzapur and Grameen replicators as SHARE Microfin Ltd.

Some of the leading alternative microfinance institutions in this segment are SEWA Bank in Gujarat which also runs federations of SHGs in nine districts of Gujarat ASA in Tamil Nadu and BASIX in Andhra Pradesh MACTS promoted by the Cooperative Development Foundation (CDF) MYRADA in Karnataka which has promoted a company of its village Sanghas known as Sanghamitra. These alternative microfinance institutions have come up to bridge the increasing gap between the demand and supply of financial services. A vast majority of them function just as NGOs they remain scattered and isolated without any cohesion or information dissemination between them. They confront funding and financial problems due to inappropriate legal structures. The main source of funds for NGOs is grants or contributions received from foreign donors under the Foreign Contribution Regulation Act (FCRA) these are not necessarily either sustainable or consistent fund flows.

NGOs are registered as Non Profit Organisations or charitable trusts if they became extremely profitable and begin earning large amounts from lending activity they stand to violate section 11(4) of the Income Tax Act and can lose their charitable status under Section 12. Moreover NGOs do not have the appropriate financial structures for carrying out microfinance activity as they are registered as societies and trusts they can never be capitalised adequately or possess equity capital which can be leveraged for borrowing.

**Cooperatives remain highly politicised hence most NGOs**

Exercise the choice to morph to NBFCs but they confront stiff entry level capital requirements. Borrowing from foreign institutions to beef up capital is not feasible as they have to obtain two credit ratings. Liquidity has almost dried up abroad.

Most foreign institutions are reluctant to give rupee denominated loans and the MFIs are also subject to exchange risks which they find difficult to handle.

## CHALLENGES OF SMALL LOAN ADMINISTERATION

The costs of administering micro finance loans are very high relative to the value of loans and deposits at stake. Financial transactions bear significant overhead and fixed costs independent of the size of the transactions. These costs include the administrative costs of making payments, keeping offices open, cost of loan monitoring, cost of payment of salaries etc. The ratio of expenses may not typically decline with portfolio size increase. Several of the loans may be impaired as the borrower's ability to pay back depends on the borrowers income stream.

1. Poor borrowers income streams are inherently unstable and risky as the exposure to exogenous shock is higher (as weather/macroeconomic fluctuations etc.).
2. The activities of the borrowers are not well diversified
3. The borrowers are not able to provide collateral
4. the loans are bound up with their personal finances business may collapse if a large medical bill is to be paid this often leads to bunched NPAs after a harvest failure or natural disaster Though most MFIs still manage to achieve very high recovery rates the potential danger of the loan turning into NPA is ever-present.

**Funding for Micro Finance Agencies And Activities.** Foreign Investment by way of equity is permissible to US $500,000 Government owned Banks in the provision of financial services to poorer households and smaller enterprises. MFIs promise to provide assistance directly to disadvantages sections of society in a relatively cost effective manner they thus play an important role in financial sector development and in overall development. The emerging role of MFIs as institutions other than Banks engaged in providing financial services to the poor has been recognised and the Banking sector has advanced loans to the MFIs for on lending to the SHGs. During the year 2006-07 Bank loans amounting to Rs 1152 crore were disbursed to 334 MFIs taking the total outstanding toRs 1584 crore to 550 MFIs as on March 31, 2007.

**Table V.8: Bank Loans provided to MFIs**
(as at end march 2007)

(Amount in Rs. Crore)

| *Agency* | *Loans Disbursed by Banks to MFIs during 2006-07* | | *Outstanding Bank Loans to MFIs as on March 31,2007* | |
|---|---|---|---|---|
| | *No. of MFIs* | *Amount* | *No. of MFIs* | *Amount* |
| (1) | (2) | (3) | (4) | (5) |
| Commercial Banks | 327 | 1,151 | 541 | 1,584 |
| Regional Rural Banks | 7 | 0.2 | 8 | 0.2 |
| Co-operative Banks | - | - | 1 | 0.01 |
| Total | 334 | 1,152 | 550 | 1,584 |

- Nil/Negligible.

*Note*: (1) Figures may not add up to their respective total due to rounding off.

(2) The actual number of MFIs would be less as some MFIs have availed loans from more than one bank.

**Source: NABARD**

Loan Basis to MFIs to be used by them for on-lending to SHGs or individuals. This loan has to be repaid along with service charge, within a period of 5 to 6 years. During the year 2007-08, RFA amounting to Rs. 8 crore was sanctioned to six agencies taking the cumulative credit sanctioned to Rs. 36 crore covering 35 agencies.

**RATING OF MFIS**

In order to identify, classify and rate MFIs, NABARD introduced a scheme for commercial banks and RRBs to enable them to avail the services of accredited rating agencies for rating of MFIs. Banks can avail the services of credit rating agencies like CRISIL, M-CRIL, ICRA, CARE and Planet Finance for rating of MFIs and avail financial assistance by way of grant to the extent of 100 per cent of the total professional fees of the credit rating agency, subject to a maximum of Rs. one lakh. The assistance is available to the first rating of MFIS with a minimum loan outstanding of Rs. 50 lakh and maximum loan outstanding of Rs. 500 lakh. During the year 2007-08, rating support amounting to Rs. 3 lakh to four agencies was provided.

**MICROFINANCE DEVELOPMENT AND EQUITY FUND-**

The objective of the MFDF is to facilitate and support the orderly growth of the micro finance sector through diverse modalities for enlarging the flow of financial services to the poor, particularly for women and vulnerable sections of society, consistent with sustainability. As per the Union Budget announcement for the year 2005-06, the MFDF was re-designated as 'Micro Finance Development and Equity Fund' (MFDEF) with an increased corpus of Rs. 200 crore. The fund is being managed by a board consisting of representatives of NABARD, commercial banks and professionals with domain knowledge. The Reserve Bank is a member of the Advisory Committee of the MFDEF.

The MFDEF maintained by NABARD is used for promotion of micro finance through scaling-up of the SHG-bank linkage programme; extending RFA and capital support to MFIs and undertakes various promotional initiatives. During 2007-08, Rs. 27 crore was utilised from the fund towards micro finance related activities.

The objective of the MFDEF, which was set up following the announcement in the Union Budget 2005-06, is to facilitate and support the orderly growth of the micro finance sector through diverse modalities for enlarging the flow of financial services to the poor, particularly to women and vulnerable sections of the society consistent with sustainability.

**Activities to be supported out of the MFDEF**

The Fund would be utilised to support interventions to eligible institutions and stakeholders. The components of assistance will include, inter alia, the following purposes:

Capacity Building

(i) Training of SHGs and other groups for livelihood, skill up-gradation and micro enterprise development.

(ii) Capacity building of staff of institutions involved in micro finance promotion such as banks, NGOs, government departments, NABARD, among others.

(iii) Capacity building of MFIs.

Funding Support

(i) Contributing equity/other forms of capital support to MFIs and service providers, among others.

(ii) Providing financial support for start-up and on-lending for micro finance activities.

(iii) Supporting self help promotion initiatives (SHPI) of banks and other SHPIs.

(iv) Meeting on a selective basis the operational deficit of financial intermediary NGOs/MFIs at the start up stage.

(v) Rating of MFIs and self regulation.

Management Information Services (MIS)

(i) Supporting systems management with regard to MIS, accounting, internal controls, audits and impact assessment.

(ii) Building an appropriate data base and supporting development thereof.

**Regulatory and Supervisory Framework**

Recommending regulatory and supervisory framework based on an on-going review.

**Studies and Publications**

(i) Commissioning studies, consultancies, action research, evaluation studies, etc., relating to the sector.

(ii) Promoting seminars, conference and other mechanisms for discussion and dissemination.

(iii) Granting support for research.

(iv) Documentation, publication and dissemination of micro finance literature.

**Others**

Any other activities recommended by the Advisory Board to Fund.

**Eligible Institutions**

The following types of structures, community based organisations and institutions, would be eligible for support from the Fund:

(i) Training: SHGs, community based organisations (CBOs), NGOs, banks, MFIs, NABARD, training establishments, networks and service providers.

(ii) Funding Support: NGOs, CBOs, MFIs, and Banks.

(iii) MIS: SHGs, NGOs/voluntary associations (VAs). Banks, MFIs, NABARD.

(iv) Regulatory and Supervisory Framework: banks, MFIs, Self Regulatory Organisation (SROs), NGOs, MFI Networks, NABARD.

(v) Studies and Publications: Banks, MFIs, NABARD, training and research organisations, academic institutions and universities.

(vi) Any other organisation as may be decided by the Advisory board from time to time.

**Mode of Assistance**

Mode of assistance from the Fund would include the following:

(i) Promotional support for training and other promotional measures
(ii) Loans and advances including soft loans
(iii) Revolving Fund Assistance (RFA) to NGOs/MFIs.
(iv) Equity and quasi equity support to MFIs.
(v) Administrative subsidies and grants
(vi) Administering Charges.

**Management of Fund**

The Fund is being managed and administered by NABARD. The interest accrued/income earned from the fund is ploughed back to the fund. The administrative charges incurred by NABARD in conduct of Advisory Board meeting and salaries, allowances of the NABARD staff involved in micro finance programmes will be met out of the Fund on such basis as may be determined from time to time. As per extant practice, meetings of the banks contributing to the MFDEF will be convened from time to time in which they will be informed regarding the status and utilisation of fund.

**Advisory body to MFDEF**

The Advisory Board guides and renders advice on the various aspects relating to the microfinance sector. The Board determines its own procedures for day to day working including constitution of committees and task forces among others for examination of various issues. The advisory board meets at such intervals as deemed necessary but in any case once in a quarter to review the status and progress of outflow and to render policy advice for orderly growth and development of the sector.

**ROLE OF SIDBI**

Small Industries Bank of India has launched its microcredit scheme (MCS) to assist individual borrowers or SHG with microfinance programs through NGOs creating self employment opportunities is one way of attacking poverty and solving the problems of unemployment.The scheme of microcredit has been found an effective instrument for lifting the poor above the level of poverty by providing them increased self employment opportunities and making them credit worthy in the field of Industry Service and Business. Under the program NGOs/MFIs are required to provide equity support in order to avail of SIDBI finance. Government provides funds to SIDBI called 'Portfolio Risk Fund" (PRF) This fund is used for meeting the security deposit requirement of the loan amount from MFIs/NGOs and to cover the interest loss. At present SDBI takes fixed deposit equal to 10% of the loan amount. The share of MFIs/NGOs would be 2.5% of the loan amount (i.e. 25% of security deposit) and balance 7.5% (i.e. 75% of security deposit) would be adjusted from the funds provided by the Government of India. The MFIs/ NGOs may avail the loan from the SIDBI for further on lending on the support of the security deposit.

(i) The recovery of loan/interests will be the sole responsibility of the SIDBI. In case of non recovery of loan, SIDBI would first adjust fixed deposit and interests accrued thereon for 2.5% security deposit of the loan pledged by the MFIs / NGOs and thereafter adjust 7.5% security deposit of the loan amount provided by the Government of India and the interest accrued thereon with the approval of Committee of Govt. of India.

(ii) After full recovery of loan from the MFIs/NGOs, the 7.5% security deposit of the loan amount provided by Govt. of India and interest accrued thereon would be rotated further as a security deposit for MFIs/NGOs with the approval of Committee of the Govt. of India or the same will be returned to the Govt. of India.

(iii) As SIDBI is already running the Micro-Credit Programme, they will monitor the scheme. They would also provide the monthly/ quarterly progress report along with details of beneficiaries, utilization of funds provided by Government of India and loan sanctioned/ utilized by the beneficiaries.

(iv) The activities covered under the scheme are manufacturing, service sector and non-farming activities.

(b) *Training and Studies on Micro-Finance Programme*: The Government of India would help SIDBI in meeting the training needs of NGOs, SHGs, intermediaries and entrepreneurs and also in enhancing awareness about the programme. This task would be performed through National Level Entrepreneurship Development Institutes (EDIs) and Small Industries Service Institutes (SISIs). The Research Studies would also be arranged through reputed agencies.

Institution Building for 'Intermediaries' for identification of viable projects : The Government of India would help in institution building through identification and development of 'intermediary organization', which would help the NGOs/SHGs in identification of product, preparation of project report, working out forward and backward linkages and in fixing marketing/ technology tie-ups. The SISIs would help in the identification of such intermediaries in different areas.SIDBI offers customised financial support through its Foundation for Microfinance Development.This assumes the form of loans, Capacity building grant, equity and quasi equity and comprehensive capacity building support to the Micro finance institutions.

## RASHTRIYA MAHILA KOSH RMK

The Rashtriya Mahila Kosh RMK was set up following the recommendations of GOIs Shram shakti report (1988) to accelerate the flow of credit to women to support self employment particularly to those in the unorganized sector. The specific mandate was to lend through the NGO sector apart from regular lending activity the fund possess considerable resources for capacity building activity. The National Credit Fund for Women or the Rashtriya Mahila Kosh (RMK) was set up in March 1993 as an independent registered society by the Department of Women and Child Development in Government of India's Ministry of Human Resource Development with an initial corpus of Rs. 310,000,000 - not to replace the banking sector but to fill the gap between what the banking sector offers and what the poor need.

Its main objectives are :

- To provide or promote the provision of micro-credit to poor women for income generation activities or for asset creation.
- To adopt a quasi-informal delivery system, which is client friendly, uses simple and minimal procedures, disburses quickly and repeatedly, has flexibility of approach, links thrift and savings with credit and has low transaction costs both for the borrower and for the lender.
- To demonstrate and replicate participatory approaches in the organisation of women's groups for thrift and savings and effective utilisation of credit.
- To use the group concept and the provision of credit as an instrument of women's empowerment, socio-economic change and development.
- To cooperate with and secure the cooperation of the Government of India, State Governments, Union Territory administrations, credit institutions, industrial and commercial organisations, NGOs and others in promoting the objectives of the Kosh.
- To disseminate information and experience among all these above agencies in the Government and non-government sectors in the area of microfinance for poor women.
- To receive grants, donations, loans, etc., for the furtherance of the aims and objectives of the Kosh.

## Regulation of Micro Finance Institutions

The rapid growth of the micro finance sector and varied number of micro finance providers influencing the lives of millions of clients have necessitated the need for regulating the sector include banks (including commercial banks RRBs and co-operative banks), primary agricultural credit societies. SHGs linked to banks and MFIs that include NBFCs, Section 25 companies, trusts and societies as also co-operatives (under MACS). Currently, banks and NBFCs fall under the regulatory purview of the Reserve Bank. Other entities are covered varying degrees of regulation under the respective State legislations. There is no single regulator for this sector. In this context, for the orderly growth and development of the sector, the Government of India has proposed a legislation and formulated a Micro Financial Sector (Development and Regulation Bill), 2007 which is under consideration of the Parliament. The Bill envisages NABARD to be the regulator and provides that all micro finance organisations desirous of offering thrift services may get registered with NABARD.

## Micro Insurance

Social security in the form of micro insurance can be a boon for the poor, when the income raising ability of the bread winner is impaired. In India, the micro insurance schemes are mostly implemented by the MFIs as a compulsory element along with the micro credit provided. Micro insurance schemes can be considered as a stepping stone to social protection. One of the best examples of micro insurance scheme is the one which is linked to the Grameen Bank scheme in Bangaladesh. Grameen established a separate organisation called Grameen Kalyan (village welfare) which uses the women groups for the collection of annual premiums for micro insurance.

offering insurance, with life insurance being more widespread than non-life insurance. Insurance Regulatory Development Agency (IRDA)'s micro insurance regulations of November 2005 formally recognised NGOs, SHGs and MFIs as 'micro insurance agents" for acting as intermediaries between insurance companies and beneficiaries. The Committee on Financial Inclusion (Chairman: Dr. C. Rangarajan), which submitted its report in January 2008, highlighted the importance of micro insurance and made wide ranging recommendations in this regard.

Generally, micro insurance schemes cover health care, life accident expenses, maternity protection and disability. Both the public sector and private sector insurance companies have tied up with various MFIs in the country to offer micro insurance schemes. One of the difficulties in the implementation of micro insurance scheme is that poor have a lesser understanding of risk pooling and are often reluctant to join schemes where payments have to be made with no immediate returns.

**Progress of Micro Finance in India**

Linking self-help groups with banks is easily the largest and fastest growing microfinance programme in terms of its outreach and sustainability. They feel that banks should have to change their mindset as e-Banking offers a huge opportunity to leapt-frog bankers' traditional concerns about 'high volumes of low value transactions' and 'investing bricks in bricks and mortar', and will increase volumes while driving down marginal costs. micro finance movement has come a long way since its inception in the early 1990s and has assumed enormous significance in the delivery of credit to the hitherto excluded sections of the population. While the SBLP has emerged as the most dominant model, the MFI model has also been gaining importance.

Mainstream Institutions for Microfinance delivery are The National Bank for Agriculture and Rural development (NABARD) Small Industries Development Bank of India (SIDBI) Housing Development and Finance Corporation (HDFC) Private Banks ICICI and Foreign Banks as ABN Amro Bank Commercial Banks Regional Rural Banks (RRBs and credit cooperative societies are some of the mainstream financial institutions involved in extending microfinance. The Committee on Financial Inclusion has estimated that the number of SHGs will have to be doubled to cover all the 50 million poor households in the country, it is timely and apt that Government in consultation with the RBI should create enabling environment, to :

1. Expand outreach in remote locations to cover small/ marginal and tenant farmers, share croppers, oral lessees, landless labourers and households residing in dry land, desert, drought prone, hilly and tribal areas of the country, in a cost-effective way and achieve sustainability of their methodology. Different types of Rural Financial Institutions (RFIs) possess comparable advantages in terms of sustainability, quality, and scope of products and services being offered.
2. incorporate operational solutions to reduce transaction costs and mitigate portfolio risk, such as using remote operating models and outsourcing services [mobile banking, ATMs, mobile phone and internet banking, correspondent retail outlets and agents]; accepting alternative collateral [warehouse receipts, assured contracts, third party guarantees]; and employing portfolio securitizations and loan guarantees

RBI conducted an MFI survey in December 2007 through its officials who held discussions with officials of district administration, branch managers, borrowers and MFIs. The objective of the study was to gain an insight into the activities of MFIs, especially in rural areas, to assess the financial services needs of the rural households and the informal products and processes that currently meet these needs. The study was aimed at gaining a better understanding of the operations of the MFIs and explore the possibility of linkages with banks resulting in extending banking outreach to the poor. In all, 77 MFIs were surveyed in the State of Karnataka, Orissa, Andhra Pradesh, Madhya Pradesh, Bihar, West Bengal, Kerala, Maharashtra, Rajasthan and Tamil Nadu.

The survey revealed that MFIs were adopting various models for micro finance such as through the SHGs, Grameen model/joint liability groups (JLGs) model, individuals as well as through cluster associations of the SHGs. The loan range varied widely across MFIs and across states. The loan range also varied across individuals and across SHGs. For individuals the loans ranged from as low as Rs. 1,000 to Rs. 20,000. For the SHGs, the range was between Rs. 30,000 to Rs. 2 lakh.

The number of clients served by the MFIs during the survey varied significantly across the States and ranged from as low as 79 to more than 10,0000. The average loan range per client was between Rs. 4, 000 to Rs. 5, 000 for individuals and between Rs. 60,000 to Rs.1,3 lakh for the SHGs.

Majority of the loans given by the MFIs in the surveyed States were for work or occupation related purposes. Occupation related loans ranged from 46 to 100 per cent of the total loans in most of the states. This was followed by other purposes like consumption, social events, health, travel and education. The duration of the loans ranged from 6 to 20 months. The interest rates charged by the MFIs were not uniform and varied widely across MFIs and across States. While some MFIS charged flat rates of interest others charged diminishing rates. The flat rates ranged between 10-27 per cent. Besides, many MFIs charged flat processing fee in the range of 1 to 1.5 per cent.

Apart from the loans some of the MFIs offered other services such as health insurance and life insurance. In many cases, asset insurance was compulsory, especially when it related to loans for animal husbandry.

Almost all the MFIs reported good recovery percentage of the loans, i.e. more than 90 per cent. Most of the borrowers also reported that the MFIs adopted fair practices for recovery. The MFIs have a close monitoring system which ensures that there are minimum defaults.

Only a few MFIs were providing performance related incentives to their staff. Some of the parameters used for providing the incentives were (i) business turnover; (ii) maintenance of clientele (low customer dropout rate); (iii) reaching the annual target about number of customers; (iv) recovery performance; (v) percentage of insurance coverage; and (vi) loan utilisation.

Only in the States of Karnataka and Andhra Pradesh, MFIs reported that the money lending legislations were applicable to them. In other States the MFIs reported that they were not bound by the money lending legislations. Almost in all States surveyed, the enforceability of money lending legislation was very poor.

Commercial banks remained the most important source of funds for almost all the MFIs. Some of the MFIs also received funds from other financial and developmental institutions and donor agencies.

The survey attempted to find out what additional support the MFIs expected from banks. Some of the suggestions and expectations were (i) low interest loans; (ii) loans for operational and infrastructure expenses; (iii) flexible banking products; (iv) continuous lending support; (v) better customer service; (vi) simplified access; (vii) capacity building by banks; (viii) IT and EDP support; (ix) sharing establishment costs; and (x) training.

Almost all the MFIs were willing to work as business correspondents (BC) of banks. One MFI however suggested that it was unwilling to work as a BC because it would lose focus on its core activity. Another MFI was unwilling to work as a BC because of the stringent conditions stipulated by banks for their BCs.

In most of the States surveyed, district administration was not maintaining the details of MFIs in the district as it was not compulsory. Furthermore, there were only very few complaints against the MFIs received by the district administration. In Krishna district in Andhra Pradesh there were complaints against MFIs for charging high rates of interest and forcible loan recovery. In Madhya Pradesh also there were some complaints pertaining to high interest rates.

The survey also attempted to obtain the response of clients with respect to the ease of availing loans from MFIs. Most of the borrowers surveyed reported that it was easy or a easy to get a loan from MFIs.

Almost all the bank branch managers opined that MFIs were good customers of banks and they could be used as business facilitators or correspondents.

The study also observed that 30 per cent of SHGs in the sample were involved in community actions. These involved improving community services (43 per cent of the total actions, including water supply, education, health care, veterinary care, village road), trying to stop alcohol sale and consumption (31 per cent), contributing finance and labour for new infrastructure (12 per cent), protecting natural resources and acts of charity (to non-members). The most common type of action taken up by SHGs was the attempt to close down local liquor outlets.

In a joint fact-finding study on microfinance conducted recently by a few major banks, the following observations have been made:

(i) Some of the microfinance institutions (MFIs) financed by banks or acting as their intermediaries/partners appear to be focusing on relatively better banked areas, including areas covered by the SHG-Bank linkage program. Competing MFIs were operating in the same area, and trying to reach out to the same set of poor, resulting in multiple lending and overburdening of rural households. Many MFIs promoted by Banks were not engaged in capacity building and empowerment of groups to the desired extent they were disbursing loans to the newly formed groups within 10-15 days of their formation, in contrast to the practice obtaining in the SHG - Bank linkage program which takes about 6-7 months for group formation / nurturing / handholding. As a result, cohesiveness and a sense of purpose were not being built up in the groups formed by these MFIs.

(iii) Banks, as principal financiers of MFIs, do not appear to be engaging them with regard to their systems, practices and lending policies with a view to ensuring better transparency and adherence to best practices. In many cases, no review of MFI operations was undertaken after sanctioning the credit facility.

Even though the branch network of the formal financial institutions had expanded substantially, during the past about four decades, they have not been able to cater completely to the small and frequent credit needs of the majority of poor. This led to the search for alternative policies and reforms for reaching out to the poor to satisfy their felt needs.

## THE ROLE OF THE RBI IN MICROFINANCE

Recognizing the potential of microfinance to positively influence the development of the poor, Reserve Bank has been providing a facilitating environment for orderly development of the microfinance sector in the country.

Reserve Bank provided policy support by advising banks, to actively participate in the pilot project of NABARD. To study further about the potential of the microfinance movement, Reserve Bank had constituted in 1994 a 'Working Group on NGOs and SHGs' under the Chairmanship of Shri S.K. Kalia, the then Managing Director, NABARD. Based on its recommendations, banks were advised, inter alia, that financing of SHGs should be included by them as part of their lending to the weaker sections and that SHG lending should be reviewed at the SLBC level and by the banks at regular intervals.

- To further promote the Self Help Group momentum in the country, banks were advised in 1998 that SHGs which are engaged in promoting the savings habits among their members will be eligible to open savings bank accounts and that such SHGs need not necessarily have availed of credit facilities from banks before opening savings bank accounts. Subsequent to the Monetary and Credit Policy announcement for the year 1999-2000, banks were also advised that interest rates applicable to loans given by banks to micro credit organizations or by the micro credit organizations to SHGs/ member beneficiaries will be left to their discretion. RBI allowed the establishment of Local Area Bank in 1996.

- LABs are registered as public limited companies under the Indian Companies Act 1956.
- Minimum capital requirement for a LAB is Rs 50 million
- Are allowed to operate in three geographically contiguous districts.
- Can mobilise deposits from public Prudential norms related to banks are applicable but rules relating to liquidity and interest rates applicable to RRBs are applicable.
- At present only four LABs are functioning and no new licenses are being issued.
- Regional Rural banks are also engaged in microfinance. Established by the Central Government through a notification in the official gazette.
- Minimum capital requirement is Rs. 2.5 million.
- The share capital of the RRBs is required to be held by the Central Government, State Government and Sponsor Bank in the ratio 50:15:35.
- From the financial year 2006-07 RRBs have been brought under Income Tax net.
- RBI has also stipulated that RRBs need to maintain disclose CAR starting March 2008.
- Several NBFCs and RNBCs also started entering the microfinance sector, gradually recognizing the potential in the sector. Companies registered under Indian Companies Act 1956 can apply to RBI to carry on the business of an NBFC.
- NBFCs are required to have net owned funds of Rs. 20 millions.
- Ownership can be defined precisely and they can raise equity.
- Mobilization of public deposits, though allowed, is almost impossible given strict guidelines of the RBI.

- Banks are comfortable lending to NBFCs which are well-capitalized and well-performing.
- Act, 1934. Section 25 Companies are promoted for the purpose of promotion of commerce, arts, religion, charity or any other useful purpose.
- They are prohibited from payment of dividends.
- RBI has exempted NBFCs licensed under section-25 of the Indian Companies Act from registration, maintenance of liquid assets and transfer of profit to Reserve Funds, provided.
- They are engaged in micro-financing activities (Rs 50,000 for small businesses and Rs 125,000 for housing).
- they do not mobilize public deposits.
- Section-25 NBFCs find it difficult to mobilize equity owing to restrictions on payment of dividends.
- NBFCs are for-profit entities and are taxable.
- FDI through automatic route is allowed subject the following limits.
- FDI up to 51% - US$0.5 million to be brought upfront.
- FDI between 51% and 75% - US$ 5 mn to be brought upfront.
- FDI between 75% and 100%- US$50mn out of which 7.5 million to be brought up-front.
- NBFCs are subject to prudential regulations regarding income recognition, asset classification and provisioning, prudential exposure limits and accounting/disclosure requirements provided.
- they are mobilizing public deposits, or.
- they are systemically important.
- All non-deposit taking NBFCs having asset size of Rs 1bn (Rs 100 crores) or more as per last audited balance sheet will be considered as systemically important NBFCs.
- Non-deposit taking and systemically important NBFCs will be subject to capital adequacy regulations, single/group exposure norms and disclosure pertaining to derivative transactions.

- Capital Adequacy Ratio (CAR) requirement is now 12% and will be increased to 15% from April 2009 for systemically important NBFCs.

Based on the recommendations of the Advisory Committee on Flow of Credit to Agriculture and Related Activities from the Banking System, it was announced in the Annual Policy Statement for the year 2004-05 that in view of the need to protect the interests of depositors, MFIs would not be permitted to accept public deposits unless they comply with the extant regulatory framework of the Reserve Bank. However, as an additional channel for resource mobilization for them, the Reserve Bank has enabled NGOs engaged in microfinance activities to access the ECBs under approval route.

12 Banks have been permitted by RBI to use the services of NGOs/ SHGs, MFIs and other Civil Society Organisations as intermediaries in providing financial and banking services through Business Facilitator and Correspondent models. Business Facilitators.

Business facilitators can be used by the banks for various pre-disbursement and post-disbursement activities pertaining to lending.

Does not include disbursement and collection activities.

No approval is required from the RBI for using Business Facilitators.

Business Correspondents can undertake disbursement of loans as well as collection of principal. They can also accept deposits on behalf of the banks. Banks can compensate BCs but BCs cannot charge anything from the consumers. Transactions need to be accounted for and reflected in bank's books by end of day or next working day.

The gathering momentum in the microfinance sector has brought into focus the issue of regulating the sector. A draft Micro financial Sector (Development and Regulation) Bill, 2007 is under consideration of the Union Government which envisages regulation of the sector. The Bill was tabled in the

Lok Sabha on March 20, 2007. The Bill proposes NABARD as the regulator for the micro financial sector. On its enactment, the Bill makes registration of microfinance organizations with NABARD mandatory. Bill to promote and regulate the microfinance sector. NABARD to be made the regulatory authority.

- Microfinance is defined to include loans, savings, insurance and pension services. Loans cannot exceed more than Rs. 50,000 (Rs. 150,000 for housing purposes)
- The bill defines an MFO as any organization that provides micro-finance services and includes societies, trusts and cooperative societies.
- All MFOs that accept deposit from 'eligible clients' need to be registered with NABARD. Minimum experience of three years and minimum net owned fund of Rs. five lakhs has been fixed as condition for registration. Different legal structures reflect diversity within the country and represent various stages of evolution of the financial sector
- Each legal structure has a purpose, has its pros and cons and is more effective in a particular situation. A plurality of approach has ben adopted to meet the diversity of needs of poor borrowers.

Microfinance suppliers are broadly divisible in three categories, firstly there are the traditional and informal providers as moneylenders, pawn shops and rotating savings and credit institutions and indigenous associations as the Bishis. Secondly there are formal institutions which are unlicensed as the NGOs and SHGs which are delivering microfinance and thirdly there are licensed financial intermediaries as the commercial banks private banks foreign banks and Public sector Banks, Regional Rural Banks, Local Area Banks Cooperative Banks and also Non Bank Finance companies.

The crucial elements of sustainability of rural financial Institutions are :

Autonomy and flexibility in all understanding the market penetration, growth and performance of these varied delivery models is an important part of assessing how the financial system as a whole works for the poor. Sharper understanding will also throw up the gaps and lead to an understanding of what needs to be done to address them.

## References

1. Microfinance in India (2008) ed KG Karmakar.
2. RBI Trend and Progress of Banking in India 2007-08.
3. BANCON compendium of papers presented 2005.
4. Microfinance Emerging Trends and Challenges 2008 ed Suresh Sunderesan.
5. Microfinance Regulation in India Sa DHAN 2001.
6. Taskforce on Supportive Policy and Regulatory Framework for microfinance National Bank for Agriculture and Rural Development (NABARD) Mumbai, 199.

# 3

# "The NABARD Sponsored SHG - Bank Linkage Program - Progress Prospects"

Social Banking, post nationalization led to the creation of a quantitatively impressive mainframe rural financial architecture with widening geographical spread and penetrative reach of Banks, hampered however by the Imperfect Information paradigm. Due to asymmetries of information Banks find it difficult to screen and select borrowers while ensuring repayment of loans (moral hazard). The strengths of SHGS operating at the grassroots, are that they self select members, ensure repayment through peer pressure and are flexible and innovative though they lack resources and the managerial, and financial expertise of the Banks. The SHG Bank linkage program bridges this gap through financial linkages between the SHGs and the Banks. The specific efficiency gain for Banks is externalization of part of the credit cycle. The extensive network of branches has been leveraged successfully in this approach.

SHG Bank linkage is the country's dominant system of mass banking. Measured on Jacob Yaron's twin criteria of evaluating the efficacy of rural finance institutions, Subsidy dependence Index of financial sustainability and outreach the program is an unqualified success. Broad based and decentralised growth is the only route by which the bulk of the poor can be provided livelihood and food security.

The central thesis is that micro policies enrich and empower the poor and the needy culminating in macro level initiatives and policies which lead to poverty alleviation, women's empowerment and promotion of the public good.

The Banking sector has extensive penetrative outreach a large number of people still remain beyond the frontiers of formal finance due to cultural /perceptual factors which inhibit the formal financial agencies on the supply side and the borrowers on the demand side some of the reasons are :

For Banks and formal financial agencies stay away due to the :

1. Perception that the poor are not bankable.
2. Loan amounts are too small to be of interest to bankers.
3. Bankers transaction costs of servicing a large number of small transactions of the penny economy are prohibitively high.
4. Geography distances areas to be serviced are too far flung to enable the bank to effectively service the loan.
5. Banks are not able to monitor income stream, cash flow capacities which determine the credit absorption capabilities of the borrowers.
6. Banks lack firsthand knowledge of borrower's behaviour they are handicapped due to the prevailing Information asymmetries inherent in the situation.
7. There are no credit histories or data base of those "without means".
8. Migrant populations make it difficult for borrowers to furnish address proof and for Banks to extend loans completing their formalities.

9. There is an absence of extension services.
10. An inadequacy of forward and backward linkages to ensure that the loans extended by the Banking system would remain productive.
11. Repayment remains ambiguous dependent as much on the borrower's character as on the success of the enterprise.
12. Human resource constraints most rural branches are staffed by one manager and one clerk pressured as they are by the need to run the branch it is humanly impossible for them to go into the field to locate and service borrowers. The experiment of treating one day of the week as the Non Public Business Working Day coinciding with market day shandy has not been an unqualified success as Banks used it either as a half day holiday or for updating of their books and records.

**Borrowers Perception**

These are powerful inhibiting factors from the borrower's side too constraints are operable which lead to Voluntary exclusion from formal institutional sources of credit :

1. The costs are perceived to be and often are too high in terms of travel time, waiting time, loss of a day's wages, incidental expenses.
2. Interminable paper work is daunting for the illiterate borrower.
3. Fear of the Bank, its legal formalities of defaulting on the loan of the police of dispossession.
4. Lack of awareness of economic opportunities.
5. Absence/Lack of collateral security.
6. Small value of transactions are not encouraged by the Bank.
7. Lack of defined address or occupation on the part of borrowers who may be migrant workers who take up whatever employment opportunities present themselves in the unorganised sector.

8. Failure of earlier attempts to obtain a loan from the Banks
9. Lack of empathy of the Bank Staff
10. Inability to articulate his needs by the borrower
11. Fear of rejection at various psychological levels
12. Availability of alternate channels of finance (doorstep delivery) through the money lender with no forms to fill or deeds to sign.

The SHG Bank linkage program avoids the pitfalls and builds on the strength of both these approaches, the structured and the unstructured the formal and the informal.

In the year 1992 NABARD started a pilot project on Self Help Groups (SHGs) for providing microfinance. In order to encourage banks to take part in the microfinance movement, Reserve Bank provided policy support by advising banks, to actively participate in the pilot project of NABARD. To study further about the potential of the microfinance movement, Reserve Bank had constituted in 1994 a 'Working Group on NGOs and SHGs' under the Chairmanship of Shri S.K. Kalia, the then Managing Director, NABARD. Based on its recommendations, banks were advised, inter alia, that financing of SHGs should be included by them as part of their lending to the weaker sections and that SHG lending should be reviewed at the SLBC level and by the banks at regular intervals. Though there are different models for purveying microfinance, the SHG-Bank Linkage Program - Progress Prospects.

SHG-bank linkage programme has emerged as the major microfinance programme in the country. It is being implemented by commercial banks, RRBs and co-operative banks. As on March 31, 2007, total number of 28,94,505 SHGs were having outstanding loans of Rs.12,366.49 crore.

The SBLP has made considerable progress since its inception in the early 1990s, both in terms of the number of SHGs credit linked with banks as also the bank loans disbursed by SHGs.

During the year 2008-09, 16,09,586 SHGs were credit linked with banks taking the cumulative number of SHGs credit linked to 42,24,338 as on 31 March 2009. Since inception of the micro-finance (MF) programme, it has enabled an estimated 8.6 million poor households to gain access to MF from the formal banking system.

Bank loan disbursed to SHGs :

16,09,586 new SHGs were financed by banks during the year 2008-09, as against 12,27,770 financed last year.

Per SHG bank disbursement has increased from Rs. 72,076 as on 31 March '08 to Rs.76,128 as on 31 March '09, with a growth rate of 5.62%.

Bank Loans outstanding against SHGs :

7,98,397 new SHG were added in the outstanding bank loans to SHGs during 2008-09 with growth rate of 16.5%. (Total outstanding SHG loan accounts with banks were 42,24,338 as on 31 March 2009 as against 36,25,941 as on 31 March 2008).

Amount of outstanding bank loans to SHGs grew by 33.4% (Total outstanding bank loans to SHGs' were Rs.22,679.85 crore as on 31 March 2009 as against Rs. 16999.90 crore as on 31 March 2008).

## SHG BANK LINKAGE TYPOLOGY -MODELS

Three models of SHGs credit linkage with Banks have emerged SHGs formed and financed by Banks.

SHGs formed by NGOs but directly financed by Banks.

SHGs financed by Banks using NGOs as financial intermediaries.

Of the three models under the SBLP, the Model II, viz., SHGs promoted by NGOs/Government agencies and financed by banks has emerged as the most dominant model in the case of India.

## OUTREACH

'The program launched in 1992 has enabled the formal banking system to reach 11.6 million poor households through the conduit of 1.17 lakh SHGs. Micro credit thus emerges as the most appropriate and economically feasible modus operandi for attaining the twin objectives of growth and poverty eradication. The institutional architecture of the rural financial system must move to spread this model. The cumulative number of SHGs credit linked with banks increased sharply from 33,000 in 1992-99 to 264,000 in 2000-01 and further to 2,239,000 in 2005-06. During the above period, the cumulative bank loans disbursed to SHGs also witnessed a sharp increase from Rs. 57 crore in 1992-99 to Rs. 481 crore in 2000-01 and further to Rs.11,398 crore in 2005-06. As on March 31, 2007, the number of SHGs maintaining savings bank accounts with the banking sector was 4.2 million with outstanding savings of Rs. 3,513 crore, thereby covering more than 58 million poor households under the programme. Commercial banks had the maximum share of the SHG's savings (53.9 per cent) followed by RRBs (32.9 per cent) and co-operative banks (13.2 per cent). Among the commercial banks, the public sector banks accounted for the largest share of savings, while private sector banks accounted for marginal share. It is noteworthy that around 87.3 per cent of the savings were by exclusive women SHGs.

## FINANCIAL SUSTAINABILITY HIGH RECOVERY PERCENTAGE OF OUTSTANDING LOANS

About 37 per cent of banks reported recovery of above 95 per cent under the programme, 36 per cent banks reported recovery in the range of 80-94 per cent and another 20 per cent banks reported recovery in the range of 50-79 per cent. Some differences were observed in recovery rates of commercial banks, co-operative banks and regional rural banks. While the recovery rate of public sector banks varied between 52 per cent and 99 per cent, the same of private sector banks varied between 60 per cent and 100 per cent. Out of the 26 private sector banks, the recovery rate of four banks was 100 per cent.

## PROGRESS

· The provisional data available so far indicates that during the year 2007-08, 552,992 new SHGs were provided with bank loan and 186,883 existing SHGs with repeat loans. Total bank loans disbursed during the year were at Rs. 4,228 crore, of which repeat bank loans to existing SHGs were at Rs. 1,686 crore. The growth of number of SHGs has decelerated in recent years, particularly in the southern region, where rapid progress was made earlier. The scheme is catching up slowly in the northern region. The MFIs have also expanded their operations, which might have impacted the growth of the SBLP to some extent. Many groups promoted under various Government sponsored programmes also constituted a part of the SBLP. As on March 31, 2007, the number of SHGs having.

· outstanding bank loans under the Swarnjayanti Gram Swarozgar Yojana (SGSY) were at 700 thousand constituting 23.7 per cent of the total SHGs under the SBLP. The loan amount outstanding under these SGSY loans were Rs. 3,273 crore which constituted 26.5 per cent of the total amount outstanding under the SBLP. During the year 2006-07, 6,86,408 new SHGs were credit linked with banks taking the cumulative number of SHGs credit linked to 29,24,073 as on 31 March 2007. Since inception of the micro-finance (MF) programme, it has enabled an estimated 409.5 lakh poor households to gain access to MF from the formal banking system. NABARD continued to emphasise scaling-up of the SHG-bank linkage programme in 13 priority States, which have large population of the rural poor. The cumulative number of SHGs credit linked in these States increased from 10.05 lakh during 2005-06 to 13.75 lakh during 2006-07 constituting 54 per cent of the number of SHGs credit linked across the country during the year. The regional spread of the programme reveals that the share of non-southern regions improved significantly from 29 per cent as on 31 March 2001 to 48 per cent as on 31 March 2007.

A grant assistance of Rs.1,403.96 lakh was sanctioned to promote 59.662 SHGs to 8 co-operative banks. 1 RRB, 352 NGOs and 23 IRVs during the year, taking the cumulative sanction to Rs. 4,749.96 lakh for the promotion of 3.09 lakh SHG - Bank

Linkage Program - Progress Prospects groups. An amount of Rs. 1980.77 lakh was released and 1,52,928 SHGs were credit linked as on 31 March 2007. Under NABARD's capacity building programmes for its partner institutions, 70 exposure / field visits to SHGs and institutions pioneering in MF for 1,864 bank/ NGO officials, 682 training and awareness programmes for 23,964 participants from banks and NGOs, 155 sensitisation programmes covering 6,395 government officials and elected members of PRIs were arranged during the year. NABARD also extended support for conducting 3,494 awareness creation and capacity building programmes covering 2,01,854 SHG members. To support the MF programme, NABARD selectively extends Revolving Fund Assistance (RFA) to MFIs for on-lending to SHGs. During the year, RFA of Rs. 1 crore was sanctioned taking the aggregate support to Rs.27.98 crore as on 31 March 2007 for 31 agencies. In addition, to enable rating of MFIs and empowering them to intermediate between the lending banks and the clients, NABARD provides financial assistance to commercial banks and RRBs to avail the services of credit rating agencies for the purpose. The Bank also introduced a scheme to provide capital / equity support to MFIs during 2006-07 to enable them to leverage capital / equity for accessing funds from banks, providing financial services at an affordable cost to the poor, and achieve sustainability in their credit operations over a period of 3 to 5 years. During 2006-07, three agencies were sanctioned total capital support of Rs. 3 crore.

## SHARES OF DIFFERENT AGENCIES

In terms of relative shares of different agencies, commercial banks continued to account for the largest share, both in terms of number of SHGs credit linked and bank loans disbursed, followed by regional rural banks and co-operative banks. Among the commercial banks, public sector banks accounted for the largest share of loans disbursed to SHG sector (88.8 per cent) in 2006-07. Out of the total loans disbursed by the commercial banks, 86.9 per cent of the loans were disbursed exclusively to women SHGs.

Under the SBLP, as on March 31, 2007, 2.9 million SHGs had outstanding bank loans of Rs. 12,366 crore.

The region-wise pattern of SHGs linked to banks showed greater concentration in the southern region, although the spatial disparity has declined in the last few years with some increase in the share of other regions, particularly the eastern region.

## UNEVEN GROWTH

In order to scale up efforts and reduce the regional imbalances in outreach, 13 non-south Indian States (Assam, Bihar, Jharkhand, Gujarat, Himachal Pradesh, Maharashtra, Madhya Pradesh, Chattisgarh, Orissa, Rajasthan, Uttar Pradesh, Uttaranchal and West Bengal) with high incidence of rural poverty and where the micro finance movement had not taken roots were identified by NABARD. Special efforts by NABARD resulted in an increase in the number of SHGs credit linked in these States from 100 thousand as on March 31, 2002 to 1.4 million as on March 31, 2007. Thus, the spread of the programme in the 13 States led to a significant decline in the share of the southern States in SHGs linked to banks.

There are several instances of SHGs that have made a positive impact on the income and employment situation of the poor.

## ASSESSMENT STUDIES

A few assessment studies have been carried out on the impact of the SBLP in India at the grass root level. **Puazhendi and Satyasai (2000)** observed a shift towards higher income slabs between pre and post-SHG situation. About 74 per cent of the sample households were below an annual income level of Rs. 22,500 during pre-SHG situation. The proportion declined to 57 per cent in the post-SHG situation indicating increased income levels. Further, involvement in the group significantly contributed to improving the self-confidence of the members. The communication with other group members also improved after association with the SHGs. The members were relatively more assertive in confronting with social evils and problematic situations.

In another assessment, **Puhazhendi and Badatya (2002)** found that availing loans from moneylenders and other informal sources with higher interest rates was significantly reduced due to SHG intervention. It was also observed that consumption oriented loans were replaced by production oriented loans during post-SHG situation.

Some studies have also indicated that the size of the loans is small and is often not sufficient to take up income generating activities. As a result, the loans are utilised for consumption purposes or for taking up subsistence-income generating activities.

## EDA Rural Systems and APMAS (2006) STUDY

The study conducted by EDA Rural Systems and APMAS (2006) brought out that a significant proportion of sampled groups (40 per cent) had a weak record of account keeping. The study pointed out that financial statements are not being regularly prepared by the SHGs. Only 28 per cent of the SHGs (22 per cent in the South and 35 per cent in the North) prepared an income and expenditure statement and an equal number of SHGs prepared a balance sheet and portfolio information. While members were usually able to provide approximate figures of total savings and total SHG loans outstanding, they were not able to provide information about profits earned or loan outstanding to banks. Further, the SHGs do not have a clear policy on how to deal with defaults or with dropouts, which formed about 10 per cent of membership.

To motivate and assist members of matured SHGs to take up income generating activities on a sustainable basis, NABARD continued to promote micro-enterprise development by SHG members. Under the Micro-Enterprise Development Programme (MEDP), 297 such programmes covering 7,579 SHG members were conducted during the year. The pilot project launched during 2005-06 for developing micro-enterprises in partnership with Marketing and Research Team (MART), is being implemented in nine districts across nine States involving 14 NGOs as 'micro-enterprise promotion agency (MEPA). During the year MEPAs completed detailed surveys of the project districts and identified existing opportunities and demand / supply patterns for farm / non-farm activities in consultation with SHG members that could be taken up for sustainable income generation in the project area. Action plan finalized by each MEPA on the basis of the survey findings, is being implemented.

To facilitate matured SHGs to meet their credit requirements of production and investments in agriculture and allied activities and to enable them to diversify their income generating activities, NABARD introduced a new line of refinance for scheduled commercial banks, RRBs and co-operative banks. Under the scheme, cent per cent refinance is provided to banks under ARF for financing term loan and cash credit limits sanctioned by them to SHGs.

## PILOT PROJECTS INTRODUCED BY NABARD

NABARD continued to implement the pilot projects launched during the earlier years. Based on its experience and in response to the Union Budget 2006-07) announcement for financing of tenant farmers by banks, NABARD formulated the scheme for financing Joint Liability Groups (JLGs) of such farmers. NABARD designed a pilot project for collaboration with Post Offices for financing SHGs which is under implementation in five districts of Tamil Nadu. As on 31 March 2007, 530 SHGs have opened saving bank accounts, of which 46 have been credit linked by the participating post offices. A pilot project for proving a social security system for SHG members was also sanctioned for implementation in two villages covering 500 poor households from Betul district of Madhya Pradesh and is being implemented through an NGO. Organisation for awareness of Integrated Social Security (OASIS) with a grant assistance of Rs. 8 lakh. During the year, Rs. 11.18 crore was utilized from the Micro-Finance Development and Equity Fund (MFDEF) for MF related activities. The Micro Financial Sector (Development and Regulation) Bill 2007 was introduced in the Lok Sabha on 20 March 2007.

The rapid development of the sector necessitated addressing the various issues associated with the sector. In October 2002, Reserve Bank set up four informal Groups to look into issues relating to: (i) structure and sustainability; (ii) funding; (iii) regulations; and (iv) capacity building of micro finance institutions. Taking into consideration the recommendations of the groups, banks were advised that they should provide adequate incentives to their branches for financing the SHGs and that the group dynamics of working of the SHGs may be left to themselves. **Innovative Approaches of SHGs.**

The self help group movement in India has gained momentum in recent years and it has been responsible for bringing in a qualitative change in the lives of thousands of people. Some of the innovative experiments in this regard are:

**Sheetal SHG. Saharanpur**, is an excellent example of people who have brought transformation in their socio economic status by determinative and collective efforts. This SHG was formed in September-2006 with the joint motivation of the Punjab National Bank and a social organisation named "SANKALP" which has been working for mainstreaming the disabled and their families. Fourteen dalit women had volunteered to become members of this SHG, of which two were disabled. They started saving Rs. 100 every month and opened their bank account with bank's branch in October 2006. NABARD helped in providing 30 days of vocational training in commercial candle making with exposure to market for purchases and sales. They were also given training for making dhoop battis and agarbattis.

Four members of this group have now started a candle making unit with the help of loan from the bank. The women now work in their spare times and are earning additional income for their families. They have become self-dependent and are confidently meeting the bank and Government officials and also travelling independently for the business requirements. The SHG has now multiplied into eight women SHGs and have recently formed a 'Mahila Manch", which is exclusively working for the economic and social upliftment of their families.

**Annapurna SHG of Tidhara village in Navsari tehsil in Gujarat** supported by Bank of Baroda consists of eleven women members from below poverty line. They were working as daily wage labourers in the village and started saving from their little earnings and opened an account with the bank branch. The group after managing to save a decent corpus of fund started catering service in the village with guidance from the bank branch. The group opened a canteen at the village panchayat office with a loan of Rs. one lakh from the bank. They also gained additional income by extending their services to various ceremonies and other occasions in the village and neighbouring areas. The group has gained popularity in the area for providing tasty and hygienic food to the locals and each group member earns a minimum of Rs. 2.500 per month.

**Pragati Mahila Sakthi Sangham of Kurakapalli village in East Godavari district of Andhra Pradesh** comprises members who worked as agricultural labours. The members took an initial loan of Rs. 25,000 from Bank of Baroda which was used for internal loaning purposes. The members then ventured into agriculture with another loan of Rs.1,80,000 after repaying the earlier loan. They took agriculture land on lease and prospered by cultivating and distributing the profits among themselves. The group has become a role model for other landless agriculture labourers in the village.

The study also pointed out that such community actions inculcated a new boldness and confidence amongst women, often putting pressure on the authorities (panchayat, district officers and police) to do their jobs, whether through petitions or by staging rallies and blockades.

Some of the States like Andhra Pradesh are trying to implement various developmental and poverty alleviation schemes through SHGs.

Micro finance has come of age in India. Although it is not a panacea for the poor, it has now developed into an important delivery mechanism for reaching the poor and achieving financial inclusion. Studies have brought out the positive impact of micro finance on participating clients. As such, its role in enhancing human capital in the long-term would be considerable. It has particularly helped women to become owners of assets, have an increased say in decision making and take up leadership positions. The challenges facing the sector are being addressed on a continuing basis, in consultation with all stakeholders.

**The World Development Report**

The World Development Report 2004 "Making Services Work for Poor People" states that often key services fail poor people in access quantity and quality. The report documents three ways in which these services can be improved. Firstly by increasing poor clients choice and participation in service delivery, so that they can monitor and discipline providers. Secondly, by raising poor citizens voice through the ballot box, and thirdly by making information widely available to all.

The SHG Bank Linkage program is a step in this direction. Microfinance is an intervention resting on social capital, a process of social intermediation whereby poor people can mobilise their savings leverage those to avail of credit, use the credit for setting up income generating projects. It rests on the pillars of compulsory savings, linking credit with savings. lending decisions by the SHG based on consensus and collective wisdom, using peer pressure and group cohesion as collateral substitutes absence of margin unit costs etc.

Loans increase incomes and savings of the poor, the taking investing and repayment of loans is transformational and empowers the poor from a sense of helplessness I can do nothing to one of "I Can", it quite simply enables the poor to work their

**Table 1: Estimates of Informal Employment in India**

| *Sl. No* | *Sector* | *Estimated number (Million)* | | |
|---|---|---|---|---|
| | | *Male* | *Female* | *Total* |
| 1 | Agriculture | | | |
| 1.1 | Rural | 138.67 | 88.06 | 226.73 |
| 1.2 | Urban | 4.91 | 3.28 | 8.19 |
| | Total | 143.58 | 91.34 | 234.92 |
| 2 | Non- Agriculture | | | |
| 2.1 | Rural | 47.46 | 13.91 | 61.37 |
| 2.2 | Urban | 53.43 | 12.36 | 65.79 |
| | Total | 110.89 | 26.27 | 127.16 |
| 3 | All India | | | |
| 3.1 | Rural | 186.13 | 101.97 | 288.10 |
| 3.2 | Urban | 58.34 | 15.64 | 73.98 |
| | Total | 244.47 | 117.61 | 362.08 |

own way out of poverty. The new paradigm in contrast to the old rural development models does not fight shy of charging

market related rates of interest, taking compulsory savings giving loans as a proportion of savings getting borrowers to repay with the lure of larger future loans and emphasising simpler procedures and the virtues of flexibility simplicity and convenience to borrowers, it enables the asset less and hard core poor to access credit from formal financial institutions to start small businesses. Studies have been conducted by GTZ, NABARD, to assess the significant role of micro finance in

**Table 2: Distribution of Employment between Organized and Unorganized Sectors Estimation of informal Employment in India Data Source ISS)**

| *Sector* | *Employment (Million)* Formal | Informal | Total |
|---|---|---|---|
| Organized | 30.66 | 25.79 | 56.45 |
| Unorganized | 4.02 | 336.29 | 340.31 |
| Total | 34.68 | 362.08 | 396.76 |

poverty alleviation. Discern the link between microfinance and the socio economic empowerment of women. To provide a comparative picture and interstate variation of performance of self help groups in India. The extent to which SHGs contribute to income smoothing and Sustainable Income generation. The degree to which it creates self employment and promotes productivity through direct income generation in the informal sector. The largest numbers of informal workers are in Agriculture. In fact, 98.84 percent of the employment in agriculture is informal. In the non-agricultural sector, the highest numbers of informal employees are in retail trade, construction, land transport, textiles etc.

Though the employment in the informal sector in India is about 340.31 million, the informal employment in the country is 362.08 million. Out of 56.45 million employees in the organized sector, about 25.79 million are informal employees. Among 340.321 million informal sector employees, 4.02 million are formal employees. The relationship between informal sector employment and informal employment is indicated in Table 2.

## SHG Post Office Linkage Programme

A pilot SHG-post office linkage programme was launched by NABARD in December 2003. This programme envisaged credit linking 200 SHGs in select 5 districts. viz., Sivaganga, Pudukottai, Tiruvannamalai, Tanjavur and Tiruvarur districts of Tamil Nadu. The objectives of the pilot programme were to (i) examine the feasibility of utilising the vast network of post offices in rural areas for disbursement of credit to rural poor on agency basis; and (ii) to test the efficacy of Department of Posts in providing micro finance services to rural clientele. The salient features of the scheme are :

(i) Post offices open savings accounts in the name of SHGs promoted by identified NGOs.

(ii) The SHGs with savings accounts in the post office and which are six months old are provided loan by the post office, in multiples of their savings, based on the rating exercise on the lines of those adopted by banks.

(iii) Post offices provide term loans to SHGs repayable within two years in 24 monthly instalments.

(iv) Post offices charge an interest of 9 per cent per annum on the loans given to SHGs using a reducing balance method.

(v) Post offices do not collect any loan processing charges or any other charges from SHGs.

(vi) Project Implementation and Monitoring Committee (PIMCs) at district and State level are constituted by the post office.

(vii) The district PIMC is responsible for smooth grounding of the project, sorting out operational issues and identification of appropriate NGOs. The PIMC meets on a quarterly basis.

(viii) State level PIMCs review overall implementation of the project, suggest new initiatives and recommend release of funds by NABARD to the Department of Posts.

(ix) Department of Posts maintain separate books of accounts for all transactions relating to utilisation and operations of Revolving Fund Assistance (RFA) from NABARD.

Under the project, NABARD would provide financial support for capacity building programmes of postal officials. While loans are given at interest rates of 9 per cent per annum to SHGs by post offices, post offices would be allowed to retain an interest margin of 3 per cent. The amount of actual interest collected from the SHGs would be shared between NABARD and post offices in the ratio of 2:1.

As at end-March 2008, an aggregate of 1,963 branch post offices/sub post offices in the identified districts are implementing the project. A total of Rs. 100 lakh has been sanctioned as FRA to the post offices by NABARD. So far 1,142 postal staff have been given training and Rs. 49 lakh has been released as loans to SHGs as of March 2008. Roll out of the pilot project in a few other States is under consideration.

## Sa-Dhan's Voluntary Mutual Code of Conduct for its Member Institutions

Sadhan is an industry body of microfinance institutions in India. It functions as a say regulatory organisation for the microfinance sector and its mentors have come together voluntarily.

In January 2007, Sa-Dhan issued a voluntary mutual code of conduct applicable to all the categories of member micro finance institutions.

## Objectives

The member institutions agree to promote and strengthen the micro finance movement in the country by bringing the low income clients to the mainstream financial sector. They also agree to build progressive, sustainable and client-centric micro finance institutions in the country to provide integrated financial services to the clients. Their aim should be to promote cooperation and coordination among micro finance institutions and other agencies to achieve higher operating standards and avoid unethical competition in order to serve the clients better.

## Integrity

The member institutions agree to:

(i) Act honestly, fairly and reasonably in conducting micro finance activities.

(ii) Conduct micro finance activities by means of fair competition, not seeking competitive of advantages through illegal or unethical micro finance practices. No officer, employee, agent or other person acting on their behalf shall take unfair advantage of anyone by manipulation, concealment, abuse of privileged information, misrepresentation of material facts or any other unfair practice.

(iii) Prominently display the core values and code of conduct on the notice board of head office and all branches and put systems in place to ensure compliance.

(iv) Ensure that their staff and all persons acting for them or on their behalf, are trained or oriented to put these values into practice.

**Transparency**

The member institutions agree to:

(i) Disclose to clients all the terms and conditions of the financial services offered in the language understood by the client.

(ii) Disclose the source of funds, costs of funds and use of surpluses to provide truthful information to clients.

(iii) Provide information to clients on the rate of interest levied on the loan, calculation of interest (monthly/quarterly/half-yearly), terms of repayment and any other information related to interest rates and other charges.

(iv) Provide information to clients on the rate of interest offered on the thrift services provided.

(v) Provide information to clients related to the premium and other fees being charged on insurance and pension services offered as intermediaries.

(vi) Provide periodical statements of the MFI's accounts to the clients.

**Fair Practices**

Member institutions are committed to follow fair practices built on dignity, respect, fair treatment, persuasion and courtesy to clients. Member institutions agreed to :

(i) Provide micro finance services to low income clients irrespective of gender, race, caste, religion or language

(ii) Ensure that the services are provided using the most efficient methods possible to enable access to financial services by low income households at reasonable cost.

(iii) Recognise their responsibility to provide financial services to clients based upon their needs and repayment capacity

(iv) Promise that, in case of loans to individual clients below Rs. 25,000, the clients shall not be asked to hand over original land titles, house pattas, ration cards, etc., as collateral security for loans, except when obtaining copies of these for fulfilling "know your customers" norms of the Reserve Bank. Only in case of loan to individual clients of Rs. 25,000 and above can obtain land titles, house pattas, vehicle RC books, as collateral security.

(v) Interact with the clients in an acceptable language and dignified manner and spare no efforts in fostering clients' confidence and long term relationship.

(vi) Maintain decency and decorum during the visit to the clients' place for collection of dues.

(vii) Avoid inappropriate occasions such as bereavement in the family or such other calamitous occasions for making calls/ visits to collect dues.

(viii) Avoid any demeanour that would suggest any kind of threat or violence.

(ix) Emphasise using social collateral which includes various forms of peer assurance such as lending through groups and group guarantees at the village, hamlet or neighbourhoold level, or guarantees by relatives, friends, neighbours or business associates; and explain clearly to clients what the obligations of social collateral are.

**Governance**

(i) Observe high standards of governance, ensuring fairness, integrity and transparency by inducting persons with good and sound reputation, as members of board of directors. The MFI should ensure that the majority of the directors are independent directors and/or duly elected representatives of the community served, and that the board would be involved in all policy formulation and other important decisions.

(ii) Ensure transparency in the maintenance of books of accounts and reporting/presentation and disclosure of financial statements by qualified auditor/s.

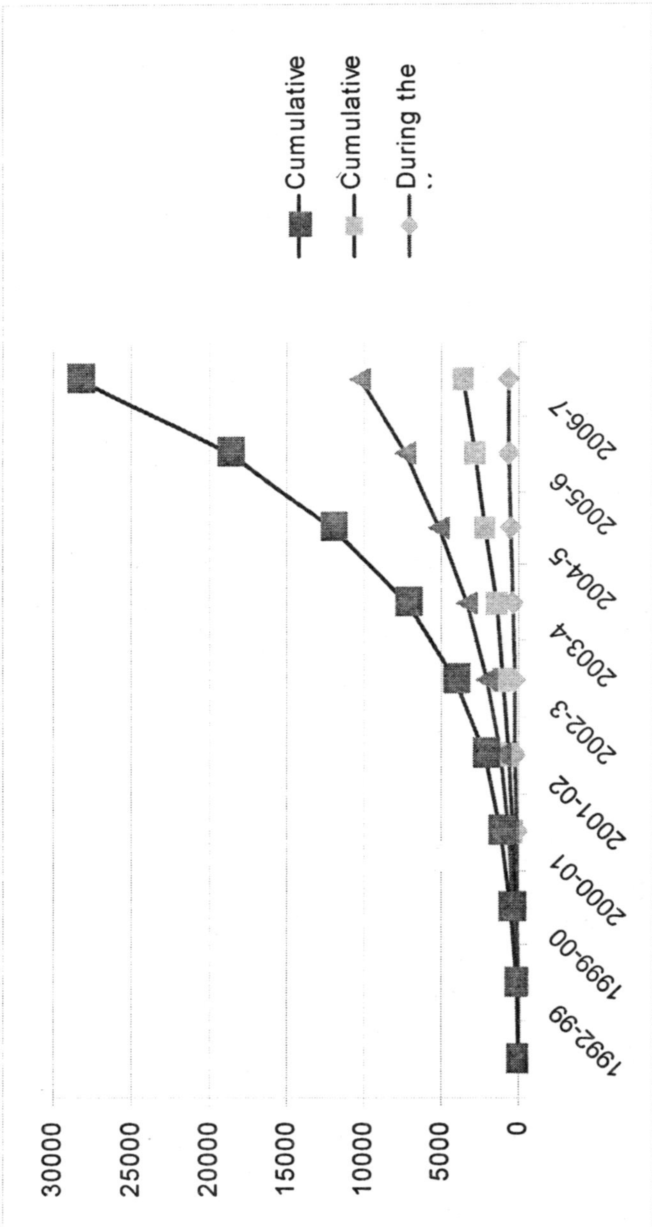


*Source*: NABARD

The engagement of banks is showing a steady increase.

(iii) Put in the best efforts to follow the Audit and Assurance Standards issued by the Institute of Chartered Accountants of India (ICAI).

(iv) Place before the board of directors, a compliance report indicating the extent of compliance with this voluntary mutual code of conduct, specifically indicating any deviations and reasons therefore, at the end of every half financial year.

**Feedback/Grievance Mechanisms**

(i) Establish effective and efficient feedback mechanisms.

(ii) Take steps to correct any errors and handle complaints speedily and efficiently.

Wherever a complainant is not satisfied with the outcome of the investigation into her complaint, she should be notified of her right to refer the matter to the Ethics and Grievance Redressal Committee constituted by Sa-Dhan.

Thus the basic objectives of the SHG Bank linkage program are as follows.

To evolve a supplementary strategy for meeting the credit needs of the poor by combining the flexibility, sensitivity and responsiveness of the informal credit system with the strength of administrative and technical capabilities and financial resources of the formal credit institutions.

To build mutual trust and confidence and bridges of understanding between the bankers and the rural poor.

To encourage banking activity both on thrift as well as credit in a segment of the population that the formal financial institutions usually find difficult to cover.

SHGs help to generate and collect small thrift amounts from a cross section of the people hitherto considered incapable of possessing the ability to save.

SHGs have facilitated the rural poor in fulfilling their credit requirements both for meeting emergent consumption needs as well as production requirements requiring a small outlay of funds.

The government sponsored poverty alleviation programs have a structured format unlike those under SHG linkage program hence the SHGs have been able to undertake self chosen activities.

SHG lending is treated as Priority sector lending for weaker sections this has encouraged Banks to treat the linkage program as a business opportunity and part of corporate strategy.

## EMERGING POLICY CONCERNS

1. The group promotion process is very long and the poor have to wait for a long time before they are able to get a loan of reasonable amount to enable them to utilise it gainfully for setting up an Income generating project initially only small loans are admissible which go in consumption or in meeting lifestyle needs. The group promotion process is arduous and a costly exercise it requires grants and other assistance as also a capable NGO who can enable this facilitation. The functioning of the group depends on group dynamics peer pressure etc. conflicts have to be managed and can arise for the most trivial reasons it becomes difficult to maintain group cohesiveness if there are major fault lines appearing hence the NGO has to be especially skilled. Exclusively women's groups face interference from male members sometimes leading to group breakdowns several NGOs have a broad agenda for taking up a variety of programs and a lack of focus on microfinance can also sometimes serve to dilute the primary purpose of the group.

   There is Inadequate handholding support to SHGs which is needed in the areas of Financial literacy and numeracy, basic book keeping and maintenance of records/registers Book keeping, is a critical though neglected area Groups mintain base books but need assistance to draw up P&L A/cs and Balance Sheets. Training and Capacity Building remain major issues.

2. Groups need help in setting up Income generating projects and in deployment of idle cash funds assistance is also needed in Project formulation, Undertaking economic activities to ensure that groups are able to take up sustainable Income generating projects one of the major reasons for groups breaking up and defaulting in repayment of their instalments was the inability to engage in sustainable income generating projects. The loans must translate to profits more than the equivalent of the minimum wages. Marketing linkages are necessary to enable groups to scale up. Small SHGs fail to capture markets for their products hindrances can range from transportation, to packaging, to incorrect marketing strategies.
3. The interest rates are high some instances of ever greening and bullet repayments from savings accounts of groups by banks have been reported. in few cases of the present sample (14%) pernicious practices as ever greening and Bullet repayment have been reported but due cognizance must be taken of these so they remain the exception rather than the norm.
4. Interest Rates on internal loans are high, these are set by groups and contribute to group corpus but multiple membership of groups has to be guarded against as that can make the burden of debt unsustainable.
5. The groups perception that internal loans are cheaper and easier to avail than the Bank loans due to their convenience, reliability, flexibility and sustainability needs change Banks must work to simplify their lending procedures, minimize paperwork and create better awareness of their products and services. They need tie ups with insurance companies and to offer composite insurance productslife, health, livestock, asset suited to the needs of m SHGs sensitization of Bankers is essential.
6. The Social impact of the program is higher as compared to its Economic impact.

Efforts must be made to increase the economic impact through income generating projects and scaling up the average size of the loans.

7. **The Pressure of Multiple Loans.** Easy availability of loans from various sources puts inordinate pressure on the borrowers and proves to be exploitive as the borrower is unable to service the daunting mountain of debt.
8. **Target Orientation of Banks/Ngo/MFI**
Most Banks, NGOs, MFIs Facilitators, animators etc. engaged in the sector are target oriented and willing to give the heave ho to actual levels of poverty alleviation or empowerment. Grant funds depend on quantifiable factors measured in terms of the number of participants, money saved repayment rates the degree to which as the root cause of marginalisation, the deprivation of power, the lack of control over resources remain sadly unaddressed.
9. **Actual Profitability of Micro Enterprises**
None of microenterprises set up with the loans availed have translated to profits in excess of the minimum wages.
10. **Lack of Extension Support**
In some instances the Loans are not backed by broader supports as technical assistance and business planning forward and backward linkages so essential to turn all loans to success stories.
11. **Marketing Support** Small SHGs fail to capture the market for their products. Difficulties extend from the lack of ability to envisage and formulate appropriate marketing strategies to packaging and transportation. Credit requirement of the marginalised especially those considered as "Below the Poverty Line" [BPL] are tried to be addressed through different schematic tie ups with a tagged in subsidy component. Thinking process in the planning and execution of such schematic linkages goes in a line of making BPL families, as unit of intervention, economically viable through such links and promote income-generating activities. But frequent household

credit needs for various reasons remained out cf purview of such operations in-spite of broad network of regional rural banks [RRB] and cooperatives.

Formal institutional credit availability and in time credit accessibility for commons remained a distant possibility in most of the rural areas. Such hindering factors gradually pushed "the families at the need of credit" to informal money lending system resulting indebtedness and repayment of usurious rate of interest with the cost of their prevailing family asset base

12. The success of the program clearly rests on the quality of groups and the task of promoting, nurturing monitoring and strengthening groups remains critical for sustainability, empowerment and development.

After the micro credit summit 1997 and after Mohd Yunus secured the nobel prize in 2008 a revolution of interest has been awakened in the microfinance movement bringing it firmly to the center stage. "If you are extremely poor ,you don't care for anything because your survival is an overriding concern. Once you go beyond that level and don't worry about your immediate survival, then you look around and help in preserving the environment, the community and the nation."

## References

1. Report on Trends and Progress of Banking 2007-08.
2. Sa-Dhan, 2007, Core Values and Voluntary Mutual Code of Conduct for Micro Finance Institutions, available on www.sa-dhan.net/Resources/corevalues/pdf.
3. SHG Bank Linkage in India Empowerment and Sustainability Meera Lal (20007).
4. Marguerite S Robinson The Micro finance revolution Sustainable Finance for the Poor.
5. Hulme David and Paul Mosley 91996) Finance Against Poverty Vol. I and II london Routledge.

6. Harper Malcolm (2002) Indian Self Help Groups and Grameen Groups A comparative analysis Freinds of Womens World Banking Ahmedabad.
7. Rurtherford Stuart (2000) The Poor and their Money Oxford University Press new delhi.
8. Social Banking Deepali Pant Joshi Foundation Books (Cambridge Books) 2006.
9. Employment and Poverty Alleviation Programmes in India An Appraisal editor KK Bagchi.
10. SHG BANK Linkage in India Empowerment and Sustainability Meera Lal.
11. Bhattacharya D Jayal N Mohapatra B Pai S ed (2004) Micro studies in Rural India Sage Publications.

# 4

# "Banks Delivery of Microfinance through the District Central Cooperative Banks and the Regional Rural Banks"

Reserve Bank issued comprehensive guidelines to banks in February, 2000 for mainstreaming micro credit and enhancing the outreach of micro credit providers. These guidelines, inter alia, stipulated that micro credit extended by banks to individual borrowers directly or through any intermediary would henceforth be reckoned as part of their priority sector lending. The banks were given freedom to formulate their own model[s] or choose any conduit/intermediary for extending micro credit. Banks were also permitted to prescribe their own lending norms so as to provide maximum flexibility in regard to micro lending. Such credit was to cover not only consumption and production loans for various farm and non-farm activities of the poor but also include their other credit needs. Banks were asked to delegate adequate sanctioning powers to branch managers and to keep the loan procedures and documents simple for providing prompt and hassle-free micro credit. The lesson from Indonesia was that banks could also work well with small borrowers, provided the interest rates were remunerative and deregulated.

The Indonesian experience shows powerfully that DCCBs and Regional Rural Banks as they operate at the grassroots level, close to and familiar with the rural clientele can serve as ideal vehicles for the delivery of microfinance to the poor clientele as they have a feel and familiarity with the rural areas and also possess the commercial knowledge and managerial expertise of formal banks. Their strength also lies in that they are closely regulated institutions and thereby attract borrowers.

**Regional Rural Banks**

Post-merger, RRBs, with 14494 branches 84 RRBs also add given the strategic positioning of the Regional Rural banks (RRBs) the Reserve Bank has advised their sponsor Banks to speedily and fully implement core banking solution (CBS) in all RRBs and commit to a firm timeline not later than September 2011, the adoption of CBS will enable the RRBs to make greater progress under the SHG linkage program and this will increase their role in the Microfinance segment, represent a powerful instrument for financial inclusion. Their role and relevance in financial inclusion is crucial as:

In rural areas, they account for 37% of total offices of all Scheduled Commercial Banks.

91% of the total workforce in RRBs is posted in rural and semi-urban areas as compared to 38% for other Scheduled Commercial Banks.

In rural areas, RRBs account for 31% of deposit accounts and 19% of deposit amount of all Scheduled Commercial Banks. Lower average deposit amount per account in RRBs as compared with commercial banks implies their better reach to small depositors.

Share of RRBs in loan accounts is an impressive 37% in rural areas.

Of all the scheduled commercial banks, RRBs account for 34% of branches in NE, 30% in Eastern and 32% in Central regions. Incidentally, these regions manifest financial exclusion of a high order.

Of the total 29.25 lakh SHGs credit linked by the banking system (as on 31 March 2007), 31% linkage is done by RRBs. More significantly, the more backward a region, greater is the share of RRBs. In North Eastern Region, it is 56%, Central region 48% and Eastern region 40%.

RRBs have also played a significant role as Self Help Promoting Institutions (SHPIs). As many as 104 RRBs (31 March 2006) are functioning as SHPIs with grant assistance from NABARD.

Keeping the above in view, the following recommendations are made for RRBs by the **Rangarajan Committee.**

Recommendations:

RRBs should extend their services to unbanked areas and increase their credit to deposit (CD) Ratio. The post merger scenario of RRBs poses a series of challenges for them and these are to be addressed. The following areas would require attention from the point of view of financial inclusion:

Setting exclusive targets for microfinance and financial inclusion

Providing funding support and

Providing technology support.

Strategic microfinance plan with NABARD support

RRBs have the potential and capability to emerge as niche operators in microfinance. They are playing a major role in the SHG-Bank Linkage Programme especially also as SHPIs. Their dual role has special meaning in areas which face severe financial exclusion and which do not have a sufficient presence of well performing NGOs. However, to upscale the programme to a level where it can really make a visible impact, RRBs need handholding particularly in the areas of training, promotion and development. NABARD may provide required assistance.

NABARD should prepare a strategic action plan RRB-wise, for promotion and credit linkage of SHGs. RRBs may be asked to form, nurture and credit link at least 3,000 SHGs in districts covered by them in North-Eastern, Eastern and Central Regions. a Memorandum of Understanding (MoU) may be signed by RRBs with NABARD for a period of 5 years - with NABARD providing the promotional and development assistance out of the "Financial Inclusion Promotion and "Development Fund" and RRBs forming, nurturing and providing financial services to SHGs. RRBs may accomplish the task with the support of individual rural volunteers, Business facilitators, their staff members, etc. NABARD may closely monitor the programme - with focus on qualitative aspects.

## NATIONAL RURAL FINANCIAL INCLUSION PLAN (NRFIP) for RRBs

The strategy recommended for NRFIP for commercial banks would be equally applicable for RRBs. They would require promotional, funding and technology support in different areas as outlined below. RRBs may endeavour to cover a large part of their incremental lending through the group mode (SHGs/JLGs) as it will enhance their outreach to financially excluded. Lending through group mode would also keep NPAs at low level.

Pilot testing of BF/BC Model by RRBs The RRBs should adopt the major model of BF/BC as a major strategy of financial Inclusion as also a technologically relevant model. RRBs may need some handholding for implementing the proposal. The committee has suggested that the NABARD may identify 10 RRBs across the country giving greater weight age to regions manifesting higher levels of financial exclusion and work in strategic alliance with these RRBs and their sponsor banks in implementing the proposal. The RRBs would also need a core banking software for integration of the technology model proposed RRBs operating in predominantly tribal areas with high levels of exclusion may prepare annual credit plans with a separate component for meeting the needs of excluded groups.

**Computerisation**

To facilitate the seamless integration of RRBs with the main payments systems there is a need to provide computerisation support to them. Banks are eligible for funding from the Financial Inclusion funds on a matching contribution of 50% in regard to districts other than tribal districts and 75% in case of tribal districts located under the sub plan.

**Strengthening Boards of Management**

Post merger the boards of RRBS need to be strengthened and powers delegated to them on policy and business operations.

**Cooperatives in SHG Bank Linkage**

There are a large number of PACS (Primary Agricultural Credit Societies) and primary cooperatives located in rural areas where there are no other financial service outlets many of the cooperatives are in districts where the District Central Cooperative Banks DCCBs are moribund or defunct Such PACS provide valuable services to their members if they get access to a commercial bank This is feasible as RBI has deemed cooperatives as eligible institutions under the BC/BF model. The BF model can also be used to organise vulnerable groups.

**Rural Credit Cooperatives in India**

Rural credit cooperatives in India have a very long history. Democratic in features, the cooperative movement was envisaged as a mechanism for pooling the resources of people with small means and providing them with access to different financial services. In the backdrop of the reform process underway for cooperative banks, they have a very significant role to play in facilitating greater inclusion.

In 14 states the Cooperatives are active under the SHG Bank linkage program. In Kerala the cooperatives are extremely active they have successfully meshed the sensitivity and responsiveness to the needs of poor borrowers of the informal credit system with the administrative capabilities of formal financial systems. Some successfull and not so well known examples are of Shreyas which is the official social development organization of the Malankara Catholic Diocese of Bathery to uplift the poor and marginalized. It is one of the leading NGOs working in South India for the development of Marginal Farmers, Tribal, Women, Children and Senior Citizen. It was started in the year 1979 and got registered in 1986 under the Societies Registration Act, 1860. The program area of Shreyas spread over 15 civil districts of Kerala, Tamil Nadu and Karnataka. The whole operational area is divided into 11 Regions consisting of 107 Units for effective management and active participation. At present 2760 Self Help Groups are catering the needs of 46646 poor and marginalized families There are several examples of successful micro finance delivery through Banks and DCCBS.

The Urban Cooperative Bank Model is almost synonymous with the Self Employed Women's Association the SEWA Bank in Ahmedabad and the Cuttack Urban Cooperative Bank in Orissa. The Mutually Aided Cooperatives Societies Act has also considerably facilitated the process of cooperatives active engagement with microfinance.

The MACs Act essentially allows greater flexibility to cooperatives to frame their own bye laws and the operations and management of cooperatives is then conducted as per those bye laws it drastically reduces the role of the Registrar of cooperative societies.

1. Greater flexibility to cooperatives to frame their own bye laws operations and management of cooperatives to be conducted according to Bye laws.
2. Role of the Registrar of Cooperatives reduced.
3. Rule making power of the government abolished.
4. Admission, disqualification and expulsion of members are the sole prerogative of cooperatives.

Members alone can contribute share capital non member including government share capital forbidden greater flexibility in mobilisation and utilisation of funds cooperatives allowed setting up subsidiary organisations. The SEWA Bank is registered as an Urban Cooperative Bank with a license from the RBI. It commenced operation in 1974 with 4000 shareholding members. Self-employed women (like hawkers, vendors, weavers, potters, beedi-rollers, agarbattirollers, pappad-rollers, manual laborers and service providers) have insecure employment and earn much less than organized sector workers. They also have no support for their work, or for themselves in times of difficulties. SEWA has enjoyed spectacular success. A cooperative Bank definitely has several advantages over an NBFC still it is not wholly an untrammelled subject as it is under the dual control exercised by the RBI and the Registrar of Cooperative Societies. Among the Local Area Banks active in this area of microfinance delivery. The Krishna Bhima Samruddhi Local Area Bank headquartered in Mahbubnagar extends microfinance in its areas of operations. Among the District Cooperative Banks as BIDAR DCCB have shown the way for active involvement under the SHG Bank linkage program about 40% of SHGS in district Bidar are promoted by Bidar DCCB utilising the grant assistance extended by NABARD for promotion of SHGs in order to take up training and capacity building on a regular basis. The bank has also established a separate training centre Sahakara Rural Development Academy (SAHARDA) at its headquarters in Bidar the Primary Agricultural Credit societies are also engaged in the exercise which has had a very salutary effect on their business development. An in-house study conducted by the Bidar DCCB in 2002 which studied the operations of four PACS at Dhannur, Koutha, Kolar (K) and Andura found positive correlates in DCCB business growth commensurable with their engagement with the SHG Bank Linkage program. In the model the PACS earn a commission of 1 per cent on SHG loans. The deposits outstanding in the SHG accounts were low cost resources

**Grant Support to Cooperative Banks Functioning as SHPIs as on 31.3.08 Rs. lakh**

| *State* | *District* | *Year of sanction* | *SHG to be promoted* | *Grant sanction* | *Grant released* | *SHG promoted* | *SHG Linked* |
|---|---|---|---|---|---|---|---|
| Rajasthan | Barmer | 2006-7 | 500 | 7.50 | 1.74 | 239 | 239 |
| Sikkim State Cooperative Bank West Geyzing | West Sikkim | 2004-05 | 10 | 0.11 | 0.04 | 11 | 0 |
| West Bengal | Burdwan | 2003-4 | 1000 | 6.00 | 4.45 | 1080 | 492 |
| Madhya Pradesh | Mandsaur | 2004-05 | 1000 | 7.00 | 3.28 | 1046 | 186 |
| Uttaranchal | Nainital | 2003-04 | 300 | 3.00 | 0.60 | 300 | 300 |
| Gujarat | Mehsana DCCB | 2005-06 | 500 | 5.00 | 3.88 | 500 | 172 |
| Maharashtra | Gadchiroli | 2003-4 | 500 | 3.50 | 3.39 | 500 | 500 |
| Karnataka | Uttar Kannada | 2004-05 | 500 | 5.00 | 4.17 | 510 | 275 |
| Kerala | Alapuzha | 2004-05 | 500 | 4.75 | 3.53 | 500 | 500 |

**Data Source NABARD Stastics Micro Finance in India 2007-08 pp. 169 and 170.**

available to PACS which they could effectively utilise for business development yielding an interest margin of 10% The growth in total deposits of PACS from 1998 to 2002 was higher than that of the DCCB branches SHG savings constituted more than 90% of total savings bank deposits of PACS as PACS members found the SHG members came regularly to deposit funds their Microfinance DCCBs /RRBs customer service bar was raised and the number of profit making PACs increased from 91 to 131 the overall recovery percentage also climbed to 95%. In sum the PACs became the Banks for the SHGs. We find across the country DCCBs are fast emerging as SHPI in the SHG Bank linkage program as per table.

Thus there is great hope for the success of the DCCB model.

- Microfinance is an ideal approach for reaching the poor for providing the requisite amount of credit without the hassles and paper work associated with the conventional loan sanction but also to provide other support services to bring about improvement in the socio-economic status of poor.

The BIDAR DCCB included SHGs as nominal members of PACs to extend its outreach under the SHG Bank Linkage Program. It created an SHG cell at its Head Office. 3 Officers of the NGO, MYRADA were appointed to manage it. NABARD provided grant assistance of 5.54 lakh for establishment of an SHG Cell in the DCCB and promotion and linkage of SHGs through the DCCB, for the purpose of loans were given in Bhogsa branch (villages in the command area of the branch and in Basavakalyan Taluka area. The bank also took a major policy decision to cover all the poor families in the district.

1. Criteria adopted by bank in SHG formation by DCCB.
2. Homogeneity and affirming of the members while forming the groups.
3. The number of members in each group should be between 15 and 20.

4. Only one member per family should be covered in the SHG.
5. For the first 3 months emphasis is placed on regularity of meetings - 100% participation, regular savings and regular remittance to the bank.
6. The concept training of 3-6 months is arranged for all group members in the training emphasis is placed on internal lending and book writing.
7. Grading of groups is done before group linkage.
8. All transactions and discussions should be done in the meetings only.

   Maintenance of Books of Account
   (i) Membership Admission Register
   (ii) Receipt Book
   (iii) Minutes Book
   (iv) Cash Book
   (v) Savings Register
   (vi) Individual savings cum loan book
   (vii) Loan Ledger
   (viii) General Ledger

Literate members of the group maintain books or an animator from the village maintains the books.

Microfinance has emerged as an important mechanism to reach out financial services to the poor. There are interesting lessons from this for the banks to adopt. There are problems for the microfinance institutions in the form of regulatory and supervisory apathy. This leads to financial exclusion of large segments of the poor. There is a huge market for financial services — both loans and savings. Innovations across the world indicate important breakthroughs in delivery of financial services. These can be implemented provided the regulatory impediments are removed. The issue of risk management has to be systematically addressed. The role of the state, wherever positive, has been effective and, therefore, this should be sharply defined to see how the state could contribute to this sector.

Barriers to access to finance continue to be vexatious and need to be addressed. Rural finance has suffered from

**Barriers to Financial Intermediation**

| *Formal Financial Intermediation* | *Barriers* | *Clients* |
|---|---|---|
| | Physical Factors<br>Few roads, rails etc | Women<br>Landless and small holders resettled persons indigenous persons low income persons in remote or subsistence areas |
| Banks | Few Markets<br>Few bank branches<br>Subsistence economy with little market activity<br>Low population density rugged terrain<br>Socioeconomic characteristics of clients<br>Illiteracy cannot read or fill out forms, Absence of numeracy skills<br>Poverty no land or other assets to pledge as collateral<br>Caste ethnicity hinders interaction with formal structures gender seclusion or restriction of interaction with non kin no land to offer as collateral | |

| *Formal Financial Intermediation* | *Barriers* | *Clients* |
|---|---|---|
| Lack of Business Model | There is an Absence of Margin of profit in such poor banking. While loan administration Costs of Small loans are high and Overheads Cost of a brick and Mortor bank branch, salaries of Staff are also high. | |

interventions from the state in the past. While some interventions have been positive, they have harmed the sector when compromises such as write-offs have been made. Microfinance has emerged as an important mechanism to reach out financial services to the poor. There are interesting lessons from this for the banks to adopt. There are problems for the microfinance institutions in the Microfinance DCCBs /RRBs in the form of regulatory and supervisory apathy. This leads to financial exclusion of large segments of the poor. There is a huge market for financial services — both loans and savings. Innovations across the world indicate important breakthroughs in delivery of financial services. These can be implemented provided the regulatory impediments are removed. The issue of risk management has to be systematically addressed. The role of the state, wherever positive, has been effective and, therefore, this should be sharply defined to see how the state could contribute to this sector.

The issue of interest rates continues to be vexatious and needs to be addressed.

PACS –SHG linkage Holds promise to extend this outreach in a country dominated by small or marginal landholdings the reach of the cooperative system is much deeper than other institutional arrangements in the rural areas the uniqueness of the PACs SHG model are that it takes an already rural member owned institution and further broadens and deepens its access the linkage also expands the coverage for women especially of the lower castes As the institutional credit delivery system expands it brings down the compulsion for the poor to turn to the informal sector for credit a combination of micro lending by larger and more efficient MFIs and direct lending by the Banks would help meet the financial needs of the vast majority of the poor.

Regional Rural Banks have an important role to play in extension of microfinance post merger there are 86 Regional Rural Banks with 14494 branches 91 per cent of their total workforce is posted in the rural and semi urban areas as against

38 percent of other scheduled commercial banks RRBs have played an important role as Self Help Promoting Institutions (SHPIs) with grant assistance from NABARD Regional Rural Banks should extend their services to hitherto unbanked regions RRBS had savings banks accounts of 13,86,838 SHGs 27.7 per cent and savings bank amounts of 1166.49 crore (31%) Of the total 29.25 lakh SHGs credit linked by the banking system as on 31 March 2007 31 per cent linkage is attributable to the RRBs the more backward a region the greater the share of RRBs In the North eastern region it is 56 per cent Central Region 48 per cent and Eastern region 40 per cent. They should formulate a microfinance plan and extend penetrative outreach in the districts under their command areas and exploit their natural knowledge feel and familiarity with the rural areas to extend outreach. A few studies have examined lending to self-help groups by some commercial banks and regional rural banks and found it to be profitable. For instance, Bank of Baroda, one of the largest public banks most involved in lending to self-help groups, had a regular repayment rate of nearly 100 per cent and reasonable transaction costs, so the total cost of this lending was not higher than for large loans. Oriental Bank of Commerce, a small public bank, has also developed profitable lending to self-help groups Bank of Madura, an old private commercial bank, has found the self-help program so satisfactory that it has made it part of its strategy for achieving viability in its 104 rural branches. Bank of Madura, now part of the large private ICICI Bank, highlights the importance of finding innovative solutions to cut the costs associated with the program and confirms the privileged role played by the private sector in innovating. Bank of Madura expects its self-help group lending to become profitable even without using NABARD refinancing.

## References

1. Report of the Committee on Financial Inclusion January 2008.
2. Joshi Deepali Pant The Financial Inclusion Imperative Foundation Books 2009.

# 5

# "Microfinance and Empowerment of Women –Key Issues and Challenges"

Microfinance programs have proved very effective in improving women's access to financial resources and a cost effective way to bring down household expenses thereby ameliorating poverty and helping to ease the dual burden which women bear of being poor, and being women. Studies of the Grameen Bank in Bangladesh have shown that the net benefits of lending to women are far greater than those of lending to men. The benefits of lending to women have been computed by researchers and have shown the marked impact on lives of women in terms of increased household expenditure, improved nutrition for their families, access to education for their children, better access to housing hygiene and sanitation, better housing and reduced rates of birth and of infant child mortality. All of this leads to empowerment and the increasing confidence of women giving them a voice in their families, their communities, in social and political activities. Their major constraint was lack of access to institutional finance rather than the wage labour market; microfinance dramatically eases that constraint this is the signal achievement of microfinance. Self employment opportunities for women create economic and social empowerment in the long run.

A large number of the very poor especially women remain outside the ambit of the formal financial system caught in the vicious cycle of low savings, low investment capacity and low income generation.

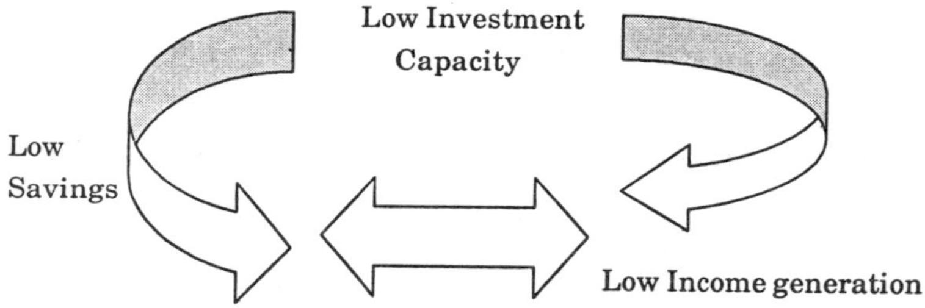


Banks and formal finance institutions are hesitant to lend down market to serve the needs of low income women headed households. Due to lack of access to property women are unable to furnish collateral required by Banks. Access to land credit, cattle and technical know are determinants and the central indicators of the economic position and development status of women. SHGs are participant oriented and collective /group initiatives that enable women to become more self reliant. For poorer women staying home as a personal preference is no longer viable they move in and out of employment as financial need, domestic circumstances and job opportunities dictate. Microfinance works on Social Capital. The World Bank has now recognised social capital as the fourth capital in the production function with physical, natural and human capital Robert Putnam 1993 has defined social capital as having features of social organisations such as trust, norms of reciprocity and networks of civil engagement that can improve the efficiency of society by facilitating coordinated actions. According to Sebstad 1996 an important aspect and development at the community level involves the building of social capital whereby members of the community mutually encourage each other. Social capital links individuals, enterprises and households to each other through two related channels information and reputation. The building of social capital further increases the contribution of savings and credit provision to women's empowerment. Through enhancing their ability to increase incomes, negotiate change in the household and engage in collective social and political activity. Social capital enables access to the limited resources for the rural poor. Women in particular are more anxious about access rather than the cost of credit Group based microfinance has significant positive externalities favouring women. It aids in poverty eradication and women empowerment in equal measure through a series of interlinked contracts and mutually reinforcing virtuous spirals. Official data show that the very poor possess few natural physical and financial assets consequently they remain severely dependent on their human and social capital to survive and improve their livelihood position. Due to high illiteracy, high drudgery irregular casual employment accumulation of human capital is rendered difficult. Through reliance on those similarly placed.

They are enabled to escape poverty and the poverty ratios which historically are high among the scheduled castes tribes and the traditionally marginalised. National Sample Survey Organisations 43rd survey revealed that rural women combine a wide range of other occupations along with household work to supplement the income of the household. The NSSO survey reflects that a large percentage of rural women in the age group of 15 years and above who are usually engaged in household work are willing to accept work at their household premises 29.3%, in activities such as dairy 9.5% poultry 3% cattle rearing, spinning and weaving, 3.45 tailoring 6.1 percent and manufacturing of wood and cane products etc. Amongst the women surveyed 27.55 rural women were seeking regular full time work 65.3 per cent were seeking part time work to start or to carry such work forward 53.6 per cent women wanted initial finance on easy terms and 22.2 per cent wanted working capital facilities as can be seen from Table.

| *Assistance required by women marginal workers seeking work at household premises* | *Percentage of women seeking assistance* |
|---|---|
| No assistance | 2.1 |
| Initial Finance on easy terms | 53.6 |
| Working Capital facilities | 22.2 |
| Raw materials availability | 4.6 |
| Marketing | 1.7 |
| Training | 10.5 |
| Accommodation | 0.4 |
| Other assistance | 4.9 |
| Total | 100 |

*Source.* NSS 43rd round.

This is corroborated by the 2001 census which showed that of 89.23 million marginal workers 54.96 million were women of 80.92 million rural marginal workers 51.11 were females. Thus women form a large segment of microcredit clientele.

Since the 1950s, various governments in India have experimented with a large number of grant and subsidy based poverty alleviation programmes. Studies show that these mandatory and dedicated subsidised financial programmes, implemented through banking institutions, have not been fully successful in meeting their social and economic objectives:

The common features of these programmes were:

(i) targetting

(ii) based on grant/subsidy, and

(iii) credit linkage through commercial banks.

These programmes

(a) were often not sustainable

(b) perpetuated the dependent status of the beneficiaries

(c) depended ultimately on government employees for delivery

(d) led to misuse of both credit and subsidy and
(e) were treated at best as poverty alleviation interventions.

Banks too never really looked on them as a profitable and commercial activity.

According to a 1995 World Bank estimate, in most developing countries the formal financial system reaches only the top 25% of the economically active population - the bottom 75% have no access to financial services apart from moneylenders- Success stories in neighbouring countries, like Grameen Bank in Bangladesh, Bank Rakyat in Indonesia, Commercial and Industrial Bank in Phillipines, etc., gave further boost to the concept in India in the 1980s. The Global Summit on Micro Finance held in Washington in Feb '97 gave an additional boost to the movement.

In India too the formal financial institutions have not been able to reach the poor households, and particularly women, in the unorganised sector. Structural rigidities and overheads lead to high cost of making small loans.

## Organisational Microfinance and Empowerment of Women

The credit culture especially of the formal financial institutions has not been oriented towards recognising the poor as credit worthy. The problem has been compounded by low level of influence of the poor, either about their credit worthiness or their demand for savings services. Micro-finance programmes have often been implemented by large banks at government behest. Low levels of recovery have been further eroded due to loan waiver programmes leading to institutional disenchantment with lending to small borrowers.

Women have traditionally been treated inequitably and denied equal access to resources. **Resources provide the material levers through which gender asymmetries are sustained**. Thus women are not a part of the formal credit markets SHG'S enable a mass participation of women from the poorer sections at the grassroots level and allows women to pool together small savings and access large sums leading to economic social and eventually political empowerment. With both peer pressure and peer support they can monitor the use of loan proceeds and enforce repayment of loan. All this has led to the popularity of the concept of micro-credit for the poorest segment along with a new set of credit delivery techniques. With the support of NGOs an informal sector comprising small Self Help Groups (SHGs) started mobilizing savings of their members and lending these resources among the members on a micro scale. The potential of these SHGs to develop as local financial intermediaries to reach the poor has gained recognition due to their community based participatory approach and Microfinance and empowerment of women.

Sustainability - recovery rates have been significantly higher than those achieved by commercial banks inspite of loans going to poor, unorganised individuals without security or collateral. SHG banking program, leveraging the strength of the formal banking system and the flexibility of informal self-help groups in providing adequate financial services to the rural poor. Through NGOs, government agencies and banks, vast numbers of self-help groups have been established in recent years: as self-reliant autonomous local financial intermediaries. 85% of the members are women; they have proven to be the better savers, borrowers and investors. Most of them are from the lowest Strata and other disadvantaged groups. The SHGs mobilize their own savings, transform them into loans to members and plough their earnings from interest income back into equity. On that basis, SHGs and banks enter into commercial relations of mutual benefit, with low bank and client transaction costs and negligible risks. In the absence of interest rate restrictions and with repayment rates >99%, SHG banking is highly viable. SHGs play a major role in poverty alleviation in rural India As poor women bar those belonging to migratory tribes, due to societal obligations, do not have the freedom to migrate in search of wage employment it is essential for them to have employment avenues and income generating opportunities in situ. The savings credit focus of the SHG Bank linkage program enables them to enjoy some control over capital this is albeit limited but better than no control.

## DEMAND FOR MICROFINANCE

The poor in India define the micro-finance market. The Planning Commission estimate of 1993-94 says 36% of the population or 320 million people live below the poverty line - there would be 140-150 million women alone living below the poverty line. Assuming that only 30% of the country's poor women are ready to adopt micro-finance as a method of poverty alleviation, it is estimated that 40-45 million poor women would need credit.

As against this, it is estimated that all agencies in India engaged in the provision of micro-finance services, would have together covered barely 1 million poor people by the close of 1998-99.

The most prominent national level micro-finance apex organisation providing micro-finance services for women in India is the National Credit Fund for Women or the Rashtriya Mahila Kosh (RMK).

## CONCEPT AND FEATURES OF MICRO-FINANCE THROUGH THE RASHTRIYA MAHILA KOSH

Micro-finance, as is being practiced by the National Credit Fund for Women or the Rashtriya Mahila Kosh (RMK), could be defined as a set of services comprising the following activities :

(a) *Micro-credit:* Small loans; primarily for income generation activities, but also for consumption and contingency needs.

(b) *Micro-savings*: thrift or small savings from borrowers'own resources.

The main features of the micro-finance services being provided by **RMK** are:

1. It is a tool for empowerment of the poorest; the higher the income and better the asset position of the borrower, the lower the incremental benefit from further equal doses of micro-credit is likely to be.
2. Delivery is normally through Self Help Groups (SHGs).
3. It is essentially for promoting self-employment; the opportunities of wage employment are limited in developing countries - micro finance increases the productivity of self-employment in the informal sector of the economy - generally used for (a) direct income generation (b) rearrangement of assets and liabilities for the household to participate in future opportunities and (c) consumption smoothing.
4. It is not just a financing system, but a tool for social change, specially for women - it does not spring from market forces alone - it is potentially welfare enhancing - there is a public interest in promoting the growth of micro finance - this is what makes it acceptable as a valid goal for public policy. Because micro credit is aimed at the poorest, micro-finance lending technology needs to mimic the informal lenders rather than the formal sector lending. It has to:

(a) provide for seasonality
(b) allow repayment
(c) and empowerment of women
(d) flexibility
(e) eschew bureaucratic and legal formalities
(f) fix a ceiling on loan sizes.

## THE CERTITUDES OF MICROFINANCE FOR WOMEN

Microfinance approach is based on certain proven truths which are not always recognised. These are:

That the poor are bankable; successful initiatives in micro finance demonstrate that there need not be a trade off between reaching the poor and profitability - micro finance constitutes a statement that the borrowers are not 'weaker sections' in need of charity, but can be treated as responsible people on business terms for mutual profit -

- That almost all poor households need to save, have the inherent capacity to save small amounts regularly and are willing to save provided they are motivated and facilitated to do so -
- That easy access to credit is more important than cheap subsidised credit which involves lengthy bureaucratic procedures - some institutions in India are already lending to groups or SHGs at higher rates - this may prevent the groups from enjoying a sufficient margin and rapidly accumulating their own funds, but members continue to borrow at these high rates, even those who can borrow individually from banks as the ease of access to loans appears more important than bureaucratic delays associated with the formal financial institutions -
- 'Peer pressure' in groups helps in improving recoveries.

## REASONS FOR FOCUS ON POOR WOMEN

Microfinance and empowerment of women

The National Credit Fund for Women or the Rashtriya Mahila Kosh (RMK) is working exclusively for poor women. Its loans are available solely and entirely to this target group. The reasons for this are several:

- Among the poor, the poor women are the most disadvantaged - they are characterized by lack of education and access to resources, both of which are required to help them work their way out of poverty and for upward economic and social mobility -
- The problem is more acute for women in countries like India, despite the fact that women's labour makes a critical contribution to the economy - this is due to low social status and lack of access to key resources -
- Evidence shows that groups of women are better customers than men - they are better managers of

resources - benefits of loans are spread wider among the household if loans are routed through women - mixed groups are often inappropriate in Indian society - record of all-male groups is worse than that of all-women groups, everywhere -

The SEWA Bank opened in 1974, to provide banking services to the Self-Employed Women's Association's trade union members in Ahmadabad. It was intended to operate as a cooperative bank, owned by its members. All of SEWA Bank's clients are self-employed women. The bank offers them varied services including savings, secured loans, unsecured loans and several types of insurance. SEWA has been advancing loans to women involved in various trades like block printing, handloom weaving, embroidery, fish and vegetable vending, etc. SEWA has empowered them to improve their skills, income and self-esteem. Solidarity among urban microcredit group members can help them solve many of their common problems of security, drinking water, sanitation, sewerage, etc. effectively. In July 1993, SEWA Bank started banking activities in the rural districts of Gujarat. This activity is carried out through the formation and development of women's savings groups, known as self-help groups (SHG). These groups, regularly meet, collect the saved money from their members and deposit it in SEWA Bank. Financially stable groups are facilitated with credit options for their individual members. Eventually, a district level savings and credit.

Federation of unregistered savings and credit groups (SCGs) is registered at the district level. The operational strategy of the SEWA Bank is based on: financial sustainability by using surplus funds for developmental activities of SEWA.

SEWA believes in borrowing and lending at market rates and not in subsidies or grants.

It has high Institutional and managerial sustainability and is regulated by the Reserve Bank of India.

There is a coporate social responsibility and Board control with regular stocktaking during annual meeting of shareholders.

Regular elections to the Board ensure that the Board is vibrant and participatory.

So it is led by a capable professional management team.

**Results**

It is the first bank of its kind in India to demonstrate that poor women do save, use loans productively and repay loans in a timely manner (in fact better than others).

SEWA Bank, which started with 4000 depositors, has 2,00,000 poor women poor women in 10 districts of Gujarat. Women as depositors and a working capital of Rs. 62.54 Crore in 2002. They can obtain loans ranging from Rs. 5000 to Rs. 25000.

**Sustainability**

Both the urban and rural banking operations of the SEWA Bank are self-sustaining. The services of the Bank are being increasingly sought after and such services have helped a large number of self-employed women by empowering them economically and socially.

**Lessons learnt**

(a) Poor women can save, if motivated and facilitated.

(b) Poor do Repay Loans.
Poor women can and do repay loans provided their repaying capacity is assessed properly.

(c) Poor do pay market rates of interest.

(d) Poor need suitable delivery mechanisms like door to door services, simple procedure, Assistance in filling forms, matching of collection schedule with cash flow and irregular income streams.

(e) Continuous contact is the key for success.

(f) They need to be informed and educated about all the services, products and processes and procedures to be followed. Microfinance leads to empowerment of women.

(g) There is a need for a handholding service, created for them.

(h) They need financial counselling for four types of financial services.
Savings services for the events which they can plan, Insurance Services for uncertainties Credit for business needs and Counseling for planning ahead.

(i) Banking with the poor can be financially viable.

(j) When the poor own the organization, they feel more responsible towards it.

(k) Controls, regulations and inspections often help institutions to improve efficiency and procedures, which ultimately leads to the growth of the organization.

(l) Poor women need a suitable environment and integrated support to come out of vulnerability and poverty. Other support services like health care, child care, marketing support, capacity building, legal aid, policy interventions, and backward and forward linkages are required for achieving the overall objectives of poverty alleviation and empowerment of the poor.

**Replicabilty**

Many other groups have taken training at the SEWA Bank and have subsequently started saving and lending cooperatives, for instance, the Cooperative Development Foundation,Working Women's Forum and Indore Mahila Cooperative among many others. One of the main demands of self- employed women workers was for credit at reasonable rates, which they were unable to obtain from normal banks. The SEWA Bank was started with the specific objective of providing credit to the self-employed women with a view to empower them and also to minimize the uncertainty of availability of credit through money sharks at exorbitant interest rates. It has been financially viable and self-reliant from the beginning, and uses its surplus to further strengthen individual workers as well as their movement. The self-employed women as shareholders own the bank. Their own elected Board makes policies. Qualified managers hired by the board professionally run the Bank. The bank aims at providing all finance-linked supportive services to SEWA members. The bank offers several schemes both in urban and rural areas. All the schemes are directed towards empowering self-employed women for improving their businesses and income, improving their housing and infrastructure, improving their knowledge and skills. The majority of SHGs consist of women, as self employment through microfinance is perceived as a powerful empowerment weapon which puts money in the hands of women and thereby makes them economically independent other freedoms follow leading to empowerment. World Bank in its report Engendering development through gender equality in right resources and voice 2001 has observed that gender equality is a necessary condition for economic development where there is gender discrimination it is found that economic growth is retarded, governance is looser populations remain mired in poverty while independent incomes howsoever modest contribute to the self confidence of women enabling them to better combat the restrictive circumstances of their lives and of being born poor and born women. Gender composition of SHGs shows clearly that SHGs are weighted in favour of women. Activity wise classification of SHGs also shows that they take up activities as care of milch animal and dairy activity which are women centric activities. Process of functioning of SHGs shows that their leadership profile is weighted towards women and membership in SHGs enlarges the autonomy and choices exercised by women in their autonomous roles as participants in these activities.

The initiatives for managing the money of the group and balancing its liabilities and assets are undertaken by the poor women at the micro level of the group.

Funds are gathered together and distributed among the women members by themselves and these decisions are taken by women themselves.

The responsibility of Self Selection of group members rests with women.

Similarly the identification of the activity, Products and Services for women.

Unit cost, loan size norms and procedures for repayment.

Within the SHG the women are able to articulate their view points and leadership positions are assigned on a revolving basis. They are able to extend support to each other and empathise with each other.

Recovery of loan recycling of funds for repeat loaning to the group members Joint liability of the group for its decisions are taken by women themselves.

SHGs are a forum for self reliance and self determination of the members and one of the major interventions for empowering poor women. SHGs take various forms they may be Savings Affinity Groups of poor women i.e. SAG or rotating savings and credit associations ROSCAS lending to the poor women by themselves based on a perception of need out of the small sums accumulated by the group, functioning as savings and credit associations and also engaging in social activity and larger groups may graduate to setting up suitable sustainable income generating products. Thus the whole process of active engagement with the group has a transformational impact on its members. The members of SEWA say that visiting the Bank for them is like "going to their mothers house."

## Products and Services for Women

Microfinance has a positive impact on improving the economic and social conditions of poor women as it works through credit delivery mechanisms that meet women's specific needs and barriers. Women are viewed primarily as housewives despite the fact that they often work outside the home they enjoy very limited control over their incomes even though women provide 70% of agricultural labor. They have extremely limited decision making power in matters of land ownership or politics and rarely control the wealth they produce. However there is perceptible change some of the older credit groups in India are emerging as the role model for women entrepreneurs of the adjoining areas. The Grameen Bank in Bangladesh highlighted the crucial role that women play in household management "Women are expected to be the household Bank." Perhaps due to this role another respondent from Bangladesh was able to report that women's access to loans had produced a positive change in gender relations among its client base, by compelling the men to depend on the women for credit. Microfinance has a definite impact on the economic and social conditions of poor women. Significant efforts have gone into the setting up of financially stable reliable institutions capable of reaching large numbers of low income women with financial services. A range of Banks, self help groups and multi service NGOs provide great depth and breadth of outreach by serving a range of clients from the poorest of the poor to low income entrepreneurs with growth oriented micro and small enterprises. Microfinance tries to design and deliver financial services to meet women's needs especially in the area of credit. However women are still marginalised even as microfinance clients signalling the need for continued efforts in the area of outreach. A deepened understanding of the multiple roles of women as economic agents as producers and as household managers leads to a further need for designing varied types of credit and financial services more than enterprise credit as women have a need for different types of credit products and microfinance methodologies have to be tailored in flexible ways to meet the range of women's various needs.

## Intersectoral Linkages

Financial services are important in that access to these services of savings and credit helps poor women to build assets and create a hedge against economic shocks. In the times of natural disaster as Tsunamii, floods, drought crop failure the need of the poor for small amounts of credit has been well recognised and microfinance loans have to be suitably structured and in such situations have proved to be of considerable help.

Microfinance programs also address the issues of women's health the effect of HIV/AIDS pandemic on the sustainability of microfinance programs also brings the issues related to health of women to the fore as part of microfinance. Thus we see that microfinance has developed several intersectoral linkages with other public health and development disciplines.

## BARRIERS TO ACCESS

Most formal financial institutions insist on formal collateral as a guarantee for loans to be advanced and women have no title to land and have poor asset ownership this is a major problem in India as also in most other countries of South Asia. Formal financial institutions insist on guarantees documentation such as property titles, birth certificates identification cards which many poor women do not possess serve as barriers to credit access. Joint Liability groups are able to address the problem of physical collateral which is substituted by the guarantee of the group. There are several other factors that hamper the development of women's enterprises.

There is a lack of regard for women's informal sector activities. There are spousal consent problems they have a lack of decision making power they face financing difficulties especially with regard to high interest rates and obtaining repeat loans Women suffer from a lack of self esteem /confidence. They are hampered by a lack of information and access to markets, the problems are further compounded by illiteracy and lack of education, which make exploitation by middlemen greater and these are compounded by poorly developed business skills.

Basically women's needs are finance related and centre around a lack of collateral formal guarantees and credit awareness. Flexibility, accessibility and ease of operations are emphasised as important traits in financial services aimed at women entrepreneurs. The other barriers which prevent women from accessing financial services are Lack of credit awareness and knowledge of financing issues.

## EMPOWERMENT

Microfinance enables women to cross the threshold of their homes and transact in the public space and thereby has an empowering effect on women. Women have immediate practical needs which microfinance addresses as savings and credit services which help to establish self sustaining income generating projects which enable the needs of shelter, housing, childcare to be met The feminisation of credit is inalienably associated with microfinance as per this aspect, conceptually if you advance credit to women you are uplifting the whole family as women will tend to address the nutrition and schooling and health needs of their families first and then their own needs. Women also have structural needs embedded in an unequal and largely patriarchcal society needs which arise out of unequal aspects of gender roles such as educational opportunities and access to and control of resources. Microfinance thus builds capacities of women to exercise control over their own lives, to satisfy family individual needs and contribute to the development of their societies. The most important example of an institution that addresses both immediate and longer term needs of women borrowers is of the SEWA Bank which links products and services to maximise the benefits for women, the signal contribution of SEWA Bank led by the redoubtable Ela Behn a Gandhian and trade activist is to bring women into the economic mainstream. SEWA the self employed women's association, provides loans to encourage activities in which women participate or which women manage exclusively as well as promote women's knowledge and skill development in activities traditionally considered men's. It has helped bring the market to women and encouraged them to develop their market knowledge SEWA Bank addresses both the immediate needs and the long term interests of women it uses an integrated strategy of economic development through its credit and savings cooperatives and joint action Grameen Bank provides another such example groups Grameen Banks housing loans require that the land the house is built on is registered in the women's name. Thus such products have the potential to initiate a process of broader societal change while also contributing to the microfinance institutions sustainability. There are hierarchies of empowerment of women which begin at the level of individual self and then graduate to societal levels. Empowerment as a process is psychological, economic, social and ultimately political. There are various examples of women organising around collective issues or sectors in order to bring about change. These efforts can be a powerful complement to services provided by the microfinance industry when women are viewed as economic agents of change.

The moral strength, confidence and empowerment levels are definitely higher among women who have become confident decision makers, investors and mentors for their families, "Organisation of women around thrift and credit groups has emerged as an effective means to their empowerment and alleviation of poverty SHG groups enable poor women to come together and work for social and economic empowerment In Andhra NABARD Basix CARE and Vikas Darshini have come together to establish the Andhra Pradesh Mahila Abhivruddhi society which is a membership body of cluster federations and acts as a specialised credit and capacity building unit for its members.

SHGs either directly provide or enable poor women to access financial services like savings credit and insurance these enable them to escape the money-lender who is the only other source of credit :

(1) Rescue their mortgaged/pledged assets such as land, ornaments and cattle.

(2) Create their own assets as house, savings equipment.

(3) Avail of productive credit to expand their business.

(4) Improve living conditions.

(5) Cope better with the challenges - life throws up from time to time.

(A) Credit thus helps repay old debts without having to incur new ones, as the credit availed of from the SHG is extended to them, after a realistic assessment of their irregular income streams and is linked to small instalments. Hence, it is a loan which they are easily able to service and wipe out, over time. The credit is available to them without Collateral security have to be repeated is the first demand of formal financial institution they effectively 'screen' out poor borrowers as potential default risks.

The credit is at doorstep, when needed and in serviceable tranches. As they grow more confident in their ability to 'bear'/'services' and repay the loans. They take more loans to fund their business and 'expand' it through working capital loans, to purchase 'time sowing' equipment and also to improve their own status by building houses, acquiring assets, etc.

(B) Credit serves as a hedge against predictable risks as sickness, accidents, ill-health and unpredictable disasters as floods, cyclones, drought all of which demand the ability to cope.

(C) SHGs help poor women as they have a set of :

(1) simplified procedures.
(2) enable door step banking with the poor.
(3) loans are advanced based on savings i.e. as a multiple of savings with the group.
(4) Credit is also extended on the borrowers' track record i.e. his previous repayment record.
(5) Thus a rough and ready "credit history is maintained".
(6) This is deemed adequate and loans are given without formal collateral. Illiterate women become financially savvy and able to avail of financial services which range from savings, credit, insurance, financial counselling and ATMs.

The groups are thus effective; SEWA Bank is owned and managed by its chief stakeholder's poor women. The Banks financial resources come almost entirely from their own members. Deposits owned by women form 82% ploughed back profits 8% and outside borrowing 4%. Income from net interest meets operating expenses and provides for non-performing assets. Part of the surplus is used for providing support services such as Social Security and education, training capacity building of members, the remaining is ploughed back as capital after distributing dividends to its members. There are several innovative ways in which the problems of women have been solved as these are innovative grass roots level organisations simple example is of the time of meeting if inappropriate this becomes a powerful barrier to access.

Time for SHG Meeting tailored to suit the Members' Convenience.

As observed in the groups of MYRADA, for example, the meeting of women's SHGs are held after eight in the night, when the women have finished their daily chores and the meeting can go on till late in the night. On the other hand, in the district of Howrah, the Village Welfare Society field staffs meets the SHG members in the early morning at the village hut, before the women go out to take up their daily work. Similarly, SHG members of SHARE, Hyderabad also hold their meetings in the morning in the school premises before the school opens.

Insistence on savings is a means of instilling a measure of financial discipline among the group members.

## SIMPLIFIED PROCEDURES FOR BANKING WITH SELF EMPLOYED WOMEN IN THE UNORGANISED SECTOR

- Technology especially biometric identification can play a significant role in increased access and much greater financial inclusion.

Microfinance wider definition includes provision of other financial services such as money transfer and micro-insurance products for the poor to enable them to raise their living standards and improve their income levels. Self-employed women are those workers who earn a living through their own-Small business or their own labour.

These self employed workers suffer from several disabilities Firstly there is the fear of loss of income as employment is insecure, Secondly they are able to either eke out a subsistence livelihood or have very low incomes. Thirdly their business expansion is hamstrung or stymied due to and lack of (capital) assets. They have limited or no access to institutional support and virtually negligible social security. Thus marginalised in these multifarious ways they lead a subsistence existence at the periphery of society. Neither, do they receive fair wages or adequate remuneration for the work that they do nor is their work recognised. Thus, they are not part of the economic mainstream. Their contribution, however, is significant. They are producers and consumers. They may be home-based workers, not necessarily only papad and pickle makers, they can also be weavers, potters, carpenters, agricultural labourers and craftswomen or construction workers. Being part of a group helps them to increase their bargaining power, improve their income, employment access to social security.

**THE BRAVE WOMEN OF JHABUA MADHYA PRADESH**

In homogenous groups in tribal pockets where common problems are to be confronted and the group members have greater faith in their leaders honesty and ability groups take up social issues apart from savings, credit and production issues as the battle against liquor or for water and basic sanitation "Bairani Kuldi" literally means Women's Bank. Over 25000 women have come together to organise 1748 Women and-Thrift Groups in Jhabua district and have accumulated a saving of Rs. 3.5 crores. What started as an alternative to the exploitative system of rural credit in the informal sector is now well on way to becoming a movement to empower women. The principles on which Bairani Kuldi groups operate are democratic, simple, and flexible and lend themselves to consumer friendly solutions.

• The Women and Thrift Groups in Jhabua sponsor as many as 38 activities ranging from agricultural credit, small income generating activities, to small consumer loans. The activities of the group has increased the awareness amongst its members, made them economically self reliant and more capable of combating vagaries of nature. The fact that the banks in the district have loaned Rs. 30 lakhs to 116 Bairani Kuldi groups for agricultural activity is an indication of the increasing confidence in the repaying capabilities of these groups.

**Gender and Empowerment** Since microfinance programs are targeted at women they are generally accepted as having a powerful empowerment impact on the women whose needs they serve to address. There is the generally held view that given the pivotal role of women in the functioning of effective groups the methodology and process of microfinance is genuinely empowering for women. It gives women self confidence, voice and visibility within the household and community along with economic power and benefits through an opportunity to take up microenterprises. Pitt and Khandekar study of 1998 published in the Journal of Political Economy led to an emphasis on the loaning bias towards women articulated by CGAP and International donors as the feminisation of credit. They found that when a loan of 100 taka was given to men it led to 11 taka going to food/nutrition/working tools/total household expenditure but when the same amount was lent to women 18 taka went into the household kitty this led to the concept of the feminisation of credit which meant that a loan to a women was not a loan extended to a single individual woman but to the entire Microfinance and empowerment of women household. The bulk of SHGs, i.e. 80 per cent of SHGs have women members. SHG serves a very important function they provide a legitimate platform for women to meet regularly, to represent their interests in public forums to articulate their Voice in panchayat meetings and to gain a foothold in hitherto unexplored domains as block offices, district collectorates, banks. The SHG is the first all womens organizational structure in the village.

On the principle of primacy to women food stamps in Sri Lanka and food and cash deliveries under the OPPORTUNIDADES (erstwhile PROGRESA) program in Mexico were directed at women rather than men clearly there was an apprehension that if such aid was extended to men they would sell the food stamps or barter them for alcohol or misallocate the resources on gambling tobacco alcohol Women are perceived as better customers for loans than men as the repayment rates on loans given to women are higher. Women have greater vulnerability to public humiliation and consequently succumb more easily to peer pressure with regard to loan repayments. Women have reduced access to alternate sources of finance which in turn reduces the scope for moral hazard Women are risk averse and more conservative in their investment strategies.

**Disruption of Social Relations**

As most of South and South East Asia is characterized by a patriarchical society negatively microfinance disrupts existing social patterns. Women are subject either to the threat of physical violence or to actual physical violence from male members who subject them to beatings to get money through loans from their groups. This can also happen and we cannot close our eyes to this darker aspect. Though it is not universally true.

Relative to initial lending practices by the Grameen Bank in Bangladesh the gender dimension of microfinance which emphasises the exclusion of men particularly at very low income levels may prove to be counterproductive in practice It can generate friction within households as men feel increasingly threatened as primary breadwinners within the household. Women are also surface to physical beaten to force them to get money through their groups. On the other hand there is the contrary view articulated that it does not seriously challenge patriarchcal structures of economic and political control as operating in rural Bangladesh and women become conduits for getting money used/misused by men. They become debt collectors for loans used by men and not only this it seriously hampers the power structures and becomes a source of greater oppression for women. Experience specially from Bangladesh has shown that the group methodology can also result in the "self exclusion" of the poorest families because of the limited opportunities they see for credit financed self employment and their inability to meet group savings commitments and also for social reasons. The feminisation of credit has a powerful empowerment effect which makes it an important social intervention effort. However on the upside Grameen has provided institutional access by replacing material with social collateral requirements i.e. joint liability or borrower solidarity groups. Though there are individual loans, the choice of activity and the size of the loan is vetted by the group which is also responsible for monitoring its use and providing support and advice to the borrowers. Each borrower is conscious that any default in repayment will jeopardise the chances of other group members. Gender focus of microfinance is sharp. It is also abundantly clear that while not all poor women set up successfull microenterprises all women need, use and benefit from financial services. In fact the poor in general and women in particular are exceedingly diverse and their needs vary with circumstances. Supply driven credit methodologies have targeted a narrow band of clients and has left a large swathe of the poorest of the poor and the less poor in remote geographic locations or sparsely populated areas untouched. At the very kernel of microfinance is the fundamental belief that access to financial services protects and empowers the poor by mitigating risks and offering them choices. Financial services help smoothen consumption and cushion shock. Whether they save or borrow evidence shows that when poor women secure access to financial services in the absence of emergency conditions they try to save money accumulate it and invest in assets and plough it back in their small enterprises. In sum financial services help the poor to cope with a constant feature of their lives.

Vulnerablity. Microfinance clients are overwhelmingly women microfinance is widely credited with empowering women by increasing their contribution to household income, the value of their assets, and control over decisions that affect their lives.

## References

1. Putnam Robert (2000), Bowling alone the collapse and Revival of American Community Simon and Shuster Harvard University.
2. Putnam Leonardi and Nanneti 1993 Making Democracy work Civivc Traditions in Modern Italy Princeton University Press Princeton USA.
3. Sebstad Jennifer and Gregory Chen (1996) Over view of studies on Micro enterprise credit Assessing the Impact of microenterprise services. Washington D.C. Management Systems International. Microfinance and Empowerment of Women.
4. Khandekar Shahidur 1998 Fighting Poverty with microcredit experiences in Bangladesh OUP New York.
5. Khandekar Shahidur Baqui Khalily and Zahed Khan 1995 Grameen Bank Performance and Sustainability World Bank Discussion Paper No. 306 IBRD Washington.
6. Kabeer Naila (1991) Gender Development and Training Raising Awareness in Development Planning GADU News Pack OXFAM OXFORD UK.

# 6

# "Microfinance and Empowerment of the Poor"

Extensive evidence demonstrates that microfinance helps eradicate extreme poverty and address hunger. It impacts poverty and reduces it through increase in income which enable the poor to build assets and combat pervasive fragility and economic weakness. Traditionally microfinance has been considered as synonymous with the empowerment of the poor and in achievement this lies its most significant contribution. Financial services put power in the hands of the poor to pursue their own strategies for building human, physical economic and social capital to escape poverty and as microfinance services can be delivered sustainably within relatively short periods of time benefits can be delivered on a permanent basis they go well beyond government sponsored programs which are top down targeted and subsidydependent Essentially microfinance has to be seen as an important poverty intervention. A substantial number of the clients of microfinance are from poor and socially marginalised households including women headed households. Microfinance does not simply provide an alternative to the money lender rather it enhances the choices of poor people. The ideological construct posits the following "Win Win" proposition which was first powerfully articulated at the Microcredit Summit in Washington DC in 1997. This focuses on three things which mark microfinance as unique.

Firstly micro credit addresses concerns of poverty alleviation by financing micro enterprises enabling the poor to work their own way out of poverty, secondly it enables women's empowerment by routing credit directly to women and thereby enhancing their status within their families, communities and larger societies and thirdly it ensures the sustainability of the lender institution or lender viability through securing higher rates of repayment of loans while charging cost covering rates of interest. "If we are looking for one single action which will enable the poor to overcome their poverty I will focus on credit" Mohd Yunus.

- Poverty reduction is at the center of the development agenda access to finance is a key component of this. Through microfinance access to financial services and credit is simplified and poverty alleviation effected thus microfinance is an essential component of the process, of poverty alleviation. Distribution of the SHG members by caste indicates that SCs/STs and OBCs account for 22.3 percent of total SHG members these findings have been corroborated by several studies.
- The percentage of SHGs that only have SC/ST members is 21 per cent.
- More than 60 per cent of SHGs consist of members belonging to BPL families.
- Changes in net household income between pre-SHG and post-SHG registered a significant growth per year at 6.1 per cent.
- Across different income activities of households, livestock registered highest growth at 11.2 per cent. The annual growth rate of per household consumption expenditure

on food and non-food items recorded 5.1 per cent and 5.4 percent respectively.

- Per household annual expenditure on education and health recorded 5.6 per cent and 5.5 per cent growth respectively.
- Net change in the value of consumer durable assets per household was Rs. 4,329 between pre-SHG and post-SHG periods and the annual growth of assets recorded a high growth between the two periods at 9.9 per cent.
- The average level of savings (financial and physical savings) per households registered 14.2 per cent annual growth between base level and 2006.
- On an average, per household borrowed an amount of Rs. 14,640 in the post-SHG period compared to Rs. 5,384 in the pre-SHG situation. The average loan amount per household grew at an annual rate of 20.5 per cent between the pre-SHG and the post-SHG periods.
- About 93 per cent of households reported that loans were taken in the post-SHG situation as compared to that of 46.5 per cent.
- On the issue of repayment of loan, the findings show 96.4 per cent of households reported regularity in repayments of loans.
- The share of households living below the poverty line reduced from 58.3 per cent in the pre-SHG period to 33 per cent in the post-SHG situation.
- About 92 per cent of households reported that the social empowerment of women had increased after attaining membership in SHGs over a period of time.
- More than 70 per cent of women respondents reported improvements or even significant improvements in their ability to face health related problems and financial crisis.
- More than 60 per cent of the households indicated that there is an increase in the ownership of productive assets in post-SHG situation as compared pre-SHGs situation.
- In terms of control over money, about 21.3 per cent of the households reported a significant improvement in control

over money with respect to buying of consumer durable assets.

- 27 per cent reported increased decision-making and control over expenditure on children's education.
- The findings show 22.5 per cent of women SHG members in the households had taken decision in the post-SHG period as compared to 9.1 per cent in the pre-SHG period with respect to children's education.
- Participation of public sphere show that 49.4 per cent of households had approached government officials to solve problems in the post-SHG period as compared to 13.5 per cent in the pre-SHG period.
- The findings of Self Help Promoting Institutions SHPI suggest that the average cost of promotion and maintenance per SHG incurred by a bank SHPI is lower than that by non-bank SHPIs.
- Microfinance programs and institutions have become an increasingly important component of strategies to reduce poverty and promote micro and small enterprise development. However, knowledge about the achievements of such initiatives remains only partial and contested. At one extreme are studies arguing that microfinance has very beneficial economic and social impacts (Holcombe, 1995; Hossain, 1988; Otero and Rhyne, 1994; Remenyi, 1991; Schuler, Hashemi and Riley, 1997). At the other are writers who caution against such optimism and Microfinance and empowerment of the poor point to the negative impacts that microfinance can have (Adams and von Pischke, 1992; Buckley, 1997; Montgomery, 1996; Rogaly, 1996; Wood and Shariff, 1997). In the 'middle' is work that identifies beneficial impacts but argues that microfinance does not assist the poorest, as is so often claimed (Hulme and Mosley, 1996; Mosley and Hulme, 1998).

The MFI subsequently provides different services to a client, most commonly in the form of a loan. These services lead to the client modifying her/his microenterprise activities which in turn lead to increased or decreased microenterprise income. The change in microenterprise income causes changes in household income which in turn leads to greater or lesser household economic security. The modified level of household economic security leads to changes in the morbidity and mortality of household members, in educational and skill levels and in future economic and social opportunities. Ultimately, perhaps, these changes lead to modifications in social and political relations and structures. The complexity of such chains provides the assessor with a range of choices about which link (or links) to focus on. For microfinance, it is useful to distinguish between two main schools of thought with regard to which link(s) in the chain to focus on. For convenience, these are termed the 'intended beneficiary'[1] school and the 'intermediary' school.

The intended beneficiary school, building on the ideas of conventional evaluation, seeks to get as far down the impact chain as is feasible (in terms of budgets and techniques) and to assess the impact on intended beneficiaries (individuals or households). The intermediary school focuses purely on the beginning of the chain and in particular on changes in the MFI and its operations. Its roots are closely associated with the Ohio State School's analyses of rural finance. Generally, two key variables are focused on: institutional outreach and institutional sustainability[2] (Yaron, Benjamin and Piprek, 1997). If both outreach and sustainability have been enhanced then the intervention is judged to have a beneficial impact as it has widened the financial market in a sustainable fashion. This is based on the assumption that such institutional impacts extend the choices of people looking for credit and savings services and that this extension of choice ultimately leads to improved microenterprise performance and household economic security. While this assumption can be supported by theoretical frameworks (if a set of further assumptions are made about perfect competition and other factors) it is an assumption which has proved invalid in a number of experiences.[3] In addition, it will not reveal borrower 'cross-financing' of loans which may threaten the long term viability of an MFI.

• The social indicators that became popular in the early 1980s (e.g. educational status, access to health services, nutritional levels, anthropometric measures) have recently been extended into the socio-political arena in Microfinance and empowerment of the poor an attempt to assess whether microfinance can promote empowerment (Mayoux, 1997; Goetz and Sen Gupta, 1996; Schuler and Hashemi, 1994; Hashemi et al, 1995). This has led to the measurement of individual control over resources, involvement in household and community decision-making, levels of participation in community activities and social networks and electoral participation. The bulk of this work has focused on changes in gender relations, but there are sometimes partially-formulated assessments of class relations within it (Fuglesang and Chandler, 1993). These extensions to the types of impact assessed permit Impact Assessment IAs to be more sophisticated and to shed light on developmental impacts at a time when the goals of development have also been extended. They do add, however, to the complexity of IA Impact Assessment work and require the skills of assessors who are experienced at making judgements on social relations.

Sebstad et al (1995) usefully distinguish between 'domains of change' (e.g. household income) and the specific 'markers of change' (e.g. amount of income, number of income sources and seasonality of income) within each domain. While not fully comprehensive, the detailed sets of domains and markers, produced in their paper provide an excellent checklist for impact assessors to consider at the Impact Assessment design stage. Often the exact markers used will be shaped by the methodology that is selected. This can cause problems for multi-method impact analysis **which is not able to apply a single definition for a marker for each of the** methods used.

In recent years microfinance projects and institutions have been subjected to a vast amount of impact assessment study.

The initial emphasis on 'scientific' sample surveys and statistical analyses has shifted as multi-method Impact Assessments and most recently participatory approaches have been utilised. These studies provide a resource from which researchers draw out lessons for future practice. Much further work will be needed as the claims that microfinance is a panacea for poverty-reduction (most publicly through the Micro-Credit Summit and its follow up), and the counter-claims that caution against such enthusiasm (Rogaly, 1996; Wood and Shariff, 1997) demand rigorous empirical testing to find out what is being achieved and how more might be achieved. To design successful products the first step entails understanding the financial needs of clients and how these mesh with their money management strategies the World Development Report 2001 on Poverty highlights the importance of understanding the risk and vulnerability of poorer clients. Given the poverty alleviation objectives of many microfinance programs these findings suggest a case for innovations improving the design of products and services to better meet the needs of clients from a broad range of households namely both the extremely poor and vulnerable non poor to improve the depth of poverty outreach they must factor in risk and vulnerability.

## VULNERABILITY -RISKS THE POOR FACE ON A DAY TO DAY BASIS

There are many sources of risk for the poor. Structural factors, such as seasonality inflation or the vagaries of weather. Emergencies as sickness or unexpected death of a family member loss of employment fires and thefts and the high costs associated with lifecycle needs marriage funerals educating a child. There are also risks associated with taking a loan or operating an enterprise.

Micro-finance rests on the following principles:

(1) Self-employment is a viable means of poverty alleviation.

(2) Lack of access to credit is a major constraint to micro-enterprise.

(3) The poor are able to save despite their sporadic incomes.

The Syndicate Bank pioneered the concept of pigmy deposits through its daily/weekly savings collections and also sanctioned micro loans for its constituents. Priority sector mandated lending refocused attention on this poorest segment of the poor. Swarn Jayanti Gram Swarozgar Yojana SGSY is limited in that and it focuses only on investment credit ignoring the other needs especially lifecycle and consumption needs these are areas of need which microfinance addresses successfully SGSY is a program which is named it can be taken as a prototype of Government sponsored schemes and subventions.

Thus all subsidy dependent programs have failed as subsidies are cornered by better off sections, repayment is poor due to 'rent costs' incurred by borrowers and late monitoring, poor supervision and follow up by the banks.

Microfinance has an immediate appeal.

(1) Loans without collateral

(2) Groups screen/self select their own members, invest their savings

(3) Supervise their groups monitor loan repayments ensuring

(4) 100% repayment weekly/monthly collection

(5) Production-cum-consumption loans

(6) Compulsory savings for financial discipline.

The flexibility of the SHG model is also a great attraction for the poor. It enables diversity of loans, for production, trade, investments, consumption, housing, variation of sizes and compositions. It also allows flexible interest rates to be charged for diverse purposes, and easier repayment terms which can be meshed with the borrowers present or anticipated future income stream.

Members use their 'own money' (warm money as opposed to 'cold' funds injected from outside). The members judiciously control the use of their own funds and after estimating individual loan risks price their portfolios accordingly.

There is a reduction in transaction costs for banks and borrowers.

For banks there is an externalisation of part of the credit cycle.

For borrowers once they learn to operate a bank account responsibly, loan screening process time as also costs for the bank are reduced.

Over time individual SHG members are enabled to graduate from microfinance to microenterprise.

The International experience from a few examples of business strategy to be adopted.

**The flow of Strategic and Operational Planning**

| *Strategic Planning* | *Operational Planning* | *Financial Modelling* |
|---|---|---|
| Articulating the mission and goals | | |
| Defining markets and clients | Defining Products and Services | Analysing credit and savings products |
| Analysing the environment<br>Competition<br>Collaborators<br>Regulatory factors<br>Other external elements | Specifying marketing channels | Projecting credit and savings activity (Overall or by branch) |
| Institutional Assessment | Planning Institutional Resources and capacity | Estimate loan loss provision, reserve and write offs |
| Credit and Savings Program<br>Board and Management Issues | | Estimating required case load<br>Projecting Branch level expenditure |
| Human resources Management<br>Administration | | |
| Financing | Developing a financing strategy | Analysing financing by source<br>Cost of funds<br>Liquidity and Investment Analysis |

*(Contd.)*

*(Contd. Table)*

| *Strategic Planning* | *Operational Planning* | *Financial Modelling* |
|---|---|---|
| Financial Management | Analysing Financial Projections | Analysing projected financial statements<br>Income statement<br>Adjusted income statement<br>Balance sheet<br>Cash Flow<br>Financial Indicators |
| Developing a strategy | Using Business Planning and financial projections as ongoing management tools | Performing variance analysis |

**Examples from across the world show the positive externalities generated by Microfinance which have made it a public good.**

**Reforming savings and Credit Cooperatives (SACCOs) in Tanzania**

In upland areas of the United Republic of Tanzania, IFAD has supported the transformation of Savings and Credit Cooperatives CARD Cooperative and Agricultural Development SACCOs from credit channels into genuine self-help organisations. They have vigorously mobilized savings and diversified their lending to the agricultural and microenterprise sectors, including women traders. Results in terms of impact include: empowerment of the poor, including women, as user-owners; substantial improvements in food security and income; and enhanced institutional sustainability.

**How an Unsustainable Credit NGO in the Philippines First Turned into a Grameen Replicator and then into a Rural Bank**

- Agriculture and Rural Development (CARD) has changed from an unsustainable credit NGO to a viable rural bank with rapidly growing outreach to very poor women. By mobilizing its own resources from

- poor and non-poor clients adopting a variety of financial products and enforcing a strict credit discipline, it has substantially increased its lending outreach to its target group: 28500 very poor women (December 1999). With support from IFAD, CARD disseminates its technology to other MFIs.

**Bank Rakyat Indonesia, the Agricultural Development Bank (AgDB)that Revolutionized Rural Finance**

Within a framework of financial deregulations, what is now the Microbanking division of BRI was cut off from subsidies and granted management autonomy in 1983. Its good practices have included: carefully-crafted financial products, high interest rates on savings and loans, staff productivity incentives, rewards to borrowers for on-time repayment, and good governance. As a result, BRI has turned into one of the most successful providers of rural financial services in the developing world. Its 3700 sub-branches serve 2.6 million borrowers at a one-year loss ratio of 1.35% and carry 25.1 million savings accounts at the village level, testifying to an overwhelming demand for deposit services among the poor (July 2000). Profits in 1999 amounted to USD 150 million, excess liquidity mobilized at the village level to an amazing USD 1.5 billion. This has set new standards for AgDBs- they can be reformed- and the microfinance industry: sustainability and wide outreach to the poor are compatible. This has inspired IFAD, the World Bank and FAO to a new initiative: the transformation of AgDBs into viable and sustainable providers of microsavings and microcredit services.

India has a large network of bank branches and most villages are within easy reach of branch. There need is a to strengthen and beef up existing institutions as DCCBs/RRBs, commercial bank branches. SHG finance can suppose their efforts not support them.

1. SHGs have ensured easy access to credit for their members they have led to the feminisation of credit and have increased the voice of women in their families and communities.
2. However, they have not lived up to the promise of encouraging micro enterprises and building microenterprises as blocks for development.
3. Microfinance has not unlashed micro entrepreneurial energies and the average size of loans continues to be small 1,766 per family (of 4) and Rs. 28,559 per SHG (of 12 members).
4. Banks do not follow consistent norms of guiding SHGs the procedural requirements are both cumbersome and variable.
5. Initial cycles of credit are used for personal consumption rather than for productive investment.
6. Essential inputs and support services to sustain rural enterprises have not been effective.
7. The number of SHGs has grown in a haphazard way.
8. Sectoral concentration in the south has okayed the movement.
9. NGOs are promoting SHGs, NABARD, and multilateral financial agencies, SIDBI and RMK Government Ministries especially Rural and Urban Development Ministry.

• The excitement about micro finance needs to be tempered by a realistic appraisal and an assessment of the spectrum of services the banks are capable of providing Microfinance for consumption smoothing will remain dependent on the generosity of donor grants. Repayment of loans in cash necessitates that the loan has to be invested in some production activity so as to generate surplus for serving debt obligations. It is also a long and arduous journey its sign posts are micro deposits to micro savings to micro credit to microfinance and then to micro enterprises. The light at the end of the time will only come from achieving an 'instamatic' target oriented approach and allowing micro enterprise to come slowly to full friction. The Self Help Groups (SHGs) which have been successfully linked to the banks and which have matured have proven their ability to manage accounts and handle money. The local flavour of the SHGs and their intimate knowledge of the areas in which they operate as also their association with banks make them a good choice to act as business correspondents. RBI may consider allowing banks to use mature SHG group leaders as BCs with IT solutions in place to ensure requisite safeguards Micro finance is of necessity a complete slow strategy marked by graduation leading to incremental growth through rural livelihood support. As most of the women SHG prefer traditional livelihoods, it is necessary to integrate livelihood skills with market related training and related but new upgraded skills. NABARD may make a detailed review of the SHG-bank linkage program and come up with revised guidelines to facilitate migration of members of mature groups to become micro entrepreneurs and increase the scale of lending through such groups. The group members should be able to access larger loans from banks in their individual capacity while retaining the group solidarity and membership. If the objective of effectively achieving banking penetration in all parts of the country is to be achieved, it is necessary that the State Governments ensure road and digital connectivity to all centers where penetration by the formal banking system is required. The achievement of such connectivity may be monitored by the sub group of the DCC referred to above. Full advantage may be taken of the special scheme offered by Reserve Bank to provide satellite connectivity through small V-SATs in remote areas. RBI has decided that, to begin with, the scheme would be implemented in the North Eastern States. It has also been decided that banks in the North Eastern States availing of this facility with 100% reimbursement for lease rental, shall be required to offer electronic funds transfer facility free of charge to their customers.

• Other infrastructure support includes ensuring conducive law and order situation, providing adequate security, uninterrupted power and water supply and irrigation. In centres where bank branches are required by the State Government for currency, Foreign exchange and government business, and banks are constrained to open branches due to lack of infrastructure, absence of viability and security concerns, State Governments will need to extend support by providing premises, security etc.

Impact on Business Development in the Bank and PACs

Identification of the Poor vide the Alappuzha Model

The Stereotyped methods of identification of the 'poor', in need of assistance from Central or State Government, do not take into account the impact of various factors on the total situation or the family. For example, a woman with a small child, is not free to go for wage work.

There is an inherent flexibility in the design of microfinance programs which enables them to target and impactthe poor. An example of the Alappuzha model will illustrate this. In the Alappuzha Model, therefore, the following nine indicators have been selected for identifying the poor. Any household having any four of these factors is identified as poor:

(i) A household with an adult illiterate member
(ii) A household with an adult unemployed member
(iii) A household without a potable water source within 150 metres
(iv) A household with katcha (mud or thatched) house
(v) A household without access to a sanitary latrine
(vi) A household with children below five years of age
(vii) A household barely managing two meals a day or less
(viii) A household belonging to a scheduled caste or tribe (SC/ ST)
(ix) A household with an alcoholic or a drug addict member

The setting up of a self help group is a long drawn out process and involves winning the trust of the community it is not an instant exercise it has necessarily to traverse the following stages.

**'STAGE I: Formation**

- When an NGO wants to start an SHG in any village or area, it has to find out, first of all, whether there are any groups already working there. The staff has to survey the area. Then a public welfare activity by the NGO is generally initiated, such as a health camp or sports competition, to secure the involvement participation and the goodwill of the people. Discussions are held with the local people in an informal manner to gain knowledge of the pattern of life being led by the poor people, their problems, and their composition.

The formation of a group can revolve initially around the solution of a common problem. The most common of the problems is poverty. The discussion can be zeroed on to solution of this problem thus microfinance helps the poor find their own solutions to poverty.

**SCREENING OF GROUP MEMBERS**

The groups should not consist of discordant members because if it is so, all their energy will be lost in settling their quarrels, rather than in progressing. After agreeing to become members and attending a few meetings, some members may join or leave the group, which is normal. The importance of a group, as a way for progress, has to be brought home. The members may be involved in a discussion about their regular savings. The question will often be raised by the members on why should they save? The answer to this question is that the regular savings provide the group with a resource to meet its expenditure. Savings also symbolise a deeper involvement of the members with the group and the issues which they together want to resolve.

Can the Poor Save?

• A common reaction is that the poor are already so poor, how can they save since they have no surpluses? Here, the distinction between savings and thrift may be brought to light; while savings are the leftover amount after fulfilling all the needs, thrift comes from sacrificing the present needs for the same of providing for the future. Again, it may be explained to them that after all, to survive from day-to-day, the members are following some economic activity and enjoy an income howsoever meagre

• **Grain Banks**. Their daily thrift may consist even of a handful of rice per member saved out of their daily consumption. This rice will in time count to be converted to their share of savings. Every member's contribution counts. Every member can look upon the amount as a basis for accessing loans from the SHG and the SHG can itself access more loans through commercial banks.

• **Equality of All Members In The Group.** No member can and should try to escape the responsibility for her regular savings, as she is an equal in position. Each woman can aspire to be the leader of the group in turn. So, why should anyone feel her capacity to be lesser than that of another. The minimum savings amount must be equal for all. The members should be mentally prepared to start saving.

**STAGE II: Stabilisation**

• When the group members struggle to cohere, automatically this leads to the screening out of some members who cannot co-exist with others. The group also has to counter opposition from family members, panchayat or community leaders, vote bank politicians, etc. This is the stage for the group to withstand pressures to survive. Many members, who have the potential of becoming strong advocates of the group, may also question the utility of the group. Impatience is expressed when the necessity of savings for the first 3 months is explained, as members expect quick results and immediate access to loans after formation. However, these stages will have to be undergone with patience and the net result will be that the real leaders from the group will emerge and when the group starts functioning, its course will be smooth.

**STAGE III: Normative**

Some groups may be able to compress the first three stages. But generally, after settling down, the group will start determining the important questions such as

(a) how much savings should the group make;

(b) who should keep the savings in custody;

(c) when should a bank account be opened;

(d) who should keep the record of the meetings;

(e) whether frequency of the meetings should be weekly, fortnightly or monthly;

(f) what is the convenient time for a meeting;

(g) what should be done with the group funds - should the entire amount be lent to individual borrowers, and if so, on what conditions, can the entire savings be withdrawn by a member at her will;

(h) should the group consider improvements in their immediate surroundings, and adopt suitable social agenda;

- Rules regarding regularity of attending the meetings also have to be drawn up whether the meetings must necessarily be attended and leave of absence on adequate grounds can be granted. How to punish a member Microfinance and empowerment of the poor

(i) Failing to attend the meetings must also be written down. Sometimes the member is fined for the absence and sometimes more interesting ways are evolved as is apparent from the strategies adopted by MYRADA groups. Time for SHG Meeting to Suit the Members' ConvenienceAs observed in the groups of MYRADA, for example, the meeting of women's SHGs are held after eight in the night, when the women have finished their daily chores and the meeting can go on till late in the night. On the other hand, in the district of Howrah, the Village Welfare Society field staff meet the SHG members in the early morning at the village hut, before the women go out to do their daily business. Likewise, SHG members of SHARE, Hyderabad also hold their meetings in the morning in the school premises before the school opens.

(j) rules also will have to be written about honorarium to be paid to the persons maintaining SHG records. It must be determined what records must be maintained;

(k) how the expenditure for meeting the cost of record maintenance or holding meetings will be met;

(l) when the group have saved for about 6 months to one year, it will have to decide further about its need for re-financing the group members for their various activities of IG; Income Generation.

(m) the SHG can also identify that in what areas it will request the NGO or the government functionaries to step in and help out a group in fulfilment of its objectives. Help and guidance from the NGOs can be sought on any problem of the SHG. The NGOs are expected to take up issues on behalf of the SHGs;

(n) when outside funding is accessible, the SHG will have to perform even more important functions. They will have to assess the real credit needs of individual women members, the profitability of the economic venture and the actual loan requirement. Thus, the project appraisal for a loan is done first of all by the SHG and only then submitted to the micro-finance institution.

**STAGE IV: Performance**

Once the cycle of loan activity has been completed, the NGO and the SHG both gain stability. They can also expand their programmes and activities as per the requirement. The performance stage can go on indefinitely in a smooth manner on the basis of sound foundations laid in the earlier stages of SHG formation.

It is generally noticed that the main hesitation in starting a programme is the fear of accounts keeping. However, this aspect is not so difficult to handle only if the various requisite records are maintained methodically in writing. The essential books of accounts and their suggested formats have been indicated in the relevant booklet of RMK. Some important issues in this context are as follows:

1. It is very essential that the records regarding the membership fee are maintained. First of all, the SHG has to determine in the first one or two meetings how much membership fee will be charged per month from every member.
2. Whether any flexibility will be given to the members to deposit a larger amount than the compulsory savings with the groups.
3. Whether the group members will be allowed to withdraw their deposits, and if so, at what stage.
4. If they do not withdraw, the money could accrue some interest to them while their money is with the group and it is to be returned to the member when she leaves the group.
5. What percentage of interest will be charged on the borrowings taken by individual members.
6. What will be the arrangement for meeting the expenses of the group.
7. The importance of maintaining the records and accounts properly may be underlined since it provides complete history and proceedings of SHGs to any lending institution or a donor agency.

Once the group starts saving, it gives the members a distinct identity and feeling of proud possessiveness about something of their own, something they can fall back upon.

Social Capital, SHGs bring together several members to think about solution to their problems. In the process, women learn to appreciate the realities of the world around them. As a form of Social Capital which is variously defined as a heuristic way of referring to elements of social structure as trustworthiness, information channels, authority relations norms and effective sanctions that serve to facilitate collective action and institutionalised endeavour. The World Bank has treated it as the fourth capital along with physical natural and human capital. Putnam (1993) had explained these processes with the analogy of the working of a choir A choir consists of a single singer and so its formation requires the surmounting of a coordination problem since choir members cannot be purchased like other capital commodities hence investment differs The choir generates an externality its members learn to trust each other even though this is not the purpose of their interaction choirs even benefit non participants as the generation of trust has externalities beyond membership of the choir. Putnam laid emphasis on a country's cultural factors in helping build social capital.

The SHGs are not in a position to keep adequate staff for updation of their accounts and individual passbooks. For such exigencies, the SHGs can do well by engaging a local person, school teacher or a student on a part-time basis for completing the passbook entries during the meeting itself, when the savings are brought by the group members. This is a vital exercise for NGOs channelizing micro-credit. Attending SHG meetings regularly should be compulsory. Leave of absence may be given only for strong reasons. The frequency of meetings should be weekly in the beginning to make the SHG come to maturity fast.

A very good example by women's SHGs was set in MYRADA. The group decided to undertake constructing a water tank in the village. They also cleaned up the village roads and drains. This activity gained them a lot of appreciation from everyone in the village. In this way, the SHGs became leaders for mobilising community participation in the rural areas. MYRADA groups are intended to be self-sustaining. The effort has been to bring them to a level of maturity and self-sustenance from where they can run their own affairs, access banks for financial support, on their own. MYRADA staff can then move on to other areas.

The usefulness of SHGs has been realised by both NGOs, State Government and Central Government agencies, which is reflected in schemes as DWACRA and SGSY. It was the success of women's SHGs in SEWA, Ahmadabad, which was responsible for Government of India's scheme entitled "Development of Women and Children in Rural Areas" (DWACRA).

Through its wider exposure and larger sympathies and possibly more varied experiences, the NGO is better equipped than the members by themselves to help the group in adopting strategies for peaceful coexistence, progress and mutual respect and support.

(a) NGO has an important role to play in stabilising the SHGs. It has to select appropriate field workers, has to train them to have the right kind of approach to problems and people and to motivate them for organising the groups and ensuring the stability of these groups. The NGO also will be in a position to take the group leaders for exposure visits to other SHGs more advanced than themselves, for a demonstration effect.

(b) The NGO can also help the SHG in identifying the issues surrounding them and prioritising their programmes.

(c) The NGO needs to teach the SHGs about the maintenance of accounts by them in an appropriate manner and in the distribution of individual passbooks. The NGO can instil in the group the sense of importance of proper accounts maintenance, opening of bank account, issuing of loans, uses of savings for group as well as individual activities, recovery of savings, calculation of interest payable, etc.

(d) The NGO can also organise a fund collection drive for pushing forward the developmental activities undertaken by the SHG.

(e) The NGO can introduce the SHG members to novel technologies and schemes, for example, sericulture for increased silk yield, use of hybrid varieties sericulture, compost preparation and initiation of new IG activities, for example, tissue culture for mushroom cultivation, hormone culture etc. After all, the SHGs are likely to provide them very strong motivation if additional income is discernible as a potential benefit from an activity.

(f) The NGO can organise skill up gradation of SHG members through better liaison with the local government department/authorities in charge of the subject. For example, non-formal education or adult literacy can be easily organised by the NGOs for SHG members. Thus, the SHGs can in fact prove to be the most effective platform for convergence of services. The women who constitute the neediest section of the society are made knowledgeable about the need as well as resources available for solving some of their problems. In fact, the village poor are known for their innate wisdom and practical sense. These are the two factors through which they have survived so far. The NGOs can make use of these, provide some coordination and use it as a springboard for a much larger level of achievement.

(g) The benefits of other schemes which presume the existence of a group of persons, for example, DWACRA or IMY, can yield their benefits to the SHG with the intervention of the NGO

The savings from members can also be used for ensuring some social security for them. For example, some groups uses the women's savings to purchase joint fixed deposits in banks. The total product is given to the member when she retires from some active participation in the economic activity. The value of money has appreciated by 8 times within this period (see box).

RBI and NABARD's Scheme of Linking SHGs with Banks

(a) RBI issued a circular in 1991 requesting the bank branches to link 500 SHGs with banks under a pilot project. In 1998, RBI issued another circular, indicating that the SHGs linked with banks under the pilot project proved to be extremely successful; the loans given through SHGs recorded a 100% rate of recovery, and Microfinance and empowerment of the poor.

Secondly, it was noticed that these loans were increasingly being used for economic activities rather than uneconomic ones. The banks were, therefore, directed that henceforth, under the "Service Area Approach" RRBs prepare detailed plans to meet the potential demand of credit in their area. They should try to encourage the SHG formation and linkage with banks, as a normal activity to encourage the weaker sections of the society. Thus, all rural SHGs can open their accounts with banks. Under the scheme, they are eligible to receive credit limits from the banks to the extent of four times of their savings. The interest rates relevant are:

| | | |
|---|---|---|
| NABARD to Banks | - | 6.5% |
| Bank to SHG | - | 12.5% |
| Bank to NGO | - | 10.5% |
| NGO to SHG | - | 12% |
| SHG to Member | - | as determined by the SHG |

SHG processes are quite sustainable even without external help, as has been demonstrated by an NGO firm of West Bengal.

## 1. ORGANISATIONAL SUSTAINABILITY

The organisational sustainability of SHGs depends on some key factors. First and foremost is the objective of group formation. Where groups are formed mostly for taking advantage of external benefits such as subsidy or other support, one finds they have a short lifespan. The second is the nurturing and training provided to SHGs. Well trained groups that are clear about their role, rules and functions, are able to sustain themselves over time. The third is the availability of need-based services, especially group maintenance services, such as maintenance of records, auditing of books, conflict resolution, etc., that help keep the group active in the long run.

Regarding the last aspect, there are some model-specific issues. While in some models, bankers and NGOs respectively are acting as financiers, they are expected to have a long-term relationship with the groups and provide/arrange for group maintenance services. However, where the NGOs are acting as facilitators, they are expected to withdraw from the groups after a period of time. Organizational sustainability of such groups is emerging as an area of concern under this model of linkage. Apprehensions have been expressed whether the groups could ever be on their own managing their affairs once NGOs withdraw from the scene.

To address the problem, some NGOs have encouraged formation of federations of SHGs in a cluster of villages federations can reduce default levels within SHGs.

NGOs like MYRADA are promoting community resource centres which provide the group maintenance services such as book-keeping, auditing, training and linkages with government programmes. The emerging need is for service providers for the group maintenance functions. NGOs are keen to promote community-based organisations such as community resource centres and federations. However, looking to the vast number of SHGs and the criticality of some of these functions, more service providers are needed. These intermediate organizations are set to become increasingly critical in enhancing the sustainability of SHGs. Capacity and Awareness building is aided through these processes. Sometimes group members are not even aware of the schemes which are available for them similarly there is a need to beef up skill upgradation and provide necessary guidance and help further in networking and linkages.

## 2. SUSTAINABILITY OF NETWORK CAPACITY OF THE FINANCIAL SYSTEM

The Reserve Bank of India, with its total support and endorsement of this programme, has created a policy environment that would ensure growth of SHG loan portfolio of banks. The keen interest of the Central government adds to the long-term stability of the programme. The policy environment is positive which induces greater participation of banks in the programme, improves sustainability and sets the ground for orderly expansion.

(a) Banks today have done a tremendous job of linking 2.24 million groups. By end of the current fiscal, this might increase to more than 2.8 million groups. The capacity of the banking system for linking more and more SHGs is not unlimited. Network capacity in the rural branches has not been expanding over the last five years. Staff strength, already reduced through a voluntary retirement scheme, is stretched to the limit with higher demands of productivity. The banks' ability to service twice the number of groups that are currently in existence by the present network of branches is suspect.

More than 4,800 entities are participating in the programme handling the tasks of promotion, nurturance and handholding. If the objective is to cover a larger proportion of rural poor, it would entail doubling the number of groups linked to the banking system. For this new NGOs and other organisations would need to be brought in as the task is an enormous one. This calls for two different sets of challenges. One is to find a large number of committed people to work in this sector in the rural areas. The other is to find training institutions and capacity-building organisations that would take up the job of moulding the manpower in the desired direction.

## 3. OPERATIONAL SUSTAINABILITY OF SHGS AND BANKS INVOLVED IN THE LINKAGE PROGRAM

Financial sustainability of the SHG-bank banking programme has to be viewed in totality and at the level of each organisation involved. The key policy issues centre around the profitability of SHG bank linkage to the banks as the banks will be interested in lending to SHGs in the long run only if they can make a profit out of it.

The methodology for measuring the profitability of linkage banking is an issue. A number of studies have yielded different conclusions. A study conducted by M-CRIL in five RRBs estimates that the cost-covering rate of interest for linkage banking is in the region of 20-22 per cent. As many banks are charging 10-12 per cent for SHG lending, the banks are incurring losses. However, another comprehensive study by Hans Dieter Seibel finds that the banks are making profits out of SHG lending as NPAs are negligible. Seibel assumes that the time of bankers carries zero opportunity cost as there is idle capacity (Seibel and Dave, 2002)

On pricing of SHG loans, there have been opinions that the groups can afford to pay high rates of interest as access to credit is their concern and not interest rates. The sustainability of the credit at borrower level depends on whether the livelihood activity produces an income that is more than the interest payable on the loan. While in the short run borrowers may be willing to pay high rates of interest out of desperation or the expectation of a windfall gain, over the long term they would not be able to do so. There are not many livelihoods in the margin that the poor pursue that produce extraordinary returns. Sustainability of the programme thus would hinge upon the ability of financial institutions to charge realistic rates of interest and of the groups in turn to fix reasonable terms for loans to their members.

(a) Banks' preference to the SHG-bank linkage model can be gauged from the fact that they are promoting groups of their own at their cost. They are continually monitoring Microfinance and empowerment of the poor expanding their SHG portfolio and are also conducting tailor-made training programmes for their staff and SHGs. The share of this model in which banks form and link groups is about 20 per cent of the groups linked. The share of bank-promoted groups in the overall linkage figures has been steadily increasing over the years. Some experts also see the present macroeconomic environment as being exceptional. Interest rates are the lowest in years, which makes other opportunities less attractive. Many banks have excess liquidity and capacity so that even a labour-intensive lending methodology with a low return becomes attractive (Bhattacharjee and Staschen, 2004).

However, many banks are looking at SHG banking with enthusiasm as with negligible NPAs, it is a safe lending methodology. Transaction and risk costs are considered to be low under this model. Many bankers report that SHG have helped in recovering past arrears from other customers in the villages. Some of the commercial banks see lending to SHGs as customer development of future business, as they expect three to four members in each group to avail larger loans and become individual customers of banks.

However, the group formation costs are at present not borne by the banks but provided by donors and governments under projects and programmes implemented by NGOs and other agencies. There is a concern that the SHGs and the banks that benefit out of microfinance services, should bear the cost of group promotion. Some commercial banks are offering incentives to NGOs for linking groups to their branches. For example, State Bank of India provides Rs.500 to the NGO (or other promoter) that opens the SHG account with SBI. Canara Bank has a scheme by which the bank reimburses the costs of promotion of every group linked with it. This is a clear sign that banks view linkage banking as a profitable business. However, how far the group development costs can be fully absorbed by the banks is a matter for further study. While commercial banks may be willing to bear the costs, RRBs and DCCBs may not be able to absorb costs of group formation in the immediate future.

## 4. QUALITY OF LINKAGE

The quality of linkages and some of the practices that are followed need improvement. The improvement of quality would make some parts of the SHG programme sustainable. Groups are currently compelled to deposit their internal savings with banks. There is hardly any new product development suitable to the savings needs of the women. Further, the time taken for processing of initial loan applications of SHGs is quite long and there is scope for reducing the same. There is also a tendency among branch managers to ration credit among the groups rather than meet credit needs after a proper appraisal.

Individuals/households being defaulters is an issue that is hampering credit flow to SHGs. Frequent transfer of branch staff also brings some uncertainties for the groups which look for a familiar face to deal with. The new branch staff needs to become oriented to deal with informal groups in their loaning operations and also achieve familiarity in the local area. Each transfer of a branch manager could slow down the linkage process as well as affect the quality of the linkage if proper follow-up or personal relations are not maintained.

## 5. POST-LINKAGE FOLLOW-UP

There are concerns expressed by bankers about the continuous monitoring needed to maintain the quality of groups. The workload on branches reflected by the 'per branch number of groups' is increasing and in some branches more than 200 groups are linked. Bankers feel a distinct need for ensuring quality and external audit of books of accounts. Post-linkage monitoring of groups is a critical requirement. Early warning systems are needed to ensure the comfort level of banks is kept high.

## 6. FINANCIAL SERVICES

(h) Many SHGs are yet to graduate to offering voluntary savings facilities to the members. Moreover, many groups do not allow withdrawal of savings by of the poor members. Loss of liquidity in their own savings proves to be a disincentive for clients who would like to save any surplus cash they have with the group.

While the savings and credit needs of members have been satisfied to some extent, formal insurance services to the poor and low-income house-holds are inadequate. Insurance, especially life and health products are required by the low income groups with which the SHG programme is closely associated. Distribution of Insurance products over a large number of people with small cover requirements could be best done though the SHPIs and SHGs themselves. There is a potential for a linkage insurance programme on lines similar to the linkage banking programme. This would make the bonding of the groups better and improve the financial content of the programme. The loan ticket sizes remain small between Rs. 2000 and Rs. 15000 which is not encouraging as with these loan sizes the loans are likely to be used for consumption purposes and not for production credit to set up sustainable income generating projects which would ensure repayments too. Even though hedged with all these caveats and uncertainities microfinance enables the poor to access basic financial services as credit, savings, insurance enabling poor households to save,access capital,and manage risk exposures of various kinds as life property and health as a prerequisite for their economic and social development. Thus it enables the effective delivery of low cost financial services to the very poor. Microfinance has its limitations however it has been found that there are significant complementarities between access to financial services and the ability of the poor to access education,health care and better technologies. The ability to secure these is certainly enhanced with increase in awareness and the upliftment which comes through engagement in gainful self employment, through income generating projects through peers.

## References


1. Benson K Institutional Finance and Rural development.
2. Basu Priya Improving access to Finance for India's Rural Poor.
3. Indira Misra Microcredit.
4. Majumdar NA Inclusive growth Development Perspectives in the Indian Economy.
5. Parthasarthy. Economic Reforms and Rural development in India.
6. Indian Banks Association Inclusive Growth New Challenges.
7. Kempson E Policy Level Responses to Financial Exclusion in Developed Economies Lessons for Developing countries paper presented at the conference on Access to Finance Building Inclusive Financial Systems World Bank Washington DC.
8. Microfinance Emerging Trends and Challenges edited Sundaresan Edward Elgar Publishing Ltd. 2008.

# 7

# "The Role of Technology in Ramping up Access to the Poor"

**Technology-intensive innovations** are acquiring an ever growing transformational role in economic growth and social development and are redefining development agendas, enabling new opportunities for the poor to bridge the digital divide and catch-up with the more affluent. New communications technologies and plummeting computing costs are shrinking distance and eroding borders over time. The remotest village has the possibility of tapping a global store of knowledge beyond the dreams of anyone living a century ago and more quickly and cheaply than anyone imagined only a few decades ago. Despite the spread of brick and mortar banking, we still have only one bank branch per 16000 people. Click and Portal banking remains a largely urban phenomenon. Yet it is widely recognized that a country which is on a high trajectory of economic growth must ensure growth with equity hence the policy focus on financial Inclusion which microfinance helps foster. Access to banking mainstreams the poor and helps bring the unorganized sector within the ambit of the formal financial system. In poorer countries barriers of illiteracy and geography have been bridged by mobile banking and smart card banking which has helped leapfrog past click and portal and enabled poorer sections to bridge the digital divide and avail the benefits of access to financial services. The advantages entailed also lie in moving in concert with the rest of the world to a cashless transaction environment minimization of physical cash in transaction reduces the opportunity for fraudulent or criminal activity reduces cash handling costs it allows the value of money to be better utilised Community network centers play an important role in successfully addressing the 8Cs of success in the digital age these are connectivity, content, community, commerce, capacity, culture, cooperation and capital.UN studies have also shown empirically that though the costs of using ICTs for development are high not using them will prove costlier.

**IT based Financial Inclusion**

Various options for IT based financial inclusion are now available in the country. These include issuing biometric smart cards, devices with the business correspondent where the account holder's finger print details are stored and banking services are rendered on basis of identification at the specific device or using mobile phones for access to banking services. Hence, in achieving banking penetration, **banks need to take the maximum advantage of available IT solutions. Since State Governments are also keen to disburse NREGA and social security funds through bank accounts, partnerships can be explored between banks and State Governments and leverage the same infrastructure for achieving financial inclusion. The funding arrangements available under Financial Inclusion Technology Fund (with NABARD) or other options such as the support offered for distribution of Government payments by RBI may be explored for this purpose.** RBI has formulated a scheme wherein it would partially reimburse the banks, the cost of opening accounts with bio-metric access at the rate of Rs. 50 per account through which payment of social security benefits, NREGA payments and payments under other government benefit program would be routed. The incentive package would be dependent on the State Governments willing to pay to the transacting banks, a mutually agreed transaction fee. The reimbursement by RBI would be available for an agreed period. Since the State Governments would in any event have to incur cost for distribution of such payments, they should be willing to reimburse the costs incurred by banks in undertaking the transactions-while the initial cost of opening the account can be partly met through the RBI offer of Rs. 50 per account.

Technology-intensive social innovations with poverty reduction objectives can be triggered, supported and sustained. One of the main unresolved issues in this field is the question why potentially useful social innovations may fail to sustain or to scale up and how this challenge can be addressed. As technology intensive innovations gain increasing influence around the world, applications for social development can be expected to gain increasing prominence and to shape future development agendas. Therefore, the questions addressed are important for understanding the role of technology in change of the financial sector landscape.

Through its guidelines on the Business Correspondent - Business Facilitator Model, RBI has created an enabling regulatory environment to foster innovation and increase the outreach of the banking system. Smart Cards and mobile telephony are part of this process which is transformational. Banks in collaboration with State Governments have successfully leveraged technology to expand the frontiers. Banks are working in tandem to take banking services to the most far flung and remote corner of the country leveraging small hand held devices and /mobile phones. New technologies, smartcard, virtual credit card, mobile phones ensure expedient banking services at affordable cost. A smartcard or chip card is a pocket sized card with an embedded integrated circuit to store data and process information. Smartcard enhanced systems are currently used in several key applications including banking, healthcare, telecommunications, secure identification, and other applications.

Under this smart card project, a customer is given a Smart Card which acts like a bank's passbook. The smart card provides customer's identity, transaction store and bio-metric data to the bank. It eases services such as opening of no-frills loan accounts, savings accounts revolving general purpose credit, government beneficiary schemes, fund transfer, remittance, recurring deposits, joint accounts, insurance premium collection and utility bill collection.

The Main barrier successfully addressed is that lack of access to markets and the last mile problem.

The approach is to create branchless banking infrastructure by establishing a network of business correspondents – a banking outpost in each village. A common service point (CSP) is identified in the project areas which offer banking facilities. The (CSP) is manned by a local person familiar with the area and able to communicate fluently, liaise effectively with the local population. A database is maintained with the help of a hand-held device and mobile connectivity. His services are utilized on commission basis. Villagers are provided smart cards with biometric identification to access their accounts. The introduction of IT-enabled financial inclusion facilitates easy payments to beneficiaries under various schemes of the state and central governments such as social security pension schemes and the National Rural Employment Guarantee Scheme (NREGS), wages payments which are directly deposited in their bank accounts on the Brazilian Pattern where payments under the "BOLSA FAMILIAS" program of the government are made to the recipients entirely through an electronic benefit card (EBT). Most microfinance borrowers are not very literate there are now ATM networks which function on the basis of fingerprint and biometric information processal and recognition Biometric teller machines and Smart cards have changed the way microfinance business can be done. The smart card on a memory chip stores customer details under the correspondent model in Brazil local post offices,petrol stations and shops are all acting as agents of banks they have barcode reading and point of sale terminals. Public Sector Banks are actively partnering state governments in the financial inclusion project among the Private Sector Banks. ICICI Bank and the HDFC Bank have been the leaders of the pack while Axis Bank and others are also making headway. The Andhra Government pioneered the initiative by providing an operational framework for increasing outreach of mainstream banking and financial services to the poorest through technology based solutions in August 2006. Rolled out as a pilot project implemented by six mandals of Warangal district and two of Karimnagar through six banks (SBI, SBH, AB, UBI, APGVB, and Axis Bank) payments commenced in May 2007 and are continuing with upscaling of the model the vision is to achieve TFI Total Financial Inclusion through smart cards. Based on the recommendations of the RBI high level committee on the subject the Government of Anadhra Pradesh (GOAP) embarked on the second phase of upscaling since August 2008 using the One District – One Bank model. The success of the project led to the identification of eight other districts where the State Government proposes to roll out the project Medak, Mahbubnagar, Chitoor, East Godavari, West Godavari, Nellore, Krishna and Vishakhapatnam districts. The State Governments vision is to upscale in a phased manner to all the 23 districts of the state. The project, disburses pensions, wages through smart card based IT enabled services provided by participating banks. On 30/11/08 the smart card project was extended to the entire Krishna district ensuring financial inclusion for 75% of the hitherto uncovered poor. Electronic benefit transfers to social security pensioners under the AP Social Security Pension Scheme (APSSP) and National Rural Employment Guarantee scheme are possible. Under the RBI incentive policy, Banks are entitled to receive Rs. 50 for every smart card account opened the Financial Inclusion Fund (FIF) and the Financial Inclusion Technology Fund (FITF) each with Rs. 500 crore have been placed with NABARD and Government of India has issued rules for administration of the fund.

Syndicate Bank, SBI and Canara Bank are launching SMART CARD ACCOUNT project in the three districts of Chitradurga, Bellary and Bagalkot in coordination with the government of Karnataka. The smart card will enable farmers to avail government pension, social security payments, National Rural Employment Guaranteee Programme (NREGP) payments and wages. The project is expected to cover the entire state in phased manner. Syndicate Bank is implementing the project on financial inclusion solutions based on IMFAST (Integra's Mobile Financial Applications Secure Terminal) system, a service by Bangalore-based Integra Micro Systems (P) Ltd. IMFAST is a platform designed to handle financial applications specifically targeted at rural customers. PNB for IT-enabled financial inclusion, the bank had identified 27 pilot projects (20 in rural areas and seven in urban areas) to be launched across 13 states in Indo-Gangetic belt. Out of the 20 rural pilot projects, six pilot projects had already been launched at Neemrana, Rajasthan, Tineri Panchayat, Patna, Bihar, Matki Jharoli, Saharanpur, UP, Gararu, Gaya district in Bihar, Mauli Jagran, Chandigarh and Kullu, Himachal Pradesh. Similarly the Indian Bank has been active in Tamil Nadu. SBI IT enabled devices and biometric scanners coupled with smart card will provide banking services to far flung areas of the state of Madhya Pradesh. Nine commercial and private banks will be allotted various districts with two blocks each. Banks have responded positively. SBI has also rolled out its Tiny card in Uttaranchal and in Mizoram in the North East.

The Raghuram Rajan Committee on Financial Sector reforms (CFSR) has advocated the early adoption of m-banking solutions to speed access. The Rangarajan Committee on Financial Inclusion has given a clear strategic direction of the way forward it is clear that branchless banking represents the wave of the future as it enables Banks and users to on the upside :

1. Cut Costs
2. Eliminate impersonation and fraud thereby plugging leakages, in transfers of wages and benefits to the poor.
3. Promote overall inclusion

There is a downside too :

1. The initial costs involved in setting up electronic infrastructure are prohibitive
2. There are also significant costs in building up a rural agent network to distribute and disseminate the information and build the competency to enable people to attain the capability of accessing the service.
3. Whether in the long run this will increase depth and actually promote inclusion remains a moot point.

Though DFID/CGAP have done research in the subject area they have found that the usage of mobile telephony or smart card banking was restricted to :

1. Receiving welfare payments
2. Making deposits/withdrawals
3. Balance enquiry

Contrary to popular belief while the possession of a mobile or a smart card increases awareness it does not automatically promote access to the entire range of Banking Services. It also leaves a question mark as to whether people who use the services primarily to get payments under NREGS or other benefits would still continue to use it beyond mere receipt and drawal of wages.

Other technical issues are of meeting the challenge of ensuring :

1. Customer safety

2. Compliance with AML/CFT guidelines- Anti money laundering and financing of terrorism guidelines norms as laid down by the Financial Action Task Force (FATF) and the Prevention of Money Laundering Act (PMLA).

In subscriber identity module sim/smart card based operations customer data /personal identification data is encrypted on the smart card, service providers merely host this information on behalf of the Banks. The two critical issues:

1. Of ensuring interoperability (across networks) while assuring.
2. Application based security also remains critical.

These are teething troubles, on a macro perspective, by leveraging technology. We can ensure financial inclusion in the years to come as Nandan Nilekani ("Imaging India-Ideas for the new century") expresses it. "A key piece of infrastructure atop an interconnected grid is the electronic flow of funds. This requires that each uniquely identified citizen or organization has a bank account into which money can be transferred from the state. This could be an account in a Bank, a post office or with a self help group within this system the ID smart card can function as a mobile, non transferable, electronic passbook. The impact on inclusive growth and India's savings rate from implementing this would be massive as 80% of Indians do not have a bank account and therefore lie outside any sort of Banking system besides perhaps the one represented by the exploitive moneylender and his steel cash box. Linking smart cards to such accounts can open up the banking system to hundreds of millions more people. It also introduces the possibility of offering direct services from pension and benefit payments to trading accounts to an unprecedented number of people."

It is an experiment which is significantly transforming banking across the globe, Russia, Argentina, South Africa, (Wizzit) Brazi (Bolsa Familias), Pakistan (Tameer Bank) Phillippines (SMART) and Ghana among others all testify to its success.

| *Nature of Financial Transaction* | *Location of transaction* | *Time to complete* |
|---|---|---|
| Cheques | Local (same bank)<br>Outstation | Three days<br>10-30 plus seven days by post |
| Demand draft | Local same bank | One to two days plus seven days by post |
| Electronic credit card | | Seven days merchant payments |
| Debit card | | do |
| Electronic clearing system | | Four days (limited coverage) |
| Postal money order | | 10-45 days |

Data Source Payment realisation for various payment modes in India Microfinance Emerging Trends and Challenges edited by S Sundaresan (2008). pg 75.

Clearly there is a pressing need to up the ante on IT based financial inclusion IBA's Approach Paper.

The IBA had brought out an Approach Paper on IT enabled FI. In the paper, it has been pointed out that technology can:

- help lower the costs of doing business by not only reducing transaction costs but also eliminating costlier, time and labour intensive workflows;
- lead to enhanced business productivity by bringing in efficiencies, effectiveness and economies of scale and scope in business processes; and
- enable structures for better management control and insight, by helping monitor and mitigate business risks in a timely manner.

The various challenges pointed out in broad basing financial inclusion include distance and reach, environmental factors, lack of last mile connectivity, suitable delivery model, storage of data, contingencies for link failure, manpower, choice

Ideal standardized technology, development of new products, lack of marketing, etc.

The paper states that if financial inclusion intermediations truly seek to leverage technology for transformational impacts, they should focus on (i) building technology-enabled interfaces that go beyond enabling transactions and (ii) using technology to capture information that goes beyond meeting reporting requirements. Further, the importance of developing and implementing a credit scoring framework has been pointed out.

It has been stated that apex bodies and banks need to play a major role to:

Develop uniform structure and modalities for inclusive growth;

Develop an actionable technology framework that the whole banking industry can leverage for the benefit of furthering Financial Inclusion objective;

Evaluate and recommend suitable technology for banking industry with acceptable standards for contactless cards/biometric facility with interoperability for using various devises conforming to defined standards;

Play an active role in implementation of various components such as (but not limited to) a centralized hub/switch for interfacing transactions with Core Banking Solution CBS systems of banks, all-purpose single card and support for both online and offline operational models;

Arrange pilot testing of transaction updation in different CBS systems and ensure that results are made available within a fixed timeframe; and

Provide support to maintain/upgrade standards and ensure conformity by stakeholders.

It has also been mentioned that IBA and IDRBT have to play a major role in synchronizing the different requirements of banks and provide technological solutions within a time frame. Broadly, the following aspects need to be addressed:

(i) A uniform structure for enrolment of customers, conforming to extant KYC norms.

(ii) Standards for the use of proximity/near field smart cards which are interoperable in different devices.

(iii) A centralized hub/switch on the lines of ATM switch for interfacing with CBS systems of different banks.

(iv) Adherence to Service Area Approach with specific villages to be allocated to specific banks for extending financial inclusion.

(v) Banks should endeavour to bring total prosperity and growth in the allotted villages, developing them into multiple and microeconomic hubs of modern India.

(vi) Qualification and training of business correspondents (e.g. similar to insurance agents).

The approach paper has also stated that if IDRBT is able to host a Centralized Financial Inclusion System (Intermediary Transaction Processing System) it would be of immense help to the industry.

It has further been suggested that an all purpose single card could be given to the account holder instead of a plethora of cards (like debit card, credit card, KCC, Swarozgar Credit Card, Artisan Credit Card, Laghu Udyami Trade Card, etc.)

A smart card is a card which is similar to a credit/debit ATM card. The distinguishing feature lines in the presence of a chip in the card which can store information. Unlike in the case of magnetic-stripe based cards, the stored information in the chip could either be permanent in nature, or may be subject to change. For instance, the passwords can be changed at any frequency by the cardholder. Because of its additional feature, smart cards find usage not only for financial transaction processing but in a number of other areas as well.

One of the greatest advantages of the smart card technology is its ability to consolidate multiple applications in a single, dynamic card. These cards simplify life for end-users, often replacing up to three other cards for payment and other transactions. Thus, there can be a single card which can function as an identity card, as a driving licence, as a health card and also for other funds related purposes. Because these cards deliver such highly personalised applications, their perceived value among end-users is much higher and helps to build stronger than average customer loyalty.

With Indian banking having embraced IT in a large way, the potential for usage of multi-application smart cards is high. Smart-card based electronic purse systems, in which value is stored on the card chip and not in an externally recorded account so that machines accepting the card need no network connectivity. Thus, the multi-application cards are beneficial for issuers as well, especially because they provide the prospect to create unique marketing opportunities. They are particularly suitable for financial inclusion in remote parts of the country. For the banks interested in introducing smart cards, another quantifiable benefit is the ability to forecast a reduction in fraud.

Multi-application smart cards also pose several challenges. Managing multiple smart card applications along with their associated scripts, data streams and cryptographic keys is more complex than issuing single-function cards. Open standards and interoperability become more critical. Life cycle management is also much more elaborate, especially post-issuance upgrades to applications. In these environments, establishing a proven, integrated smart card infrastructure will likely mean the difference between ongoing success and failure to capitalise on the most lucrative opportunities. To address these issues, the Reserve Bank has supported pilot projects which would outline the major problems which are likely to be faced and the measures to overcome them, based on which acceptable and implementable standards will emerge.

The Reserve Bank has been encouraging banks to use technology-based solutions for increased financial inclusion. Credit delivery in rural areas has often been expensive for banks with large number of small loan accounts to be serviced.

Information Technology (IT) enabled methods are being looked into as the best alternative for rural credit delivery that can increase outreach and reduce cost of delivery.

Permission to banks to appoint business correspondents (BCs) has opened possibilities of outreach which were not available earlier. The use of appropriate technology by the BCs has the potential of reducing operational costs and building up a powerful management information system (MIS) in addition to creating rural employment. The use of technology combined with an effective use of BCs has the potential of creating a banking outpost in every village which can enhance the rural credit delivery.

Several models have emerged in the last couple of years to enable technology driven rural outreach by banks. Nearly all of them converge on the following essential components: (i) a customer with a multi application smart card which can be a contact card or a contact-less card, (ii) business correspondent with a simputer/hand held terminal/mobile phone enabling banking services, (iii) a central processor unit, (iv) the banks and (v) a centralised card management for each of the above systems.

The technology application model is premised on providing financial services in the rural areas through the BC model using low cost and simple IT based solutions. A central system which could be a shared infrastructure providing for economies of scale and consequential cost benefits, and a field system which enables access to the central computer by the BCs are essential components of the model. Hand held computer devices which connect to remote servers using fixed line connectivity and mobile technology are being extensively used. Finger print method for uniquely identifying customers for extending financial services is being widely accepted. It has been observed that bio-metric identification for KYC purpose is emerging as the most popular method. Transactions in the accounts such as cash deposits and withdrawals can be carried out by customers without having to go to the bank branch. The customers are issued hard copy of transaction details facilitated by a tiny printer.

An IT enabled model for banking outreach is basically implemented as under:

Information regarding potential customer is collected by business facilitators and passed on to the bank in a prescribed format or the BC enrols the customer account for the bank.

Banks carry out KYC scrutiny and arrange for opening a savings bank account for the customer, after relevant information is captured, such as his photograph, fingerprints and signature (optional). This information is encrypted in the smart card.

While handing over the card to the customer, the BC activates the card for the customer by fingerprint identification. At the time of activation, the balance available in the bank account is recorded on the smart card.

A customer can withdraw and deposit money using his smart card at the terminal of the BC. Every time a transaction is made, a print out is provided to the customer. Transactions cannot be undertaken unless a biometric verification of the cardholder is done.

Banking transactions are freed from branch timings and can be done whenever the BC is available with a capture device.

If a BC does not have requisite money to pay the customer, a print out will be given to him stating that no cash is available at the customer's end. This information will be passed on to the bank through the central processor to facilitate immediate replenishment of cash. Incidentally, this also acts as a check to prevent business correspondents from denying service to customers.

The terminal with the BC is operated with a rechargeable battery and not dependant on steady supply of electricity.

An added facility that can be enabled is that the customer can use the smart card as a debit card at merchant establishments.

A central processor unit integrates village level terminals and identified merchant establishments with the bank.

The technology seamlessly integrates into core banking solutions of the banks concerned and supports various types of deposits and loan accounts.

Each hand held model can be used to service 500 to 1000 accounts by a BC: the device when seen in the context of its servicing capabilities and range is very cost effective. Such models have already been adopted by some private sector and public sector banks. In the Annual Policy for the year 2007-08, banks were urged to scale up IT initiatives for financial inclusion speedily while ensuring that solutions are highly secure, amenable to audit, and follow widely accepted open standards to ensure eventual inter-operability among the different systems.

If financial inclusion intermediations truly seek to leverage technology for transformational impacts, they should focus on (i) building technology-enabled interfaces that go beyond enabling transactions and (ii) using technology to capture information that goes beyond meeting reporting requirements. Further, the importance of developing and implementing a credit scoring framework has been pointed out.

It has been stated that apex bodies and banks need to play a major role to:

Develop uniform structure and modalities for inclusive growth;

Develop an actionable technology framework that the whole banking industry can leverage for the benefit of furthering FI objective;

Evaluate and recommend suitable technology for banking industry with acceptable standards for contactless cards/biometric facility with interoperability for using various devises conforming to defined standards;

Play an active role in implementation of various components such as (but not limited to) a centralized hub/switch for interfacing transactions with CBS systems of banks, all-purpose single card and support for both online and offline operational models;

Arrange pilot testing of transaction updation in different CBS systems and ensure that results are made available within a fixed timeframe; and

Provide support to maintain/upgrade standards and ensure conformity by stakeholders.

It has also been mentioned that IBA and IDRBT have to play a major role in synchronizing the different requirements of banks and provide technological solutions within a time frame. Broadly, the following aspects need to be addressed:

(vii) A uniform structure for enrolment of customers, conforming to extant KYC norms.

(viii) Standards for the use of proximity/near field smart cards which are interoperable in different devices.

(ix) A centralized hub/switch on the lines of ATM switch for interfacing with CBS systems of different banks.

(x) Adherence to Service Area Approach with specific villages to be allocated to specific banks for extending financial inclusion.

(xi) Banks should endeavour to bring total prosperity and growth in the allotted villages, developing them into multiple and microeconomic hubs of modern India.

(xii) Qualification and training of business correspondents (e.g. similar to insurance agents)

(i) Banks have been advised that their obligation to maintain secrecy in respect of customers transactions arises out of contractual relationship between the banker and customer and as such no information should be divulged to third parties except where the disclosure is under compulsion of law, where there is a duty to the public to disclose, where the interest of bank requires disclosure and where the disclosure is made with the express or implied consent of the customer.

(ii) In order to ensure that persons belonging to low income group, both in urban and rural areas do not encounter difficulties in opening bank accounts, the know your customer (KYC) procedure for opening accounts has been simplified for those accounts with balances not.

(iii) exceeding Rs. 50,000/- and credits thereto not exceeding Rs. 100,000/- in a year. The simplified procedure allows introduction by a customer on whom full KYC drill has been observed. The banks have the discretion to accept any evidence as to the identity and address of the customer to the satisfaction of the bank.

(iv) The Business Facilitators (BFs) may be used for facilitation services which may include identification of borrowers, collection and preliminary processing of loan applications, creating awareness about bank products and education and advice on managing money and debt counseling, processing and submission of application to banks, promotion of Self help Groups/ Joint Liability Groups, post sanction monitoring, follow up for recovery, etc. and no approval of RBI is required for using business facilitators for the services mentioned above.

(v) Business Correspondents (BCs), apart from the above services can disburse small value credit, recover principal/ collect interest, collect small value deposits, sell micro insurance/mutual fund products/pension products/other third party products, receive and deliver small value remittance / other payment instruments.

(vi) banks may pay reasonable commission/fee to the BFs / BCs, bank's agreement with the BFs/BCs should specifically prohibit them from charging any fee to the customers directly for services rendered by them on behalf of the bank.

(vii) Banks can use NBFCs licensed under Section 25 of the Companies Act, 1956 as Business Correspondents.

(viii) Banks may utilize appropriate technology to scale up their financial inclusion efforts while taking care to ensure that the solutions developed are highly secure, amenable to audit and follow widely accepted open standards to allow inter operability among the different systems adopted by different banks.

(ix) Banks have been advised that the adoption of customer acceptance policy and its implementation should not result in denial of banking services to general public, especially to those who are financially or socially disadvantaged. Banks were also advised that customer identification means identifying the customer and verifying his/her identity by using reliable, independent source documents, data or information to their satisfaction and that 'being satisfied' means that the bank must be able to satisfy the competent authorities that due.

(x) diligence was observed based on the risk profile of the customer in compliance with the extant guidelines in place.

(xi) Banks, while appointing individuals as BCs may ensure that these individuals are permanent residents of the area in which they propose to operate as BCs and also institute additional safeguards as may be considered appropriate to minimise agency risk.

(xii) As regards mobile banking operations, only banks which are licensed and supervised in India, having a physical presence in India and who have implemented core banking solutions are permitted to offer mobile banking transactions to their customers and /or holders of debit/ credit cards. The technology used for mobile banking must be secure and should ensure confidentiality, integrity, authenticity and non-repudiability.

**Banking Correspondents (BCs) as Delivery Channels**

The distance criteria under the BC guidelines have been reported as being restrictive. It would be necessary to take all relevant aspects into consideration before waiver of the distance criteria is recommended by DCCs/SLBCs and the same is to be strictly done on a case by case basis.

There have been demands that NBFCs should be considered for appointment as BCs.

There were also suggestions requesting banks to engage common service centre (CSC) as business correspondents (BCs). In this context, banks are presently not permitted to engage Common Service Centres (CSCs) established by Service Centre Agencies (SCAs) as Business Correspondents. However, there is no objection to CSCs, established by SCAs, being appointed as Business Facilitators.

There have been demands that Self Help Groups (SHGs) should be considered for appointment as BCs. SHGs are essentially groups formed for the purpose of self help though thrift and internal loaning. Most of the SHGs are unregistered and do not have a legal constitution. Studies have revealed that many of the SHGs rely on Self Help Promoting Institutions (SHPIs) or NGOs for their accounting and book keeping requirements. The activities to be undertaken by BCs may involve cash handling on a day to day basis. Accordingly, these entities have not been permitted to function as BCs for the present.

## Service Area Approach Concept

In Karnataka, for the pilot project for IT enabled financial inclusion, the banks have adopted the Service Area Approach (SAA) for coverage of beneficiaries. However in Andhra Pradesh, this model has not been followed. In Krishna district of Andhra Pradesh, one bank is effecting the Government payments through smart cards. While some public sector banks still find the Service Area Approach preferable, the new generation private sector banks find these restrictive.

Problems could also arise when one bank one district model is adopted for the EBT scheme as it may cause resentment on the part of other banks operating in the district. It would be necessary to arrive at a consensus between the State Governments and banks operating in the districts and adopt a model which is acceptable and comfortable to all the banks operating in the area, whether is a one district one bank model or the SAA approach or any other model through appropriate discussions involving the various stakeholders viz. State Government, Reserve Bank, SLBC convenor bank, banks operating in the districts, etc.

**Financials**

The costs involved in implementing the project would include the initial investment cost of IT infrastructure, smart card costs, service charges payable to BCs, maintenance cost of equipment, etc. There is no agreed cost sharing between the State Governments and banks in place.

**The Road Ahead**

A multi-agency approach involving close coordination/ interaction between the different entities would have to be adopted. The State Governments would be best suited to assume leadership with banks being delivery agents.

The various initiatives, especially those relating to laying the requisite technology architecture would require substantial investments and commitment from the banks. Such of these banks that are reluctant to measure up to the requirements may have to give way to other willing banks forthwith, thus ensuring that the entire process does not get delayed.

The banks coming forward to assume the responsibility of disbursement of government payments in a particular area should also give some undertaking to the DCCs that appropriate arrangements would be put in place to ensure that the various banking needs and requirements of the people in that area hitherto being catered to by other banks would continued to be satisfactorily met.

Mobile Phone guidelines were issued in October 2008 dismissed as "Overly Cautious" by critics ( cf CGAP criticism- "India's mobile phone guidelines who wins and who loses 8 Oct 2008 Kabir Kumar) has focused on the following"

The guidelines permit only licensed banks with a physical bank presence in India to launch mobile banking- By requiring physical presence for account opening, the guidelines give mobile banking a crippled start in the Indian market. Only domestic transactions in Indian rupee are permitted and are capped at Rs. 5000 per customer per day for funds transfer and Rs.10,000 per customer per day for transactions involving purchase of goods/services.

The unbanked remain un-helped because a mobile wallet service from a mobile operator would have surely reached more people faster. Millions could have had a mobile wallet account for transfers and payments, barriers to account opening for the undocumented/ unbanked in India will remain the same.

Interoperability will slow down the time to market but ultimately clients will benefit. In practice the payment realisation remains extremely poor.

1. Internet criticism of the guidelines stems from mobile service providers who view the guidelines from their perspective as "too little too late" hence the lament that No G-cash in India, or m-pesa until RBI issues new guidance on e-money. Both of those services are not backed by a bank account and will attract Section 45(S) of the RBI Act 1934.
2. The transaction caps are large enough to meet the needs of the target clientele.
3. Reliance on Banks and insistence on interoperability ensures that there is no oligopolistic dominance of any one provider dominant in the market it also leaves room for greater competition and consequent innovation and up gradation of services.
4. The guidelines go farther than most countries on customer protection issues which are a virtue.
5. As per the guidelines, Customers have to open accounts in person this measure is essential to avert impersonation and fraud.
6. Discretion to allow exceptions to the above are left to banks based on their judgment rather than putting Banks

in a straitjacket of uniform criteria. Banks can use the instructions in the spirit of the guidelines to facilitate rather than inhibit the process of financial inclusion.

7. Keeping in view that this is a nascent market and we are in unchartered waters dealing with a sensitive target group, it is best that the guidelines err on the side of caution and we gradually work to ramp up the efforts.
8. This was also the approach followed by Banks of their own volition when they initially introduced new products (credit cards) using technology nearly two decades ago.
9. Branchless banking has great potential to extend the distribution of Banking Services the real challenge is of making it a Financial Inclusion banking model that imparts depth and serves the poor by making the full range of Banking Services accessible. At present there are limitations to this and hence it can only be treated as a qualified success.
10. Dr. Rangarajan has stated that "The weakest aspect of India's economic reach is financial access" this is an indictment we have to address

Efforts are needed to beef up competency and capability of the target clientele to use the new technology and to make the SMART Card based technology an affordable household hand held device. Technological Innovations hold the key to reducing the costs of the delivery of small loans and accepting very small savings deposits.This will make the approach more scalable. In conclusion it is becoming increasingly apparent that large scale sustainable microfinance can be achieved only if financial services for the poorest are integrated into the overall financial system. Microfinance services become the lower end of the entire financial sector opening up access and markets to increasingly poor and geographically remote clients. It means enabling the financial outreach and financial sustainability through leveraging technology and streamlining business processes to increase cost efficiency in the face of competition. These policies will allow financial sector deepening and expansion and also allow the vision of Microfinance as larger than mere microcredit and microenterprises as financial services for the poor. Building both the market for these services and the local human resource base to meet market demand is a key condition for the development of the microfinance industry.

## References

1. Microfinance Emerging Trends and Challenges S Sundaresan.
2. Milbrandt J 2008 Biometrics and smartcards serve as successfull microfinance Innovations in Asia Microfinance Report January 9.
3. Global Envision 2007 Microfinance goes mobile cell phone banking revolutionises microfinance financial services for the poor www.globalvision.com library.
4. CGAP Phase III Strategy Paper Building financial Systems that work for the Poor.

# 8

# *Emerging Concerns*

The scenario of microfinance has transformed into the microfinance Industry and has undergone a sea change. Regulatory challenges deserve greater attention from policy makers. The rapid growth of the industry and the inflows of capital represent its own set of challenges at the upper end the International capital markets are growing rapidly integrated with financing and investment needs of the microfinance market in India ECB borrowing is permissible subject to regulatory caps. The rapid growth and inflows of capital present their own regulatory challenges and the implicit need to ensure compliance with the know your customer KYC and Anti Money Launder AML guidelines. At the lower end of the spectrum conversely things remain the same NGOs and SHGs are the mainstay of the poor borrowers to meet consumption and basic lifecycle needs. Median loan sizes remain miniscule and interest rates prohibitively high.

Emerging Concerns :

(1) Up scaling

(2) Capacity Building

(3) Sustainability of SHG
(4) Graduation from micro finance to micro enterprises
(5) Impact of continuous program with 'subsidy' components
(6) Interest rates
(7) Inability to graduate them from microfinance to micro credit
(8) Go beyond income smoothing and consumption credit
(9) Time is involved in all SHG activities there is no magic seed.

**Section I : Key Issues of Concern**

Interest in the regulation and supervision of microfinance institutions has been driven primarily by the desire of unregulated microfinance institutions to mobilize deposits from the general public. Trying to become sustainable, seeking to expand their outreach, these microfinance institutions apprehend difficulties in receiving funding from donor agencies in the amount and timeframe needed to meet their desired levels of expansion. One alternative that some microfinance institutions have pursued is borrowing from banks. Many other microfinance institutions, however, prefer to investigate the possibility of mobilizing deposits from the general public.

There are three major reasons why microfinance institutions are attracted to the idea of deposit mobilization as a source of funding:

(1) deposit mobilization appears to leave funding decisions in the hands of the microfinance institution;
(2) deposits appear to be a cheaper source of funds than bank loans; and
(3) there may be economies of scope between lending and deposit mobilization to the extent to which the borrowing and depositing clienteles overlap;
(4) a number of sustainable microfinance institutions in various countries have turned to deposit mobilization as

the primary source of funds for their growing loan portfolios.

Since virtually every country in the world requires the licensing and regulation of institutions that mobilize deposits from the general public. The issue of regulating and supervising microfinance institutions has become an increasingly important item on the microfinance agenda, especially for the more successful and aggressive institutions. As expected, this has led to some undesirable side effects:

1. Microfinance institutions, who wish to mobilize deposits are keen on the creation of a 'soft' regulatory environment that is more lenient toward microfinance institutions than other financial intermediaries.
2. In some instances, they want the role of the regulatory agency to be extended to cover institutions that do not yet mobilize deposits in an effort to help them qualify to accept deposits or to obtain funding from other sources.
3. The debate on regulation tends to focus excessively on the characteristics of microfinance institutions, particularly their nonprofit origins, to the neglect of the risk characteristics of clients and loan products.
4. Those who are not so enthusiastic about the new more market-oriented practices of microfinance have used the attention devoted to regulation and supervision as an opportunity to raise issues related to regulating micro lending, especially usury ceilings on Interest rates.
5. The impact of regulation and supervision on microfinance institutions that might want to undertake micro lending as a major activity has been neglected.
6. As the typical bank is much larger than the typical microfinance institution and more of the largest micro lenders are banks e.g., Grameen, Bank Rakyat Indonesia, Bancosol, many knowledgeable observers of microfinance as Marguerite Robinson have concluded that major increases in outreach will need to come from banks.

**Should there be Regulation of Microfinance Institutions?**

A regulatory agency's basic objective is to protect the financial system from unsound i.e., excessively risk practices by deposit-taking institutions and thereby to protect a country's payments system and, secondarily, to protect small and uninformed depositors. If a regulatory agency adds other objectives, it may spread its resources too thin, thus deflecting the necessary attention to meet its major objectives. In some cases, the added objectives may even conflict with the basic objective.

Except in so far as it affects risk taking by deposit-taking institutions, there is no reason for a regulatory agency to be concerned with lending behaviour. In particular, a regulatory agency should not be concerned in any way with the lending practices of microfinance institutions that do not mobilize deposits. Regulatory agencies have often become involved in dealing with fraud in lending and controlling interest rates, but with detrimental results. Fraud in lending can be handled just as well by institutions whose primary purpose is to deal with fraud. Controls over interest rates (usury laws) have been shown to be rarely enforceable and, when enforceable, to be counterproductive in that they make credit completely unavailable to high-cost and high-risk potential borrowers.

India's entire approach to credit delivery in the rural sector has been premised on the thesis of the 'Evil Moneylender'. Au Contraire the moneylender offered a valuable service in meeting credit available at the right time. He also quite literally knew his borrower. There were therefore, no information asymmetries/moral hazard issues or default risks in loan contract enforcement. For the poor the timeliness and availability of credit for meeting pressing life cycle needs (births/ weddings/ funerals) has always been more important, than the 'cost' of credit.

In fact, a key element in the sustainability of microfinance institutions has been their ability and willingness to charge market rates of interest that can cover all the institution's costs including a margin for profit. Some observers have complained that microfinance institutions pursuing this retail model and charging such high interest rates are monopolists, and are no better than the usurious moneylenders that they are supposed to replace. However, it is not clear what their source of permanent monopoly power might be and, in countries such as Bolivia where the number and outreach of microfinance institutions have been growing, competitive pressures have driven micro lending interest rates down over time.

Some donors and government funding agencies have promoted the supervision of microfinance as this facilitates the selection and monitoring of microfinance institutions for channeling their funds. Again, this can detract from the regulatory institution's basic function. Moreover, donors and government funding agencies can pay for the necessary supervisory work by hiring local qualified auditing firms/Rating Agencies or undertake the task themselves internally. In some cases, microfinance institutions themselves have attempted to promote the regulation of microfinance institutions to improve the image of the microfinance industry as a whole for their individual benefit. However, the existence of such "externalities" is a main reason for the existence of 'industry organizations' that undertake self-regulation as SROs and should not be the business of government regulatory agencies.

## Prudential Regulation

Regulation is prudential when its subject is systemic stability and safeguarding of small depositors interest. It involves the regulators in overseeing the financial soundness of regulated institutions. It also requires a specialized financial agency for operationalisation. Prudential regulation interalia implies:

(1) stipulation of minimum capital adequacy norms
(2) specification of minimum reserves and
(3) liquidity ratios

**Non-prudential Regulation**

Non-prudential regulation, on the other hand, inter alia, requires:

(i) disclosure of effective interest rates,

(ii) disclosure of controlling interest and ownership of a company and

(iii) Fit and proper screening norms.

Non-Prudential Regulation (NPR) may be self-executing and can be dealt with other than by financial authorities or a specialized financial institution. Non-Prudential conduct of Business issues and Regulatory issues span a wide spectrum. These issues include:

(i) enabling the formation and operation of micro lending

(ii) protecting consumer

(iii) preventing fraud and financial issue

(iv) setting up credit Information Services

(v) supporting secured transactions

(vi) developing policy with regard to interest rates

(vii) setting limitations on foreign ownership management services of capital

(viii) identifying poor accounting issues

(ix) a variety of cross-cutting issues for transformation from one institutional type to another.

There is a consensus on the twin objectives of Regulation, Safety of depositors' funds and maintaining the soundness of the system as a whole. As microfinance counts for a very small part of the country's financial assets it does not pose a serious threat/risk to the overall banking and payment system. In fact in case of implementation of Prudential regulation opening up of a less burdensome option, if existing microfinance institutions are not strong candidates for transforming to regulatory institutions, can result in a rash of under qualified depository institutions. This will create a serious supervisory challenge that the authorities will find difficult to fulfil.

The critical and realistic importance of supervisory issues stems from the fiduciary responsibility, which the Central Bank assumes while according financial licenses. The Central Bank effectively supervises the financial intermediary and ensures depositors protection. For institutions licensed by the RBI there is an implication that the RBI promises the stability of the institution and guarantees the security of the depositor's funds.

The argument is that if the concern is with regulating microfinance only to exclude these with poor records and 'Fly by night' operators from owning or controlling microfinance institutions, the Central Bank does not have to bear the onus of controlling/regulating MFIs. It will suffice to require registration and disclosure and special adherence to fit and proper criteria for the promoters of these institutions.

**Section II: Approaches for Microfinance Regulation**

Interest in the regulation of microfinance focused on unregulated microfinance institutions that want to transform themselves into regulated institutions so that they can mobilize deposits from the general public. The special characteristics of these institutions have thus become a primary focus, if not the focus, of any adjustments in the regulatory framework that might be required to accommodate microfinance. This, in turn, has led to concerns about the nonprofit origins of the vast majority of microfinance institutions in the characteristics of board members and the ability to raise additional capital if and when needed. It has also focused discussion on capital adequacy requirements and, in particular, whether a softer regulatory regime is appropriate to create the possibility of institutions with lower minimum capital and more limited banking powers (e.g., no demand deposits, no operations in foreign exchange, etc.) to specialize in microfinance. It is thus important to consider these issues in greater depth, as is done below. It is equally important, however, to ask questions concerning the extent to which existing regulations may also dissuade commercial banks from carrying out micro lending and, more basically, whether microfinance is essentially different from other forms of financial intermediation or is just a variant of basic banking.

**Perils of Soft Regulation**

There is a very strong argument against soft regulation. As the experience with cooperative banking shows, a soft regulatory regime relative to scheduled commercial banks, be it in terms of governance or prudential aspects, tends to attract less than truly 'fit and proper' persons to capture such institutions. Indeed it is possible to argue that our experience with bringing cooperative banks under the Banking Regulation Act 1949, in 1966 coupled with their coverage under Deposit Insurance, compared with the health and reach of the cooperative sector before such regulation came into effect, would provide some valuable lessons in this regard.

**Regulatory Arbitrage**

If new categories of institutions are added to the regulatory architecture, issues of the interplay between the existing and new rules would have to be addressed. If the new rules appear to establish a softer regulatory regime, a more lightly or benignly regulated.

Environment, many existing institutions and new market entrants may contort to qualify as MFIs such regulatory arbitrage can leave some gap under regulated. Whenever there is an expectation that existing MFIs will change their form to take advantage of a new regulatory window there should be a competent financial analysis of at least leading MFIs before decisions are made on the viability of introducing the new niche (regulatory window).

**Capital Adequacy**

The Basle agreements have established a broad consensus on appropriate ratios of capital to risk assets. Requirements have been set high to limit entry. It would seem needlessly risky to set minimum capital requirements lower than those needed to support a full-service deposit-taking institution of the size that would exhaust the major economies of scale, and needlessly anticompetitive to set them higher.

In addition to the ability to contribute capital, there are likely to be other required characteristics for the principal owners, directors, and high-level managers of microfinance institutions that want to formalize themselves so that they can take deposits. Regulatory agencies routinely apply rules concerning character (honesty) to all holders of such positions at a bank, and expertise of some degree in banking also is required. There appears to be no reason why the same criteria could not be used for microfinance institutions applying to be regulated, unless microfinance intermediation is seen to be substantially different from banking in general.

## SUPERVISORY TOOLS AND THEIR LIMITATIONS

### Can Offsite Monitoring Be Effective?

Leaving aside for the moment the question of whether off-site monitoring of microfinance can be effective without the accumulation of a substantial body of experience for comparative purposes, the standard approach to on-site bank examination, even as carried out by regulatory agencies that are highly regarded in general, and may not be appropriate for microfinance. The vast majority of bank examiner time and effort in an onsite examination traditionally is devoted to examining credit files. In particular, a stratified sample is drawn in which credit files for all loans over a certain size are examined, a high percentage of loans in the next size category are covered, and so on until only a very small percentage of credit files of loans in the smallest category are examined. The result is that, for a bank with a typical loan size distribution, more than half of total loan amounts outstanding may be covered, and thus a similarly high proportion of all risk assets, since loans are the main category of risk assets. Although such a procedure and allocation of time and effort may work well for the typical bank, this approach is clearly inappropriate for a bank that specializes in micro lending (or for a microfinance institution). First, without a very large sample, and a large allocation of time and effort, only a very small percentage of total loan amounts outstanding will be examined. Second, since micro lending decisions are not based on traditional collateral or other formal documentation, such as audited financial statements, bank examiners will find little of interest in microloan credit files besides basic information on the micro entrepreneur together with the loan officer's judgment about past cash flows and estimates of future ones.

**Costs of Operationalisation**

This is consequently a very costly approach to microloan examination, and its use may be a major reason why supervisory agencies are rarely enthusiastic about dealing with microfinance. In countries like the United States and the Philippines where there are large numbers of small banks, using the traditional approach described above results in a disproportionate share of examination time and effort being devoted to examining banks with a very small proportion of total deposits in the system. Although small loans and small banks are not the same thing, they are often found together i.e., because bank capital limits loan exposure to individual clients, and both lead to relatively high costs for bank examinations.

As discussed above, one of the main characteristics of successful micro lenders is loans with low administrative costs for the lending institution and low transaction costs for the borrower. This, in turn, implies that decision-making must be decentralized and that loan delivery must likewise be decentralized to the vicinity of the borrower.

**Bottom-Up Approach**

This approach is primarily audit based. Usually the same procedures and approaches are applied to all institutions almost equally. The primary focus is on the accuracy of the balance sheet, including the loan loss reserve, the income statement, and the adequacy of traditional internal controls that are primarily designed to prevent fraud. The primary objectives are balancing journals, reviewing large numbers of individual transactions, such as loans, and quantifying problems based on the aggregate of transactions reviewed. This approach has merit for determining the current condition of a financial institution and quantifying current problems, but it provides little insight into future performance and does not put the onus of accurate record keeping and problem identification and correction where it rightfully belongs—on management and the Board of Directors. Because it often addresses the symptoms of problems instead of causes, it frequently leads to remedies that cause institutions to reduce risks as opposed to employing techniques to manage risks better. Reducing risks is a form of avoiding risks that has a tendency to reduce the variety and volume of products and services offered to the public. This includes credit to borrowers that may be small and considered less creditworthy.

**Top Down Approach**

Top-down supervision was developed in the 1970s. This approach relies on an overall financial analysis and review of policies, procedures, systems, and management practices. These are documented and tested for integrity. Unlike the bottom-up approach, transactions' testing is done to test compliance with stated policies, procedures, systems, and practices. For example, if a loan policy defines certain underwriting criteria, a sample of loans would be reviewed to determine compliance with the criteria. These same loans would be tested for credit quality. If problems are found, they are defined and corrective actions are directed toward correcting systemic deficiencies rather than individual transaction deficiencies. If credit quality of the sample loans is found to be deficient but in compliance with underwriting standards, then changes in the underwriting standards may be appropriate. At this point, there is no attempt to quantify problems unless the examiner suspects the problems are significant in terms of the safety and soundness of the institution. In the top-down approach, systemic problems are identified and defined, and the root causes for the problem are addressed. If problems are identified that, in the opinion of the Regulator or the examiner, significantly affect the safety and soundness of an institution, then a bottom-up examination may be necessary to quantify the problems and determine the precise condition of the institution.

**CALIBRATION OF RISKS**

It can be argued that microfinance is just another market niche with its own set of distinct characteristics but that it shares a common set of risk factors with other more traditional products and services. Standard tools for examining portfolios would not work for microfinance loan documentation in microfinance will be a weak indicator of risk.

All bank and microfinance products and services have multiple risks in their profiles. One of those risks is always operational risk. To understand the differences in risk profiles for different products and services, it is necessary to break them down into their component parts. For example, there are six risks that account for an overwhelming majority of losses in financial institutions. The first and most obvious is credit risk. The others are operational risks, which includes costs, interest rate risk, liquidity risk, market risks, and foreign exchange risks. Market and foreign exchange risks are virtually nonexistent in microfinance, as MFIs in India are not allowed to borrow from the Capital Markets except to a restricted extent, as they may not be able to clearly appraise risks associated with such borrowings.

Once the component risks have been identified, it is necessary to measure them on an individual and portfolio basis.

For example, in a microfinance institution, the credit risk associated with one microloan is very little (not the same as low) due to the size of the transaction, but the credit risk for the entire portfolio could be high, depending on the systems and processes in place. For a wholesale commercial bank that makes only large loans, the credit risk associated with individual loans could be high, as well as the portfolio risk. However, in the case of the wholesale commercial bank, transaction (operational) risk may be low because of the number of eyes that look at each loan and check and double check the numbers, whereas in the microfinance institution transaction risk may be high for the opposite reasons. Therefore, by understanding the risk profiles for the two examples, it would be appropriate for a regulator to take a different approach in the two institutions. In the microfinance institution, more focus on systems and processes would be appropriate because of the small risk associated with individual transactions. In the commercial bank, more focus on individual loan transactions would be appropriate because of the higher risk associated with each loan, although operational risks would not be ignored. We conclude that while it is relatively easy and interesting to craft regulations, it is much harder and less attractive to do practical planning for effective supervision.

The main purpose of adjusting the regulation and supervision of microfinance is so that more microfinance services will be provided and so that the institutions providing microfinance services will not take excessive risks. Hence, the deposits of the general public will be at least as well protected as they were before any changes in regulation and supervision.

## MODELS OF REGULATION

### Who should bell the cat ?

(1) Where should regulation be located ? The most appropriate supervisory body is generally assumed to be the supervisory authority responsible for commercial banks.

This becomes further complicated when depository and non-depository MFIs are to be addressed within a single comprehensive regulation framework.

(2) Self-Regulation – Self Regulation of financial intermediaries has often been tried and has not proved effective it is like betting against very long odds.

(3) Delegated Supervision – Delegated supervision is effective where direct supervision is delegated to an outside body but control is retained over that body.

Before deciding on Regulation, there is a need to pay much more attention to issues of likely effectiveness and cost of supervision.

The question of whether to apply prudential regulation has also to be approached from the standpoint of weighing of costs and benefits, which again will depend on :

Timing and State of the Industry

Is there a critical mass of Depository Institutions that can be regulated ? What are the financial and administrative costs of such regulation ?

- Ability of (deposit taking) institutions to meet regulatory requirements
- Is the loan tracking system strong enough to produce reliable information ?

In fact, RBI in its comments on the draft report of the Task Force on Revival of Cooperative Credit Institutions (Vaidyanathan Committee, February 2005) has argued in favour of substituting RBI's regulatory jurisdiction with a separate independent national or State level regulatory, body broadly in line with what was advocated by Dr. Bimal Jalan in his policy statement in 2001 in regard to Urban Cooperative Banks.

Self Regulatory Organisation which disseminate best practices to regulation delegated to :

(i) External audit firms,

(ii) NABARD,

(iii) A new 'institution'

Market oriented development policy that seeks to liberalise the financial markets needs to be implemented. Microfinance regulation should not create a flawed incentive structure, which will encourage the players in the microfinance market to pressure the government for credit subsidies. Loan quotas and other subventions, which will serve to further distort the financial markets. Managerial and Technical capabilities of MFIs have to be enhanced to enable them to provide effective services.

**Objectives of Prudential Regulation and The Regulation Applicable to MFIs**

Much of the current discussion of microfinance focuses implicitly or explicitly on NGO/MFIs that have begun with a 'Credit-Based' model and now want to move to capturing deposits. As in most parts of the world these MFIs take deposits from shares and savings and are not permitted to mobilize deposit from the general public. Regulation will automatically subject them to :

- Rationing Requirements (CRR/SLR requirements), Capital Requirements (as per Basel Norms, perhaps for MFIs these may be fixed higher).
- Qualitative Institutional Assessments.

Both are stiff to restrict entry and there is a trade off between the numbers of new Depository Institution licensed and the likely effectiveness of the supervision they will secure.

The objectives of regulation are sub-served when retail deposits of the general public are protected. Thus if MFIs raise funds from depositors they will have to be subject to Regulation.

Depositor protection is not an absolute value that overrules all other considerations. It has to be borne in mind that :

- Some rules that lower risk can also lower poor people's access to financial services, an equally important value
- The regulators objective should be not the elimination of risk but rather a prudential balancing of safety and access.

Regulatory Mandates, which serve, legitimate prudential objectives will have to be complied with.

It will be difficult for MFIs to cope with the following regulatory prescription mandate :

- minimum capital requirements
- risk weights on credit portfolio which presuppose a 'stable' but not a 'volatile' portfolio
- unsecured lending limits and loan loss provisioning
- loan documentation
- frequency and contents of reporting
- reserves against deposits
- mandates statutory ownership and diversification requirements

Typical banking regulation mandates the nature of permissible shareholders, maximum number of shareholders and maximum percentage of ownership for any shareholders.

## Section III – Extant Banking Laws and Norms and their application to microfinance institutions under the SHG-Bank linkage programme

The SHGs linkage program is a normal business activity of banks included for planning and monitoring under the Service Area Approach. Banks are allowed to consider lending to SHGs as separate segment under priority sector part of their mainstream credit operations both at policy and implementation level. They may include SHG linkage in their corporate strategy/plan, training curriculum of their officers and staff and implement it as a regular business activity and monitor and review it periodically. The SHGs registered or unregistered which are engaged in promoting savings habits among their members would be eligible to open savings bank accounts with banks. These SHGs need not necessarily have already availed of credit facilities from banks before opening savings bank accounts. As per operational guidelines of NABARD, SHGs are sanctioned savings linked loans by banks (varying from a saving to loan ratio of 1:1 to 1:4). Experience showed that group dynamics and peer pressure brought in excellent recovery from members of the SHGS. Banks were advised that the flexibility allowed to the banks in respect of margin, security norms, etc. under the pilot project would continue to be operational under the linkage program even beyond the pilot phase. Keeping in view the nature of lending and status of borrowers, the banks prescribe simple documentation for lending to SHGs. The defaults by a few members of SHGs and/or their family members to the financing bank do not ordinarily come in the way of financing SHGs per se by banks provided the SHG is not in default to it.

However, the bank loan may not be utilized by the SHG for financing a defaulter member to the bank. An important step in the Linkage Program is the training of the field level officials and sensitization of the controlling and other senior officials of the bank. Considering the need and magnitude of training requirements of bank officers/staff both at field level and controlling office level, the banks may initiate suitable steps to internalize the SHGs linkage project and organize exclusive short duration program for the field level functionaries. In addition, suitable awareness/ sensitization program conducted for their middle level controlling officers as well as senior officers. Having regard to the emerging potential of the SHGs and the relative non-familiarity of the bank branches with lending to SHGS, banks have to closely monitor the progress regularly at various levels. Further the progress of the program is reviewed by the banks at regular intervals. A progress report are sent to both RBI (RPCD) and NABARD (MCID).

**NBFCs Engaged in Micro-financing Activities**

The Task Force on Supportive Policy and Regulatory Framework for Microfinance set up by NABARD in 1999 recommended that the policy and regulatory framework should give a fillip to the Self Help Groups (SHGs) or Non-Governmental

Organisations (NGOs) engaged in micro-financing activities. Accordingly, it was decided to exempt such NBFCs which are engaged in (i) micro financing activities, (ii) licensed under Section 25 of the Companies Act, 1956 and (iii) which are not accepting public deposits from the purview of Sections 45-IA (registration), 45-IB (maintenance of liquid assets) and 45-IC (transfer of profits to Reserve Fund) of the RBI Act, 1934.

Based on the recommendations of the Advisory Committee on Flow of Credit to Agriculture and Related Activities from the Banking System (Vyas Committee), in the Reserve Bank of India (RBI) Annual Policy Statement for the year 2004-05, it was announced, in view of the need to protect the interests of depositors, microfinance institutions (MFIs) would not be permitted to accept public deposits unless they comply with the extant regulatory framework of the Reserve Bank.

Vide A.P. (DIR Series) Circular No. 5 dated August 1, 2005, RBI has allowed that Non-Government Organisations (NGOs) engaged in micro finance activities are eligible to avail External Commercial Borrowings (ECBs) upto 5 million. Such NGO (i) should have a satisfactory borrowing relationship for at least 3 years with a scheduled commercial bank authorized to deal in foreign exchange and (ii) would require a certificate of due diligence on 'fit and proper' status of the board/committee of management of the borrowing entity from the designated Authorized Dealer (AD).

## Interest Rates

The interest rate applicable to loans given by banks to micro-credit organisations or by the micro-credit organisations to Self Help Groups/member beneficiaries would be left to their discretion.

## Mainstreaming and Enhancing Outreach

A Micro Credit Special Cell was set up in RBI to suggest measures for augmenting flow of micro credit as announced in

RBI Governor's Monetary and Credit Policy for the year 1999-2000. In the meantime, a Task Force on Supportive Policy and Regulatory Framework for Micro Credit was also set up by NABARD. On the basis of their recommendations, banks were advised to follow guidelines for mainstreaming micro credit and enhancing the outreach of micro credit providers:

(i) The banks to formulate their own model(s) or choose any conduit/ intermediary for extending micro credit. They may choose suitable branches/pockets/areas where micro credit program can be implemented. It will be useful to start with a selected small area and concentrate fully on the poor in that area and thereafter with the experience gained replicate the arrangement in other selected areas. Micro Credit extended by banks to individual borrowers directly or through any intermediary would be reckoned as part of their priority sector lending.

(ii) The criteria for selection of micro credit organizations are not prescribed. It may, however, be desirable for banks to deal with micro credit organizations having proper credentials, track record, system of maintaining accounts and records with regular audits in place and manpower for closer supervision and follow-up.

(iii) Banks may prescribe their own lending norms keeping in view the ground realities. They may devise appropriate loan and savings products and the related terms and conditions including the size of the loan, unit cost, unit size, maturity period, grace period, margins, etc. The intention is to provide maximum flexibility in regard to micro lending, keeping in view the prevalent local conditions and the need for provision of finance to the poor. Such credit should, therefore, cover not only consumption and production loans for various farm and non-farm activities of the poor but also include their other credit needs such as housing and shelter improvements.

(iv) Micro credit is included in branch credit plan, block credit plan and state credit plan of each bank. While no target is prescribed for micro credit, utmost priority is accorded to micro credit sector in preparation of these plans. Micro credit forms an integral part of the bank's corporate credit plan and is reviewed at the highest level on a quarterly basis.

(v) A simple system requiring minimum procedures and documentation is a pre-condition for augmenting flow of micro credit. Hence, banks should strive to remove.

(vi) all operational irritants and make arrangements to expeditiously sanction and disburse micro credit by delegating adequate sanctioning powers to branch managers. The loan application forms, procedures and documents should be made simple which would help in providing prompt and hassle-free micro credit.

**Section IV – Challenges of Micro Finance Regulation**

At the risk of repetition, we reiterate here that the generally agreed objectives of Prudential Regulation include (1) Protecting the country's financial system from domino effect preventing the failure of one institution from leading to a 'run' prompting the failure of others, (2) Protecting small depositors who are not well positioned to monitor the institutions financial soundness themselves.

The undernoted questions indicate the challenges of microfinance regulation.

- Currently there are five organizational forms of the MFIs, viz., Trusts; Societies; Cooperative Societies; Not-for-Profit Companies and Non-Banking Finance Companies. We will have to weigh the merits and demerits of recognition of one or more or all the organizational forms under the formal structured regulatory framework. SHGs are amorphous entities with no formal organizational structure. We will have to distinguish micro credit institutions from micro finance institutions. It is not clear how they will be brought under a formalized frame of regulation. There are also instances of large corporate undertaking micro-credit activity as a part of their operations. Under their corporate social responsibilities. The microfinance institutions may invite the overlapping jurisdiction of several regulatory agencies.

- The latter may need more varied skills and in any case, warrant a policy view by more than one financial sector regulator?
- How do we distinguish micro-finance institution from micro-credit institution and both these from other financial institutions? Is it by the ceilings imposed on the size of deposits, lendings and / or by defining activities? What part or percentage of the activity could be non-financial while the institution continues to be an MFI? Is there merit in differentiating between not-for-profit MFIs and the profit-seeking ones?
- There is also a need to recognise the large regional differences in the spread of SHGs and the MFIs across the country. While the issue needs deeper analysis to identify the reasons for such variation and to promote balanced growth of the MFIs, it, prima facie, appears that the MFIs have flourished more in the Southern States with well-developed banking infrastructure and outreach. Thus, the MFIs in our country would seem to be a supplement rather than a substitute for a developed banking infrastructure.
- The role of foreign capital and venture capital in regard to the MFIs would have to be carefully considered. It may be necessary to recognise here the orientation of micro-finance activity given the limitation of size and skills in the MFIs and then consistency with the risk-reward bias of such sources of commercial capital. As regards external commercial borrowings, the imperatives of exchange rate risk and the capacity of the MFIs to effectively assess and manage this risk would also need to be duly reckoned.

- What could be the scope and effectiveness of a self regulatory organisation for the MFIs and how would it mesh with the possible formalised regulatory framework under contemplation?

  Credit rating is usually assigned for specific instruments issued or for a defined purpose and often, on a continuing basis. There is merit in devising rating system for the MFIs, experience so far in regard to utility and quality of rating exercises of MFIs. How to ensure that the rating exercise adds value to the localised operations of the MFIs?
- What are the prospects for expanding the permission accorded by the RBI to the non-banking financial companies for offering credit and other financial services to not-for-profit companies ? What are the prospects for creating a separate category of NBFC-MFIs to be regulated by RBI ?

  Some of the areas where MFIs said that their best practices conflict with standard banking regulations include the following:
- The definitions of secured and unsecured lending that tend to place most microloans in the unsecured category (with the accompanying limits on acceptable volumes and risk classification). In particular, the non-recognition of standard forms of guarantee used in microfinance, such as group guarantees or non-standard collateral.

  Loan documentation requirements unsuitable for informal business – without actually improving the safety of the portfolio. In fact, post introduction of Regulation both BancoSol (Bolivia) and Mibanco (Peru) experienced resentment from clients regarding increased loan documentation requirements after they became commercial. Existing clients viewed the demand for such documentation as evidence the lenders no longer trusted them.
- Classification of microfinance in same grouping as consumer lending. Though the loan sizes and terms are similar, these kinds of lending are based on entirely

different lending techniques and repayment comes from a very different source (salary versus self-employment). Each type of lending needs its own set of norms.

- Inappropriate methods of supervising the portfolio: regulators spend too much time looking at individual loan folders and not enough testing the quality, timeliness and reliability of MIS and examining portfolio quality control systems in general.

## Deposit Insurance

There is a debate on whether public deposit insurance is effective in improving bank stability of whether it encourages inappropriate risk taking. Should such insurance be provided by Private Markets ?

If deposits in commercial banks are insured the presumption is that deposits in other prudential institutions licensed by the financial authorities should also be insured.

Finally, should all the MFIs or only a select category out of them be permitted to accept public deposits? While there is a view that only banks should be permitted to accept public deposits, currently non-banking financial companies are also permitted to accept public deposits but subject to the regulatory prescriptions of the RBI. Needless to say, it is the issue of accepting public deposits that poses major challenges, both legislative and more importantly, of moral hazard.

## Section V – International Experience of Regulation of MFIs

ACCION International, whose Latin American Network currently includes 12 regulated microfinance institutions, has a great interest in promoting mutual understanding between regulators and the regulated. In order to contribute to greater understanding, ACCION conducted a survey with detailed interviews of seven microfinance institutions, five from the Network and two outside it: BancoSol (Bolivia), Calpia (E1

**International Experience on MFIs**

| *Institution* | *Banco Sol* | *Banco Solidario* | *Cajalos Andes* | *Calpia* | *Compar tamos* | *FINSOL* | *Mibanco* |
|---|---|---|---|---|---|---|---|
| Country | Bolivia | Ecuador | Bolivia | ElSalvador | Mexico | Honduras | Peru |
| Founded | 1986 | 1995 | 1991 | N/A | 1990 | 1985 | 1969 |
| Original Form | NGO | Com Bank | NGO | NGO | NGO | NGO | NGO |
| License Date | 1992 | 1995 | 1995 | 1995 | 2001 | 1999 | 1998 |
| New Form | Com. Bank | Com. Bank | FFP | Financiera | SOFOL | Financiera | Com Bank |
| Active borrowers | 60,976 | 14,645 | 41,665 | 34,390 | 62,797 | 15,026 | 58,088 |
| Portfolio (US$ million) | 77.8 | 6.3 | 46.8 | 26.5 | 10.9 | 6.3 | 36.9 |

**Note**: Data as of end 2001 with exception of Calpia, which is end 2000.

Salvador), Compartamos (Mexico), Finsol (Honduras), and Mibanco (Peru). These institutions represent six countries (see Table). Three are commercial banks while four are 'financieras'. All, with the exception of Banco Solidario, underwent transformation from NGO into regulated institution and thus they are in a position to compare the experiences of operating in an unregulated versus a regulated environment. The purpose of the survey was to examine the views of the institutions on the experience of being supervised, including perceived costs and benefits, and to glean some recommendations on changes the practitioners would suggest to the content and implementation of supervision.

**Benefits and Costs of Regulation**

The institutions involved in this study were overwhelmingly pleased to be regulated. All reported that the benefits of being regulated outweighed the costs. None would even begin to contemplate reverting to their NGO status. This message is highly significant. It means that even when debate over specifics of regulation became heated, the underlying fundamentals are there. The process of becoming regulated has brought microfinance institutions the benefits they sought:

- Greater access to sources of funds for both equity and debt, especially commercial sources
- Ability to achieve growth and quantitative outreach goals: to serve more people
- Improved, more professional operations through meeting higher standards of control and reporting
- Greater ability to offer products beyond microcredit, especially savings and transfers
- Enhanced legitimacy in the financial sector and with clients

These very profound benefits must be weighed against very practical costs. Although MFIs cannot give exact figures, CGAP estimates that the cost of supervision is as much as 5 percent of total costs during the initial year and 1 percent thereafter. However, it is important to note that many of the initial costs involve internal improvements required to meet supervisory requirements, most of which are necessary for running a strong microfinance institution.

The only general negative factor that some institutions mentioned was a loss in ability to experiment with unconventional ideas, particularly those involving products or markets that have not yet proved their viability. This observation draws attention to the continued importance of NGOs as seedbeds for experimentation.

## Section VI – Key Policy Prescriptions

Prudential regulation and supervision should be applied only to deposit-taking institutions. Hence, microfinance NGOs that do not take deposits should not be regulated except under the general laws that deal with fraud and so forth, and this should not be the job of Bank Superintendencies.

Regulation and supervision of microfinance institutions must deal with two basic issues: how to regulate microlending by MFIs (and other existing supervised financial institutions, which may include finance companies, cooperatives, etc.) and how to regulate NGOs that want to begin to take deposits. Too much focus has been on the latter, and especially on certain characteristics of nonprofits (i.e., NGOs), to the neglect of the former and especially how to evaluate the risks associated with microlending.

Techniques of microlending have significant differences from traditional bank lending techniques. This, together with the institutional differences between microfinance NGOs and for-profit commercial banks, has led to attempts to define different standards for microfinance. However, this is a mistake because it will lead to endless proliferation of different standards and different supervision techniques for each market niche in finance.

Risk-based supervision can provide a more basic and unifying approach by focusing on risk management in all cases and by developing different risk profiles from the same underlying risks.

There has been an excessive focus on analyzing laws and norms relative to an analysis of how supervision has been carried out in practice. This is probably because it is much easier to do the former. Good case studies, however, must include the latter, which requires the consent of the Superintendency being analysed and teams that have expertise in both microfinance and regulation.

**Facing the Supervisory Challenge**

(1) A balance has to be struck between supervisory capability, operational costs and alternate consumption of services to be provided. The administrative costs of supervision will be high.

(2) For microfinance to enter the arena of licensed prudentially supervised financial intermediation regulations must be specially crafted.

(3) Portfolio testing and supervision of MFIs will require specialized skills and greater sophistication than those used to supervise commercial banks. Supervisory staff will need to be trained and specialized in order to deal effectively with MFIs.

In this regard, for microfinance regulation to be deemed effective, it must show after regulation (1) that more MFIs are actually providing savings/deposit taking services; (2) that more NGOs have transformed into formal financial intermediaries; (3) that those transformed NGOs are consequently able to reach a larger clientele; (4) that savings mobilization constitutes a major source of funding for those transformed NGOs; (5) that actual examination practices keep aligned with laws and norms; and (6) the costs and practices of microfinance supervision are congruent with the risks and volume of operations involved.

NGOs exist as Societies, Trusts, Cooperative Societies and Mutually Aided Cooperative Societies besides NBFCs and Section 25 Companies. It is a myth that as at present NGO/ MFIs are not subject to any regulation. They are depending on their form subject to the following regulation. As a 'Society' registration is required under the concerned States' Society Act. As a Trust registration is required under the Indian Trusts Act 1882, come under Regulation of "Charitees Commissioner". Cooperative Societies are registered under the Cooperative Societies Act and come under the regulatory purview of the Registrar of Coop. Societies or under the Mutually Aided Cooperative Societies Act (MACS) in some State, which have MACS as Andhra Pradesh. An NBFC falls under the NBFC Act and is regulated by RBI while under Section 25 company comes under the Company's Act.

The growth of MFIs and spread of micro finance has also been uneven across States and it is virtually absent in some States. The urgency, as of now is to build on its strengths and extend it to vast areas which are inadequately covered 13 Priority States with high incidence of rural poverty viz., Assam, Bihar, Jharkhand, Gujarat, Himachal Pradesh, Maharashtra, Madhya Pradesh, Chhattisgarh, Rajasthan, Orissa, U.P., Uttaranchal, West Bengal. In conclusion, it is of overriding importance to recognize that we have to build inclusive financial systems. At present there does not appear to be any overwhelming urgency for regulating MFIs based on the costs of regulation and benefits as analysed above.

SHG – Bank linkage: in most states it is not happening

Quality of SHGs will not improve unless they get a bank loan after they have functioned for 6-12 months

Promotional funds to promote quality SHGs?

- Capacity of the Govt./NGOs promoting SHGs needs to be improved
- SGSY implementation not synchronized with SHG model
- Livelihood promotion support for matured SHGs should address Women Empowerment SHGs more engaged in credit management

Many NGOs which traditionally promoted SHGs are transforming into Microfinance Organizations MFOs Why don't banks participate ?

- Banks don't want to absorb costs involved on grounds of impact on viability of operations.
- Lack of clarity regarding procedural complexities Movement towards individuals: ex-servicemen, retired bank officials, schoolteachers.
  For small farmers, interest rates are capped

2. Correspondents are not allowed to charge clients for their services
3. Banks can randomly inspect the correspondents of banksidentification of borrowers and fitment of activities,which are basically restricted to collection of applications and verification of primary information/data, and preliminary appraisal of credit based on standard norms set by banks and using local data/information (a simple credit scoring model may be employed).

Government transactions directly or through agents/ correspondents has statutory backing as enshrined in Section 6 of Banking Regulation Act and Section 21(A) and Section 45 of Reserve Bank of India Act, 1934. As regards non-bank model or Private Public Partnership (PPP) model which involves Government Departments entrusting the responsibility to a non banking institution to deliver services on their behalf, this may require amending various statutes or putting in place required regulations to create an enabling environment. Further, the Electronic Benefit Transfer (EBT) framework under the PPP model may involve transfer of funds to the card accounts maintained with the identified non-bank service provider which would be treated as payment system outside the banking system and the resultant regulatory overload may not make the system viable. Third party handling Government funds may also involve reputational risks for both Government and Reserve Bank in case of leakage of funds, if any, through fraudulent means at the service provider level. In January 2006, Reserve Bank permitted banks to utilise the services of non-governmental organizations (NGOs), micro-finance institutions (other than Non-Banking Financial Companies) and other civil society organisations as intermediaries in providing financial and banking services through the use of business facilitator and business correspondent models. From April 2008, banks have been permitted to engage retired bank employees, ex-servicemen and retired government employees as BCs. In August 2008, banks have also been permitted to engage companies registered under Section 25 of the companies Act, 1956, as BCs provided that the Section 25 companies are stand-alone entities or Section 25 companies in which NBFCs, banks, telecom companies and other corporate entities or their holding companies do not have equity holdings in excess of 10%. It has also been stipulated that every BC would be attached to and be under the oversight of a specific base branch and the distance between the place of business of a BC and the base branch, ordinarily, should not exceed 15 Kms in rural, semi-urban and urban areas. In metropolitan centres, the distance could be up to 5 kms. However, in case a need is felt to relax the distance criterion, the matter can be referred, on a case by case basis, to the District Consultative Committee (DCC) of the district concerned for approval. Where such relaxations cover adjoining districts, the matter may be cleared by the State Level Bankers' Committee (SLBC).

Further, it has also been advised to banks that in case the BCs of banks desire to appoint sub-agents at the grass-root level, banks have to ensure that the sub agents of BCs also comply with the relevant criteria stipulated for BCs and that the BC carries out proper due diligence in respect of the sub agent to take care of the reputational and other risks. The distance criteria, as applicable, from the base branch should be invariably be fulfilled in case of all sub-agents. In addition, where individuals under the permitted categories have been appointed as BCs, they cannot in turn appoint sub-agents.

As the sub-agents also will be handling cash and discharging responsibilities on behalf of the banks, it is of utmost importance that due diligence is exercised over their activities and hence the stipulations for BCs have been made applicable to their sub-agents also. Cash in or cash out through non-banks and non account holders are fraught with enormous risk and are not favoured.

The Committee on suggesting a Framework for Electronic Benefit Transfer (Chairman: Dr. R.B. Barman) examined three different models of EBT viz. Bank-branch model, Bank -led model and Non-bank model. In the Bank-branch model, the service delivery will be only through the banking channel, using the bank branches as the service delivery point. The Bank-led model refers to provision of banking services at the bank branches as well as through their BCs. In the Non-bank model or PPP model, the payment is made through a channel without involving the banks.

Under the bank branch model, the service delivery will be only through banking channels, which envisages the branch at the service delivery point and thus the model may not be cost effective. In the case of bank-led model, the existing framework of RBI/banks undertaking Government transactions directly or through agents/correspondents has statutory backing as enshrined in Section 6.

Banking Regulation Act and Section 21(A) and Section 45 of Reserve Bank of India Act, 1934. As regards non-bank model or Public Private Partnership (PPP) model which involves Government Departments entrusting the responsibility to a non banking institution to deliver services on their behalf, this may require amending various statutes or putting in place required regulations to create an enabling environment. Further, the Electronic Benefit Transfer EBT framework under the PPP model may involve transfer of funds to the card accounts maintained with the identified non-bank service provider which would be treated as payment system outside the banking system and the resultant regulatory overload may not make the system viable. Third party handling Government funds may also involve reputational risks for both Government and Reserve Bank in case of leakage of funds, if any, through fraudulent means at the service provider level.

Of the three models, the Bank-led, smart card-based model for adoption by banks for the purpose of disbursement of benefits to beneficiaries at or near to the place of their habitation is recommended.

The Business Facilitators (BFs) may be used for facilitation services which may include identification of borrowers, collection and preliminary processing of loan applications, creating awareness about bank products and education and advice on managing money and debt counselling, processing and submission of application to banks, promotion of Self help Groups/ Joint Liability Groups, post sanction monitoring, follow up for recovery, etc. and no approval of RBI is required for using business facilitators for the services mentioned above.

Business Correspondents (BCs), apart from the above services can disburse small value credit, recover principal/ collect interest, collect small value deposits, sell micro insurance/ mutual fund products/pension products/other third party products, receive and deliver small value remittance / other payment instruments. While banks may pay reasonable commission/ fee to the BFs / BCs, bank's agreement with the BFs / BCs should specifically prohibit them from charging any fee to the customers directly for services rendered by them on behalf of the bank.

E Choupal village internet kiosks which deliver information to enable the borrower to enable the farmers to sell produce directly bypassing intermediaries The Simputer can also be extremely useful in applications such as agriculture product marketing, contract farming, keeping track of the inputs, and for tracking the payments to contractors etc. Microcredit schemes find it to be an extremely effective tool, owing to its local-language and SmartCard facility and built-in communication capabilities. Likewise, Simputer kiosks owned by local educated unemployed youth in the villages could be an effective source of income generation by providing e-mail, voice-mail, information access, tele-diagnosis, and other services to the community members." Objective: To empower farmer communities by providing them reliable and timely agriculture related information (market prices, information about fertilisers, crop varieties etc.)

**Approach: A computer kiosk managed by a farmer at each village; One kiosk for 600 farmers who can use the system for the latest price and technical information**

**Beneficiaries: Nearly 1 million farmers in 10,000+ villages**

**Benefits to community: Better prices, reliable information, Ease in selling their products**

- **Driving Agency: ITC – a private firm Better supply chain for ITC's Food and Agri Businesses**
  **– Reduced Costs, Consistent Quality, Traceability, Efficient SCM**
- **Access to the Underserved Rural Markets**
  **– Through a Virtuous Cycle created by "Larger Incomes", and founded on "Trust" that is built**
- **New ITES Business Opportunities**
- **Emerging Challenges and Concerns**
  **– Health, Education, Entertainment**
- **Shareholder Value through Serving Society**

– **Also, the infrastructure serves as a reliable delivery mechanism for resource development initiatives (e.g. water, animal management)**

Customer Targeting- eliminating the "Unknown"

– Gather information like location, creditworthiness, customer preferences, financial position and spending patterns

– Represents the first link between the vast untapped market and the urban commerce

- Micro-finance extended to farmers enables
  Increased Yields due to better inputs
  Improved Quality
  Reduction in Transaction costs due to elimination of traditional middleman
  Power of Scale to the Small Farmer
  Customized Knowledge despite Heterogeneity
  Real time information despite Distances
  No explicit payment for knowledge and information got from e-Choupals

Relevant and Real-time Information
- Commodity prices, Local Weather, News

Customised Knowledge
- Farm Management, Risk Management

Supply Chain for Farm Inputs
- Screened for Quality, Demand Aggregation for Competitive Prices and Efficient Logistics

Direct Marketing Channel for Farm Produce
- Lower Transaction Costs, Better Value through Traceability

Distribution of Products and Services to Rural Markets
Micro marketing
- Product/Services Demos

| *State* | *Choupals* | *Hubs* |
|---|---|---|
| Madhya Pradesh | 1750 | 43 |
| Uttar Pradesh | 1750 | 42 |
| Maharashtra | 900 | 22 |
| Rajasthan | 500 | 15 |
| Karnataka | 100 | 2 |
| Andhra Pradesh | 150 | 3 |
| **Choupals** | **5,150** | **127** |
| **Villages** | **31,000** | |
| **Farmers** | **3,500,000** | |

– Marketing and Brand Building activities

Pilots

– Bhoomi
– e-Health with Private Health Service Providers
– e-Education

Rural BPO

Adding Six New Choupals Every Day

Intend Scaling up to 100,000 Villages in 15 States by 2010

- End-to-end solution is designed collaboratively
- Identify major problems and
- solve them with efficiency and transparency
- When ITC started, it was with a FMCG approach, with reliance on
- Market Research
- Focus Groups
- **... and then the approach quickly changed to** 'Prototypes' to enable experience and obtain feedback
- An iterative approach to build models to solve the real world problems of the Individual and of the Community Solution : Access to Price Information – Anytime and in the Village
- Solution : Transparency and Accuracy in Weighment
- Solution : Modern Methods for Quality Assessment
- Step 1: Leveraging ICTs for empowered access to markets (inputs and outputs)
- Step 2: Economic viability of IT infrastructure investments is justified through Win-Win business models, hence also scaleable
- Step 3: Customer responsive IT infrastructure in the villages facilitates access to supplementary Education, Health, Employment, e-Governance services
- Value through Unbundling what was bundled together earlier (Information and Transaction)
- Unbundling
- Emerging Challenges and Concerns

- Price information is now available at the door step without a necessity to go to mandi
- Has an option to fix price at the village itself. However, at the time of selling, still retains the freedom to go to mandi if he believes he gets better offer there.
- Input Transaction Value through Bundling (Information, Knowledge, Transaction) what was available unbundled earlier
- Bundles
- Information on Weather and Best Practices from the website
- Knowledge of 'what to do' from the Experts
- Efficient supply platform for inputs purchase that enables aggregation and scale efficiencies
- The scale and complexity inherent makes it a high maintenance network
- The Orchestrator has to ensure
- There is a 'Big Picture' to what is initiated
- 'Changing Needs' are tracked and are efficiently responded
- 'Continuous Innovation' of the business model is ensured for its long term relevance
- ICT Kiosk with Internet Access
- In the house of one trained farmer, Sanchalak
- Within walking distance of target farmers Link
- Warehousing Hub / Store
- 3 X 3 eChoupal Infrastructure
- Managed by the erstwhile middleman, Samyojak
- Within tractorable distance of target farmers Link
- Collaborative Network of Companies
- Orchestrated by ITC
- With a Pan-Indian presence Link
- Mobile Payments are any monetary transactions that take place with the help of a mobile phone. There are three primary types of mobile payments:

- **M-Commerce:**
- Mobile phones linked to credit/debit cards can be used to make payments typically for transportation, vending machines etc.
- **E-Money:**
- Cash loaded in the mobile phones at service provider outlets. Consumers use this virtual cash as real value for all types of transactions.
- **Banking Channel:**
- Mobile phone used for accessing the bank accounts. All payments are routed through the bank
- RBI has granted permission to transfer funds across various mobile-phone service providers, 3 public sector banks are rolling out their mobile banking solutions in the next few days.

State Bank, said it is in the final stages of its M-Banking roll-out and has scheduled its launch in late July while Bank of India and Union Bank of India plan to introduce their services by end-June. SBI, which has partnered with Mumbai-based technology services provider, Spanco Systems, is understood to have plans to tie-up with a number of service providers to take the service to the far-corners of the country Some banks offer only the option of text alerts, which are messages sent to your cell phone that alert you to activity on your account such as deposits, withdrawals, and ATM or credit card use. This is the most basic type of mobile banking.

A more involved type of mobile banking allows the user to log into his or her account from a cell phone, and then use the phone to make payments, check balances, transfer money between accounts, notify the bank of a lost or stolen credit card, stop payment on a check, receive a new PIN, or view a monthly statement, among other transactions.

- When a bank offers mobile payments service, it may be ensured that customers having mobile phones of any network operator should be in a position to request for service.

- The long term goal of mobile payment framework in India would be to enable funds transfer from account in one bank to any other account in the same or any other bank on a real time basis irrespective of mobile network a customer has subscribed to. This would require inter-operability between mobile payments service providers and banks and development of a host of message formats.

- Most Indian banks offer mobile banking facilities. RBI has cautiously encouraged the trend with guidelines on mobile banking with putting in place a Rs. 50,000/- limit on withdrawals via a mobile banking transaction to avoid fraud.

- The mobile payments market is still at its infancy in India and it is estimated that the current daily transaction volumes today will be in the range of Rs. 5-10 Million. Even if 5% of mobile bill payment and recharge shifts onto mobile payments platform the industry can grow to Rs. 200 Million a day.

- mobile transactions are as follows :

| | *Push Based* | *Pull Based* |
|---|---|---|
| Transaction Based | | * Fund Transfer<br>* Bill Payment<br>* Other financial services like share trading. |
| Enquiry Based | * Credit/Debit Alerts.<br>* Minimum Balance lerts<br>* Bill Payment Alerts | * Account Balance Enquiry<br>* Account Statement Enquiry.<br>* Cheque Status Enquiry.<br>* Cheque Book Requests.<br>* Recent Transaction History. |

- Thousands of people from rural areas across 12 states are likely to get their social security pension and wages paid under the National Rural.

- Employment Guarantee Act (NREGA) scheme with the help of mobiles over the coming few months.
- In Andhra Pradesh alone, for instance, 250,000 people have registered for mobile banking services. The state government is rolling out a programme to enroll three million people by the end of 2008.
- Mobile banking pilots and full-scale operations are being conducted across 12 states, and the entire ecosystem is being managed by the government with the help of the Reserve Bank of India, banks, leading telecom operators and technology implementation partners.
- The ecosystem is important since banking regulations in India currently do not allow cash for exchange of another 'unit' such as 'airtime' in the case of mobiles. Only banks and the Indian Post (through money orders) are currently allowed such transfers.
- Mobile banking, which is catching up fast in the cities and hinterland, is not only helping the government to take a step forward towards fulfilling its aim of having one bank account for every household, but also saving it crores of rupees by way of reduced transaction costs.
- While the government incurs a transaction cost of Rs 12-13 for every Rs 100 it shells out, mobile banking helps it reduce the cost to a mere Rs 2.
- RBI estimates that around 40 per cent of Indians lack access to formal financial services and are largely 'unbanked'.
- The mobile acts as a branch of the bank by storing a database of customers. It also has a smartcard, which biometrically stores the identity of the customer such as name, address, photograph, fingerprint templates and relevant details of the savings or loan accounts held by the issuing bank.

- Customers get a secure electronic identity via phone or smartcard, while agents take deposits and dispense cash
- Bharti Airtel, is in the process of tying up with two leading banks to extend its mobile remittance services to rural areas, according to its president (Mobile Services.
- Airtel has already partnered with the Indian Farmers' Fertiliser Cooperative Limited (IFFCO) to set up IFFCO Kisan Sanchar Limited in Rajasthan.
- Under this initiative, the cooperative department will provide mobile handsets to farmers at marginal price through its outlets in the rural areas. These handsets would be loaded with green SIM cards, which will flash daily updates on agricultural practices and weather forecast free of cost.
- ICT can be key player in reducing costs for meeting this challenge
- Technologies like mesh networks, kiosks, etc. on the client side
- Management information systems for back-office efficiency Low network penetration in villages
- There are hassles which need to be understood
- Emerging Challenges and Concerns
- Rough environmental conditions/usage
- Lack of continuous power
- Language barrier
- Regulatory issues particular to microfinance, like digital signatures, etc.
- All problems have solutions as Develop low cost network technologies like mesh networks

- Develop rugged/robust units for rough interaction (like machines in kiosks)
- Develop algorithms supporting intermittent connectivity
- Research in natural languages for localization of services
- SHGs must provide greater flexibility, avoid bureaucracy, increase convenience
- Reliability of SHGs has to be guaranteed.
- ICT capabilities to be developed and harnessed for greater outreach and sustainability of these efforts
- Regulatory support necessary

Initial government support for ICT expansion MFIs are using new information and communication technologies (ICTs) to improve their operations in three main areas: expanding their customer base and extending their reach into underserved areas, establishing secure identities for customers, and lowering transaction costs.

**Reach**

Larger banks, whose access to capital, scale, reach, and expertise could alleviate many of the problems associated with microfinance, have been reluctant to respond to the unmet demand for microfinance services due to the large costs of building and maintaining physical bank branchs, and the high transaction costs and low profit margin on small loans. With this in mind, many initiatives are currently using new information and communication technologies (ICTs), such as smart cards, handhelds devices and modified ATMs, to bypass the traditional methods of providing bank services. In doing so, they are lowering their overhead costs and expanding their reach, helping to extend the availability of microfinance.

In Bolivia, one MFI is providing ATM-enabled banking services to Bolivians that do not have access to the traditional banking system. PRODEM FFP was established as an NGO in 1986 by ACCION International. Since 1999, it has been a regulated, privately held financial fund focused on bringing microfinance services to underserved communities, both rural and urban.

In a country where 70% of the general population and 94% of the rural population are classified as poor, PRODEM has designed its own ATM, tailored to meet the needs of its rural customers. The company provides its customers with a smart card, so that the ATMs are able to verify the customer's identity and complete transactions without being electronically connected to the central office, thereby allowing PRODEM to expand its reach into remote areas.

• PRODEM finds that the ATMs allow it to serve customers who cannot come to their branches during normal business hours. Moreover, the ATMs are capable of "speaking" to their users in their local language, thus enabling illiterate customers to access their services. Audio instructions are currently available in Spanish, Quechua, or Aymara. Combined with a touch screen interface, customers are able to deposit and withdraw funds without filling out a deposit slip or withdrawal form. Additionally, the ATMs facilitate money transfers, and provide access to government programs that provide work for low-skill workers and make payments to senior citizens.

PRODEM's ATM software was developed by a subsidiary of PRODEM, Innova Empresarial, which specializes in technology and consulting services. Its features include an easy-to-use administrative interface, as well as a number of reporting options, including daily, weekly, and monthly. In addition, Innova is in the process of developing palm technology that would enable PRODEM to take their financial services, via a handheld devices into local homes and businesses of their customers.

ICTs are also being used by VOXIVA to allow MFIs located in Peru to :

• expand their reach. The company uses a phone-based system with voice prompts to expand microfinance networks into rural areas that have high numbers of illiterate people. The service reduces operating and transaction costs, resulting in savings that can be passed on to the borrower.

Rural poor people frequently lack an "identity" that allows them to access credit. Banks are reluctant to provide services to these potential customers, who are often illiterate and have no credit history. By providing secure identification, new ICTs such as smart cards and biometrics are compensating for this, allowing many to access credit from formalized institutions for the first time.

PRODEM, for example, is using ICTs to verify the identity of its customers. It utilizes a combination of smart card technology combined with biometrics to allow fingerprint ID verification at all of its branches and ATMs. The use of fingerprint verification ensures that only the account holder can complete a transaction, making it more secure than traditional ATMs that only require a PIN number. The system is also easier to use for customers not familiar with PINs, passwords, or other identifiers that require memorizing an identification code. The smart cards store all of the customer's personal and financial data. As a result, the ATMs are able to verify the customer's identity and complete transactions without being electronically connected to the central office. As of May 2003, PRODEM had 32,000 smart card account holders. The company plans to extend its network throughout Bolivia, and intends to expand into other countries in the near future.

Secure identity can also protect MFIs from customers who have proven to be bad credit risks "shopping" for loans from one branch or one MFI to the next. Addressing this problem requires sharing customers' credit histories among MFIs operating within a country—a function typically performed by a credit bureau. A new effort to explore such cooperative approaches, and the ICT tools to make them possible, is the Microdevelopment Finance Group (MFG), an initiative convened by technology giant Hewlett-Packard as part of its pro bono initiative under the

UNICT Task Force working group on entrepreneurship. The MFG is developing new "end-to-end" technology solutions for microfinance as well as new organizational forms that could increase cooperative efforts such as credit bureaus or pooling loans across many MFIs to access capital markets.

**Efficiency**

ICTs also allow microfinance organizations to increase their efficiency, thereby lowering their overhead costs, and helping them to achieve sustainability. The Dhan Foundation, for example, is streamlining its microfinance activities using a combination of handhelds and smart cards. The technology results in time savings for loan officers, while also ensuring more accurate accounting and record keeping. Because all the information is stored on a smart card, field officers can make decisions on the spot, reducing the number of visits required to complete a transaction.

BASIX, India's largest microfinance organization, is experimenting with handheld devices and smart card technology to automate the loan process and keep track of repayments, in order to reduce labor and cash handling costs. BASIX's Mobile Portfolio Management System also helps to minimize accounting errors.

Swayamkrushi, a women's lending cooperative in India, has also experienced an increase in efficiency since it computerized its operations. The computers used in the microfinance operations are also being used by members to access the Internet, providing additional benefits to the women.

Pride Africa, a cluster of MFIs currently operating in five sub-Saharan African countries, is using IT for increased efficiency and faster growth. In Kenya, it has launched an experimental portal, DrumNet, which stores information on the buying and business habits of Pride clients, in order to group the purchasing power of thousands of small entrepreneurs.

Various software packages are contributing to the increase in efficiency of many MFIs. HISAAB, for example, is a group-level microfinance designed for illiterate and uneducated users. The software is used to document transactions, and allows for more macro-level analysis of lending patterns, cash flows, and repayments. Other software features include the ability to record meeting attendance and savings/credit account transactions, and to exchange data with the central bank office. Cooptions Technologies has developed a software package, Pax@2000, which will computerize the activities of cooperative lending societies and micro-lending banks. The software features online disbursals, data transfer to managing banks, savings/credit account modules, and financial accounting systems. Another, Microfinancer MATRIX, is designed for large micro-lenders. It links the head office to branch offices, and also has built-in accounting and evaluation capabilities.

Additionally, software enables microfinance organizations to consolidate their loans. Once microloan details are stored in an electronic format, their amounts can be combined into a larger loan that can be bought by a larger bank, or securitized to capital markets, thereby providing a much needed supply of capital to MFIs. The Microdevelopment Finance Group hopes to field test some elements of a system that can potentially provide increased efficiency and other aggregate benefits to MFIs over the coming year.

MFIs often don't know what software they need, or are not culturally ready to adopt it within their organization. To address this deficiency, the Consultative Group to Assist the Poorest (CGAP) will soon begin a consulting program that helps these MFIs to decide what software they need, and then assist them in buying and implementing it.

ICTs will continue to impact microfinance operations worldwide. As prices of relevant technology like ATMs, biometrics, voice recognition, smart-cards, and PDAs continue to fall, more MFIs will be able to take advantage of the benefits they offer. New technologies and applications are constantly being developed aimed at increasing the reach and efficiency of microfinance organizations. Improvements will make operations more secure, increase transparency (and thus scalability), reduce repetitive tasks, and provide data mining capabilities that will allow MFIs to compete effectively and better manage their operations. Together, ICTs are helping MFIs to finally meet the unmet demand for microcredit throughout the developing world.

- Financial Inclusion/Microfinance
- Changing landscape (profitability, links to
- formal financial sector, scope of services)
- Potential to address financial exclusion
- Need for enabling environment
- Recommend: Launch of financial inclusion initiative as also launch Capacity-Building Measures to Strengthen and Develop Financial As Banks possess significant distribution Systems Infrastructure and ability to leverage ICT their involvement is nothing short of transformational. They also possess extensive managerial capabilities and are in a position to offer technical advice.

# 9

# *The Way Forward*

The minimalist approach stresses that Banks are equipped to ensure outreach of credit services thus their intervention is restricted to the provision of financial access. Is this enough? There is a view that says that this has to be accompanied by social intervention which is more properly the domain of the NGOs, who have both the capacity and skills for handholding hence the provision of social support services is clearly not the Banks domain. While this is acceptable, credit alone is not enough and Banks need to ensure the provision of 'integrated services', for building income - assets - sustainable livelihoods the poor also need access to savings, credit, insurance, payments and remittance facilities through the formal financial system as a public good and certain other essential services :

(1) Market information and commercial linkages

(2) Technology and ways to improve productivity leveraging technology

(3) Market Infrastructure

(4) Health and Social Security Services

(5) Information, knowhow

(6) Representation/Voice

**Appropriate Mechanisms**

Banking with the poor and illiterate requires special procedures and mechanisms suited to their culture their needs and their economy. This requires adopting procedures and designing schemes suitable to them, like collecting small daily savings from their place of business or houses providing Savings Boxes and biometric access.

They require 'Special loan Procedures' 'Special loan Products' and 'Special treatment'. Borrowers are also savers through micro savings, micro credit and micro insurance, the poor women are set on the path of self- reliance. The 'relationship' should be built between Bank and borrower beyond a 'one off' transaction. Poor women are economically active, therefore they are bankable. They are deeply concerned with livelihood issues and their family's well-being and household income - hence they are the most eligible borrowers. Door step banking is a must. As their economic enterprises are very small, they can only repay their loans in very small instalments. This method of repayment of loans 'payable as able' allows for 95% recoveries. Formal financial institutions have a bureaucratic mindset - this has to be changed. Barefoot bankers are needed and the 'mindset' requires a paradigmatic shift.

## DIVERGENCE BETWEEN STRATEGY AND OUTCOMES

Strategies of pro-poor development have not quite delivered in terms of improving access to finance for most formal sector households, particularly the poor and other small borrowers. The Government owned RBI regulated public sector banks are operationally constrained and functionally hampered as they work within a framework of perverse incentives which lead to embedded inefficiencies. Many rural banks particularly RRBs, Cooperatives (Rural Cooperative Banks) are in such a weak financial position owing to decades of poor governance and weak management in the face of perverse incentives they are unable to perform their primary task of financial intermediation. Critics aver that the measures and initiatives in the area of rural finance have had unintended consequences of "credit rationing". Banks operate on 'wafer thin' margins as loans are capped at PLR and there are floors on short term deposit rates. Banks evade the priority sector obligation by investing in Government bonds. 'Lazy Banking' enables 'safety', security of assured returns through 'Asset allocation' in Government Securities as against the need to build a diverse loan portfolio.

### New Products - Flexibla Products

The poor do not enjoy defined and steady incomes but have irregular income streams and expenditure requirements. They need to borrow at frequent rests and repay in small instalments. An immediate challenge for microfinance is to introduce products and services that are better suited to the needs of the poor.

## REQUIREMENT OF A FULL SUITE OF FINANCIAL PRODUCTS (RANGE OF INTEGRATED SERVICES)

Small borrowers are subject to various hazards and risks, require a composite range of services savings/lending services life, health, livestock, crop insurance etc.

Better staffing policies and doorstep banking staffing policies need to be revisited doorstep banking needs encouragement.

### Improving Incentives Encouraging Competition

Building a more inclusive system will require more fundamental changes to improve the incentive regime promote competition and enhance the efficiency of the rural market.

INTEREST RATES - There is an argument that caps on rural lending rates and floors on deposit rates must be dispensed with. Caps and floors have the opposite effect of what is intended- poor borrowers are cut off from access and end up paying higher interest rates to informal lenders. This measure of removing ceilings and base rates will facilitate greater efficiency of the rural financial markets. This will enable the poor to catch up with the rest of the economy as it grows. However a major controversy had erupted in 2006 Andhra Pradesh which is the state with the largest number of SHGs, in the Krishna District there was a spate of complaints received by the District Collector alleging the charging of usurious rates of interest some borrowers of MFIs committed suicide and had to resort to the extreme step due to the high rates of interest charged and the inability of the borrowers to service these loan contracts due to insufficient income. SADHAN an SRO of SHG MFIs had to step in and the MFIs were asked to adhere to a formal code of conduct to ensure that the interest rates were capped at 15% further an agreement was entered into between the State Government and the MFIs agreed to eschew forced loan recovery and usurious rates of interest. An agreement was also reached on MFI interest rates, MFI product portfolio, inter MFI competition. The problem arises as there are multiple NGOs and SHGs targeting the same set of borrowers hence there is multiple indebtedness of the borrowers leading to failure to service the loans by the borrowers which is compounded by indigence, drought, crop failure etc. The flaring up of the issue actually raises more questions than it resolves. Principally are interest rate caps justified. Are these adhered to strictly or in the breach. Is there any mechanism for monitoring. How often should these be set or reset How exactly are they to be calibrated. The median loan sizes remain miniscule how are these to be scaled up with severely pared operating margins.

The Central thesis is that micro finance is no substitute for an efficient formal financial sector and in the long run microfinance borrowers need to graduate to Banks and other formal financial institutions where they could 'access' standard individual loans of a slightly larger size.

## RECOMMENDATIONS

While microfinance has grown rapidly, further growth would take it to another orbit in rural finance. Sustainability at those scales of operation would be feasible if the stakeholders approach the programme with realism and sensitivity. There are a few issues that need to be examined and acted upon in future.

## LINKAGE WITH BANKS

Microfinance offers many advantages for banks like high recovery performance, reduction in transactions costs for banks and clients, market interest rates, reasonable margin and opportunity to the banks for developing quality future clients. In spite of several advantages, some banks are yet to appreciate this as a business opportunity. Some policy-level issues which need to be addressed are:

- Banks should develop ownership of the SHG-linkage programme. A corporate vision for the programme should be developed so as to give a clear direction and purpose that would be bank-wide.
- The increasing size of loans to groups calls for a close look at collateral requirements for large-sized loans to SHGs.
- Federations of SHGs that seek loans on behalf of the member-SHGs are dealing in large size loans. Here too the issue of collateral has to be examined.
- MIS to be strengthened in order for the financing bank to get periodic information on selected indicators on the health of the SHGs they have financed which can serve as an early warning system. At present, information to amount of savings with the groups, usage of loans, dormancy in groups, impact of government-sponsored programmes on the SHGs, is not captured at higher levels of banks as also policy level. In view of the large size of the programme, growing larger each day, it is necessary to design and implement a comprehensive MIS solution.

## BUSINESS DEVELOPMENT SERVICES

There have been calls on the NGOs and other stakeholders to provide livelihood skills and linkages to SHGs so that the members could take up remunerative economic activities and truly improve their quality of life.

But such a programme design, though comprehensive in terms of dealing with the problems of the poor, goes far beyond financial intermediation. A combination of interventions such as skills training, marketing, networking of input supply and output procurement entities, finance, etc. are involved. The road to be travelled is long-beyond financial services to business development, escort services and stabilisation of livelihoods. Whether banks would be willing to travel to travel down this road and if they do not want to what is the alternative are questions that have to be answered sometime in the near future.

## SUPERVISION AND REGULATION

The rapid expansion of this program, and the large numbers give rise to concerns about the continued stability and integrity of the movement. A modest failure in any part of the country could have a snowballing effect. Hence there is a need for effective regulation. In small groups where each member knows every other person closely, savings do not appear to be in any danger. But very often savings are entrusted to the NGO or the federation and such other intermediaries based on a continuing relationship of trust. It is here that the need for regulation is felt.

The Government of India may look into the supervision and regulation aspects of the sector in the interests of millions of the poor who access financial services through this mode. It is necessary that a flexible and Effective mechanism of supervision which is not top-down but at the same time produces sufficient quality information is introduced at the earliest.

## EXTERNAL INFLUENCE

A mass-based programme which has managed to bring in large numbers with potential for massive expansion could attract political attention. While the programme has so far managed to steer clear of political interests, the future challenge is to ward off unwanted attention, which would reduce the programme to a vote bank with all attendant ills of favoured treatment and subsidies.

Several key issues are being raised on the financial intermediation role of federations on the basis of studies and discussions. At federation level, whether it is the individuals or the groups who should be members of the federations is a serious issue as the furtherance of the interest of the primary member is central to the setting up of the additional tier. While the objectives of setting up a federation are varied, the protection of member savings is a key concern that emerges. In some cases, the objectives and activities of the federations and member-SHGs are conflicting and competing. The federation undermines the services provided by the primaries-lending to members is one such are. Illiteracy and insufficient organizational experience constrain the governance capacity and effective performance of oversight functions of Board members of the federation. Many federations are run and managed by promoter organisations and the Boards comprising grassroot leaders do not effectively oversee the affairs of the federation and give a clear sense of direction. The finance, accounts and MIS functions are weak even in well-established federations. Though there is a general claim that the repayment rates in the SHG structure are fairly high, some of the study reports on SHGs and federations indicate that default is a serious issue and is not being reported and monitored adequately. Operating cost ratio in the federations is high-ranging from 11 to 44 per cent and total cost ratio ranges from 15 to 56 per cent. One of the most empowering aspects of SHGs is the way it allows members to pick and choose between financial service providers.

Federations can demand loyalty, the price of which is essentially a loss of freedom. Overall, there are more issues and concerns on the financial intermediation role of the federations with no clear answers even after 10 years of federating experience in India.

However, there is a very strong demand from member-SHGs, bankers and other major stakeholders that federations should play a major role in group maintenance and empowerment. There is space for non-financial functions and a federation is best suited to provide services such as accounting, auditing, capacity-building, literacy, social awareness and business development/escort services. Through better monitoring and externalising the peer pressure at federation level, the federations can reduce default levels within SHG. Other services like microinsurance can be facilitated. Federations can enable SHGs achieve empowerment beyond that achieved by SHGs, on their own, being small organisations. This is rendered possible through better access to information, expertise and ability to move a larger body of people for a public/social cause.

The banks are far more comfortable in financing the poor through this mode as they find the risk and transaction cost to be low. This would guarantee their sustained interest in the programme. The sustainability of the programme from the point of view of availability of resources is clearly established.

The Indian experience has demonstrated that microfinance is a participatory exercise and the banking system can deliver it sustainably, Instead of creating new institutions to deliver microfinance, it has enabled linkage of groups of poor with the existing banking infrastructure. Though there are emerging issues which need to be addressed to make it sustainable in the long run, it shows that by involving voluntary organisations in social mobilisation and creating an enabling policy environment, which offers flexibility, autonomy and the space for innovations, microfinance can achieve a vast scale and needs to morph into

| *Formal Financial Intermediation Services* | *Social Intermediation Services* | *Clients* |
|---|---|---|
| Banks | -----Linking Approach--- | Group members |
| Public Sector Banks | Intermediary NGO | women |
| Regional Rural Banks/Local Area Banks | Local Group | Landless and small and marginal farmers low income marginalised populations shifting migrant tribal populations |
| Cooperative Banks | Specialised NGO-SHG Bank Linkage facilitator | Scheduled castes/Scheduled tribes |
| Primary Agricultural Cooperative Societies | | Other backward castes |
| Private Banks | | |
| Non Bank Finance Institutions | | |

a national movement. Studies have shown that in practice we are far from attaining this goal.

Secondly there is a reluctance on the part of the Banks to go out into the field and take up the exercise in earnest. There is a need of an attitudinal shift and of sensitization of the Bankers. They appear to have adopted the tried and tested numbers approach and completed their targets without understanding the concept of financial inclusion.

The percentage of exclusion at a median 50% is not comfortable and points to the need for more vigorous/zealous efforts.

Exclusion

- Involuntary exclusion

- 50.2% of the people queried stated that they did not have any information from the Banks or any local authority about Financial Inclusion
- Some families were not approached by banks/ agents of banks for opening of accounts.
- Voluntary exclusion
- 52.39 % people were not performing any transactions in their bank accounts though no frills accounts had been opened they were dormant and the reasons stated for this was
- Distance from the branch (79.64%)
- Do not want (10.04%)
- Illiteracy (6.60%)

1. Lack of savings
2 Perception of non availability of any benefits from the Banks
3. Difficult to complete transactions within a reasonable time leading to multiple visits
4. Non availability of Pass book
5. The migratory nature of the families

- Although there is good coverage of households under the No Frills Account (NFA) scheme, the purpose for which the account has been opened has not been achieved as majority of the accounts are not operated.

## Emerging Concerns Future Challenges and Strategy

Micro finance acts as a catalyst in the lives of the poor. It has helped them achieve a reasonable rise in their income level and improve their standards of living. Thus, micro finance is expected to play an important role in promoting financial inclusion and inclusive growth. However, there is a large gap in the demand and supply of credit to the poor. As per world Bank studies, the credit support for poor households in India has been assessed at about Rs. 4,50,000 crore. Some of the micro level studies indicate that the poor still continue to depend on informal sources of credit, accounting for 40 per cent to 60 per cent of the household demand. There are, however, several challenges faced by the micro finance system.

*Regional Imbalances*: There is a skewed distribution of SHGs in favour of Southern region. The dominance of the Southern States has, albeit, declined in recent years on account of rapid progress in promotion and credit linkage of SHGs in non-Southern States. Nevertheless, over 50 per cent of the total SHG credit linkages in the country are concentrated in the Southern States. However, in States which have a larger share of the poor, the coverage is comparatively low.

*Quality of SHGs*: Sustainability in income generation is dependent on the quality of a SHG. Therefore ensuring quality of a SHG is a big challenge. Owing to the fast growth of the SHG-Bank Linkage Programme, the quality of SHGs has come under stress. Some of the factors affecting the quality of SHGs are : (i) the target oriented approach of some of the government departments in promoting groups, (ii) inadequate incentives to NGOs for nurturing them on a sustainable basis, and (iii) low level of skills on the part of the SHG members in managing their groups.

The strength of the programme stems from the fact that the loan recovery levels under the programme are significantly higher than credit disbursed under various government sponsored programmes. However, the quality of SHGs is of paramount importance to sustain the higher recovery levels.

*Training of SHPIs, banks, SHG members:* The success of the programme depends on the role played by self-help promoting institutions (SHPIs) in the promotion of quality groups and easy hassle free availability of bank credit. The promotion of quality groups, in turn, depends on the internal strengths - managerial and financial - of SHPIs. Therefore capacity building through training programmes in respect of various stakeholders remains a challenge in the absence of quality resource centers at the district level as also lack of adequate appreciation on providing training to various personnel involved in the programme implementation.

*Graduation from credit to enterprise*: The more critical challenge is to induce SHGs to graduate into matured levels of enterprise, livelihood diversification, increased access to the supply chain, linkages to the capital market and appropriate/ production and processing technologies.

The SHG Bank-linkage programme needs to enable SHGs to also meet the non-financial requirements for setting up business and enterprises. However, there are not many viable and sustainable livelihoods in the area. This has led to groups turning morbid i.e. older SHGs not availing credit from banks after the initial few rounds of credit linkage. The job of micro enterprise promotion is further compounded because of factors like self-confidence, ability to invest, and access to market opportunities being unequal among the groups.

*Emergence of SHG Federations:* Of late, many SHPIs have started promoting federations of SHGs so that some of their functions can be performed by them in a cost effective and sustainable manner. However, no serious efforts have been made towards capacity building of federations. There is no established model which can be replicated across the country. The emergence of SHG Federations represents the aggregation of collective bargaining power and economies of scale. They are fora for addressing social and economic issues. However, every additional tier adds to its cost and thus, tends to weaken the primaries. It must, therefore, be ensured that the quality of the federations is good. To ensure the quality of federations, care needs to be taken by monitoring institutions engaged in promoting SHG Federations. One, federation should be evolved based on the felt need of the SHGs and the group should have freedom to or not to join the federation. Two, the federations need to be evolved as member-owned, member-driven institutions so that they can function in a democratic manner,

**Table 1.1- Progress of Commercial Banking at a Glance**

| *Important Indications* | *June 1969* | *March 2000* | *March 2001* | *March 2002* | *March 2003* |
|---|---|---|---|---|---|
| No. of Commercial Banks | 89 | 297 | 301 | 298 | 294 |
| (a) Scheduled Commercial Banks | 73 | 297 | 296 | 294 | 289 |
| Of which : Regional Rural Banks | - | 196 | 196 | 196 | 196 |
| (b) Non-Scheduled Commercial Banks | 16 | - | 5 | 4 | 5 |
| Number of offices of Scheduled Commercial Banks in India | 8262 | 65412 | 65919 | 66190 | 66535 |
| (a) Rural | 1833 | 32734 | 32562 | 32380 | 32303 |
| (b) Semi-Urban | 3342 | 14407 | 14597 | 14747 | 14859 |
| (c) Urban | 1584 | 10052 | 10293 | 10477 | 10693 |
| (d) Metropolitan | 1503 | 8219 | 8467 | 8586 | 8680 |
| Population per office (in thousands) | 64 | 15 | 15 | 16 | 16 |
| Deposits of Scheduled Commerical Banks In India (Rs. Crore) | 4645@ | 851593@ | 989141# | 1131187# | 1311761# |
| Of which (a) Demand | 2104 | 145283 | 159407 | 169103 | 187837 |
| (b) Time | 2542 | 706310 | 829731 | 962085 | 1123924 |
| Credit of Scheduled Commercial Banks in India (Rs. Crore) | 3599 | 454069 | 529272 | 609053 | 746432 |

*(Contd.)*

*(Contd.Table 1.1)*

| *Important Indications* | *March 2004* | *March 2005* | *March 2006* | *March 2007* | *March 2008* |
|---|---|---|---|---|---|
| No. of Commercial Banks | 291 | 288 | 222 | 183 | 175 |
| (a) Scheduled Commercial Banks | 286 | 284 | 218 | 179 | 171 |
| Of which : Regional Rural Banks | 196 | 196 | 133 | 96 | 91 |
| (b) Non-Scheduled Commercial Banks | 5 | 4 | 4 | 4 | 4 |
| Number of offices of Scheduled Commercial Banks in India | 67188 | 68355 | 69471 | 71839 | 76050 |
| (a) Rural | 32121 | 32082 | 30579 | 30551 | 31076 |
| (b) Semi-Urban | 15091 | 15403 | 15556 | 16361 | 17675 |
| (c) Urban | 11000 | 11500 | 12032 | 12970 | 14391 |
| (d) Metropolitian | 8976 | 9370 | 11304 | 11957 | 12908 |
| Population per office (in thousands) | 16 | 16 | 16 | 15 | 15 |
| Deposits of Scheduled Commerical Banks In India (Rs. Crore) | 1542284& | 1732858& | 2109049 | 2611933 | 3196939 |
| Of which (a) Demand | 245943 | 265033 | 364640 | 429731 | 524310 |
| (b) Time | 1296342 | 1467824 | 1744409 | 2182203 | 2672630 |
| Credit of Scheduled Commercial Banks in India (Rs. Crore) | 865594 | 1124300 | 1507077 | 1931189 | 2361914 |

*(Contd.)*

(Contd. Table 1.1)

| Important Indications | June 1969 | March 2000 | March 2001 | March 2002 | March 2003 |
|---|---|---|---|---|---|
| Deposits of Scheduled Commercial Banks | 56 | 1302 | 1501 | 1709 | 1972 |
| Credit of Scheduled Commercial Banks per office (Rs. Lakh) | 44 | 694 | 803 | 920 | 1122 |
| Per capita Deposits of Scheduled Commercial Banks (Rs.) | 68 | 4531 | 5221 | 5919 | 7143 |
| Deposits of Scheduled Commercial Banks as percentage of National Income (at current prices) | 15.5 | 53.5 | 58.9 | 60.7 | 65.3 |
| Scheduled Commercial Banks Advances to Priority Sector (Rs. Crore) | 504 | 155779 | 182255 | 205604 | 250989 |
| Share of Priority Sector Advances in Total Credit of Scheduled Commerical Banks (per cent) | 14.0 | 35.4 | 35.5 | 34.8 | 34.6 |
| Share of Priority Sector Advances in Total Non-food Credit of Scheduled Commercial Banks (per cent) | 15.0 | 37.4 | 38.5 | 38.2 | 37.1 |
| Credit Deposit Ratio | 77.5 | 53.3 | 53.5 | 53.8 | 56.9 |
| Credit Deposit Ratio | 29.3 | 36.6 | 37.1 | 38.7 | 41.3 |
| Cash Deposit Ratio | 8.2 | 9.8 | 8.4 | 7.1 | 6.3 |

(Contd.)

*(Contd.Table 1.1)*

| *Important Indications* | *March 2004* | *March 2005* | *March 2006* | *March 2007* | *March 2008* |
|---|---|---|---|---|---|
| Deposits of Scheduled Commercial Banks | 2295 | 2535 | 3036 | 3631 | 4204 |
| Credit of Scheduled Commercial Banks per office (Rs. Lakh) | 1288 | 1645 | 2169 | 2685 | 3106 |
| Per capita Deposits of Scheduled Commercial Banks (Rs.) | 8166 | 10440 | 13774 | 17355 | 20928 |
| Deposits of Scheduled Commercial Banks as percentage of National Income (at current prices) | 68.5 | 68.5 | 73.8 | 79.1 | 84.4 |
| Scheduled Commercial Banks Advances to Priority Sector (Rs. Crore) | 311335 | 400775 | 546774 | 703756 | 824773 |
| Share of Priority Sector Advances in Total Credit of Scheduled Commerical Banks (per cent) | 37.1 | 36.7 | 37.2 | 36.5 | 34.9 |
| Share of Priority Sector Advances in Total Non-food Credit of Scheduled Commercial Banks (per cent) | 38.8 | 38.1 | 38.2 | 37.4 | 35.6 |
| Credit Deposit Ratio | 561 | 64.9 | 71.5 | 73.9 | 73.9 |
| Credit Deposit Ratio | 43.8 | 41.6 | 35.5 | 30.3 | 30.4 |
| Cash Deposit Ratio | 5.6 | 6.9 | 6.6 | 7.5 | 8.6 |

@ Includes Resurgent India (RIB) (Rs. 17,945 crore)

\# Includes Resurgent India Bonds (RIB) (Rs. 17, 945 crore) and also India Millennium Deposits (IMD) (Rs. 25, 662 Crore)

& Includes India Millennium Deposits (IMD) (Rs. 25, 662 Crore)

* Provisional

^ Exclusive Administrative Offices

See Notes on Tables.

keeping in view the aspirations of their constituents -self-help group. Three, the process of systems of federations need to be designed in such a way that these federations do not depend on the promoter perpetually and become self-managed in a reasonable period of time.

*High Cost of Delivery:* MFI model is comparatively costlier in terms of delivery of financial services due to low volume of loan and also loan size as also the cost of funds. A good number of MFIs are subsidy dependent and only few MFIs are able to cover more than 80 per cent of their costs. High rate of interest charged by them has become an area of concern. While it is agreed that the cost of services offered by MFIs is high, there is no consensus on the floor limit of rate of interest that could be permitted to be charged by MFIs. They, therefore, need to develop strategies for increasing the range and volume of their financial services so that they can provide their services at a cost affordable by poor.

*Capacity building of MFIs.* Successful delivery of flexible, client driven and innovative micro finance services to the poor would not be possible without building up the capacities of the MFIs and their primary stakeholders. Innovations in various aspects such as social intermediation, strategic linkages and new approaches centered on the livelihood issues surrounding the poor, and the re-engineering of the financial products offered by them are the need of the hour.

*Future Strategies:* Inspite of phenomenal growth of SHG-Bank Linkage Programme achieved over the years, there is still a large segment of society that is denied access to financial services. An estimate suggests that only 20 per cent of the low income group population has access to financial services. Thus, there is an urgent need to widen the scope, outreach as also the scale of financial services to cover the un-reached population.

To be successful the Micro Finance Programs (MFP's) must be effective in outreach. Efficient in operations and sustainable in the long term over a period of time.

**Consumption smoothing v/s. Micro enterprise development**

NGO - MFIs retain savings of their members to establish a degree of control over their members who are also borrowers. NGO led MFIs achieve 'consumption smoothing' but do not possess the resources and skills to ensure micro enterprise development.

**Consumption Smoothing**

The pressure to grow rapidly to achieve financial sustainability leads them to push a portfolio of fast moving 'small' loans, for consumption/petty trade, they do not focus on enterprise development.

**Micro Enterprise Development**

Micro Enterprise Development does not tackle bottom of the pyramid hard core and asset less poor. It targets those who possess some basic skills, are able to absorb and service larger amounts of loans, take risks and establish the linkages to sustain business enterprises. Large Loan Portfolios including incomes which increase incomes through productivity, scale, genuine business initiative.

The Need is to "embed credit in a broader framework of service provision and investment that has the potential to light the poor Above Poverty Line (APL) and keep them there".

The activity for which micro loans are taken is one of several Indian Generating Activities (IGA) that households juggle to meet their daily needs throughout the year. Given the Scarce Resources, Poor Infrastructure and inability to take risks due to lack of supporting systems, poor people tend to opt for a 'bundle' of livelihood activities just as they practice multi-cropping due to the uncertainty of rain, getting involved in one major enterprise throughout the year may be considered by them as too large a risk. A genuine Micro Enterprise should be one large enough to employ the family throughout the year and feed it.

1. Credit Absorption capabilities of the poor have first to be increased within a larger developmental context.
2. Adequate supporting infrastructure is necessary to create the enabling environment for the poor to work their way out of poverty. This includes the provision of linkages for them and of savings facilities, insurance buffers, marketing channels and continuous capacity building efforts, all of the above taken in tandem can ensure successful interventions. Savings is generally managed by Savings Assets Groups (SAGs) themselves but linkages with banks are used to avail loans which become necessary for 'scaling up' the microenterprises of the poor while ensuring operational and financial self-sufficiency.
3. Competition provides the best service, where Savings Asset Groups (SAG) proliferate, rates come down as providers of financial services multiply, there is a competition for such services in the market. Doorstep banking keeping costs of credit low combined with low service costs, provides competition to money lenders in their own backyard. This is the biggest contribution of grassroots agencies working with poor communities in the villages. People should be encouraged to work on a single thematic and financial support
4. focus and financial support for a substantive period and then linking them to formal financial systems. Competent professionals can greatly assist in the endeavours.

Essentially microfinance stabilises the livelihoods of the poor by providing success to multiple credit needs which include consumption supporting existing income generating activities and creating new ones.

Large Scale Linkages with Banks, groups need to be linked to local commercial and rural banks to address the multiple credit needs of the poor and to ensure the sustainability of these organisations.

The poor have demonstrated time and again that they are able to save or borrow and invest their funds. Banks through Micro finance initiatives for poverty reduction basically help the poor to help themselves by providing :

1. Loanable Funds
2. Enabling access to Financial Services
3. Helping, the poor to establish their own financial institutions. Given their mandate of sustainable poverty reduction Banks and MFIs strengthen the self reliance of the people and of the SHG institutions and federations set up by them. They are inextricably bound together Policy interventions must serve to strengthen both individual self help capacities and institutional viability. It should not weaken them through well meaning but inappropriate interventions for instance while there should be no subsidised interest rates there should also be no caps and yet the golden mean on rates charged needs not onlty to be adopted but also to be closely monitored. The virtuous cycle of institutional and group viability through income generating self sustaining enterprises.
   1. Viable Financial Institutions
   2. Growth
   3. Viable enterprises
   4. Growth

Thus there is a linkage between viable financial institutions which in turn prompt economic growth which leads to setting up of viable microenterprises which also leads to economic growth. The poor need sustainable financial services.

Microsavings deposit facilities for

1. The safekeeping of their savings
2. Consumption smoothing
3. Emergencies
4. Accumulation of resources
5. Self financing of investments

Microcredit with access to loans of various sizes and maturities for

1. External financing of investments
2. Consumption smoothing
3. Emergencies

Microinsurance including specialised insurance services (life, health, accident or cattle insurance and non specialised services providing social protection through access to ones savings or to credit in case of emergency for :

Risk Management

Social Security

Loan Protection

Plus other financial services delivered through microfinance institutions in concert with formal lending institutions.

The objective of all institutions working with the poor is to mediate between savers and investors, allocate scarce resources for various purposes with different returns to provide these services reliably and cost effectively while helping lower transaction costs and widen and deepen financial services for the poor. The growth of outreach for sustainable poverty reduction is contingent upon the dynamic growth of self reliant institutions. The essence of self reliance of the poor and their institutions is local resources. Savings deposited and accumulated by the poor in local financial institutions are the basis of self financing and household risk management. Savings mobilised by local financial institutions are the main source of growth of funds and bring independence from external subsidies and interference. MFIs have come in for a very great deal of criticism on account of the high rates of interest they charge. Their contention is that rates of interest are pitched high to enable them to cover the costs of several large volume, small value transactions, from the point of view of the poor borrower finance at these higher rates is still attractive as rates charged by the money lender are even higher or he may not be able to have any alternative channel to access finance. MFIs are also conscious that they must make a profit to finance expansion from their returns as only viable institutions can provide financial services on a sustainable basis to the poor.

Sustainable poverty reduction requires the political will of governments and a conducive policy framework. No poverty reduction program can be sustainable without good governance and adequate policies. The purpose of MFI institutions is to increase the productivity income and food security of the poor by promoting access to sustainable financial services They attempt to cover costs, recover loans and make a profit to increase their saver and borrower outreach. Cutting edge technology can also play a transformational role in delivering financial and other services to poor borrowers.

Creating rural finance systems is not a panacea. Nor is without its challenges among them assuring the participation of all shareholders, building rural financial; infrastructures that are diversified according to local conditions enhancing institutional sustainability with outreach to the poor and fostering a conducive policy and regulatory environment. Access to finance remains an issue crucial to the task of reducing rural poverty. We do not insist on any particular institutional model the demand for financial services is very diverse among the rural poor and any sustainable response has also to be pluralistic. For the demand to be met it is essential that linkages are fostered to upstream financial institutions with a much larger capital base.It is increasingly apparent that large scale sustainable microfinance is feasible only if financial services for the poor are integrated into the overall financial system. Quite simply all this means is that financial services for the poor becomes the lower end of the entire financial sector Banks must downstream their products and services opening up access and markets to increasingly poor and geographically dispersed clients.

As a consequence of this process financial sustainability is achieved through innovation by successfully leveraging the technological advantage.

Streamlined business processes enable increased cost efficiency in the face of ever increasing competition

## COMMERCIAL MICROFINANCE

As microfinance is increasingly attracting new players including private sector debt and equity funds there is a need for greater transparency if microfiance is properly conducted it is a profitable,low risk and expanding financial activity. Bolivia first demonstrated this. The sector in Bolivia attracted private sector institutional investors seeking full market returns and in 2004 the International Capital markets began to grow into active players Initial Public Offerings, bond issues and collateralised debt obligations and securitisation of the underlying loan entered the lexicon of microfinance leading to cross border capital inflows in the sector debt and equity security issues of microfinance have raised funds in India the larger players have even in tight market conditions raised funds from International Markets as SKS Finance Data from the Micro Banking Bulletin reports that 63 of the world's top MFIs had an average rate of return, after adjusting for inflation and after taking out subsidies programs might have received, of about 2.5% of total assets. This lends to the hope that microfinance can be sufficiently attractive for investors, as well as the mainstream into the retail banking sector. Providing financial services to poor people is expensive. This cost is one of the most important reasons why banks don't make small loans. For example, a Rs. 2000 loan requires the same amount of resources as a Rs.100,000 loan.

*Microfinance is a high-personal interaction business:* At SKS, field staff managers must perform village surveys before entering a village, conduct interviews with potential members, train members on credit discipline, travel to villages by motorbike every week to collect interest and disburse loans, and follow-up to ensure the loans are being used for their intended purpose. These personnel and administration costs easily amount to 11% of our total cost structure.

In addition, they must borrow from commercial sources to lend to their members. This cost of lending is anywhere from 10-12%. The combination of this personnel/administration costs, the cost of lending, a 1-2% loan loss provision (due to default or writing off a loan), and 1-2% profit used to expand operations, translates to an interest that appears high. However, it is the lowest possible interest they assert they can charge to cover our costs. As the microfinance industry matures, and MFIs like SKS continue to scale and increase efficiency, the cost of lending may reduce. And, if commercial banks reduce their own rates, they can and will deliver these savings to our borrowers. SKS Microfinance, raised a 75 crore non convertible debenture issue on 17th May 2009 an issue of 1-year NCD at a coupon rate of 10 percent. The NCDs have been listed on The Stock Exchange, Mumbai. For the first time, a debt security issued by an MFI has been listed on the stock exchange Swayam Krishi Sangham SKS has already introduced several mainstream capital market financial products to the MFI sector and this issuance marks a new chapter in 'Funding innovation'. "This transaction enables the m MFI to diversify the sources base and access capital market funding. By listing the NCDs on the stock exchange, it also raises the bar on transparency and governance standards for the sector as a whole." Standard Chartered India is the sole book runner and lead arranger for the Issue.

The consensus which has emerged is that the poor can save invest and repay their loans they need access to financial services :

1. Depost facilities for safe keeping of their savings which are needed for consumption smoothing.
2. For self financing economic operations.
3. Insurance for social security and loan protection.
4. Only sustainable financial institutions can provide adequate financial services and continually increase their outreach to the poor. The strength of microfinance institutions lies in their ability to reduce transaction costs

| *Subject* | *Status* | *Shortfall* |
|---|---|---|
| Policy environment | Macroeconomic stability interest rate deregulation | Inadequate policy environment slow implementation of deregulation inadequate property rights and judicial processes |
| Microfinance Institutions | | Lack of an appropriate legal framework High minimum capital requirements,Interest rate caps through money lenders acts in some states as Tamil Nadu |
| Non Formal financial Institutions | Opportunities are available for upgrading to formal levels and for financial market integration | The potential for upgradation remains largely untapped due to high capital requirements and other constraints |
| NGOs | Innovative approaches to poverty lending in financially repressive environments t | NGOs are slow in mobilising local resources to reach self sustainability on their own steam. Donors support unviable NGOs |

*(Contd.)*

*(Contd.)*

| *Subject* | *Status* | *Shortfall* |
|---|---|---|
| Regional Rural Banks | Reform helped them to move towards self sustainability | Political interference in lending decisions,trade unions stymies their viability |
| MFI regulation and Supervision | Controversial discussion on the need for effective regulation and supervision of MFIs | The Reserve Bank and financial authorities as NABARD do not supervise MFIs there is a lack of mfi self supervision |
| Non Bank Finance Companies | Self financing through profits and non targeted commercial credit | High Capital and entry point requirements |
| Access of the poor to financial services | Outreach of viable mfis (including rural and other banks) to the poor as users and owners drastically increased | Vast numbers of the poor 76% as per world bank survey particularly in marginal areas lack access to savings and credit services |

make their resources grow dynamically allocate resources efficiently and manage risks. The Indian experience has shown that with sound practices and in a conducive policy and regulatory environment different types of financial institutions can be sustainable and form the building blocks of an effective rural financial system. The household cycle of savings and credit shows how the poor can through the provision of requisite necessary finance work their own way out of poverty.

Thus microfinance Industry is growing to encompass many types of actors with different objectives, roles and comparative competitive advantages. The plurality is welcome as the major bottleneck to the growth of microfinance is perceived to be the absence of strong retail institutions just as there is wide diversity in the number of poor clients there should be wide variety and a wide range of service providers. However mission drift should not take place and the focus must remain on the poor. Developing strong sustainable financial systems also requires coordination and partnership between the different actors and agencies so as to enable them to build better linkages with other development sectors. This is the only way the financial frontier can be expanded to encompass the remotest rural areas this larger vision necessitates, mapping of financial services for the poorest of the poor, advancing Industry knowledge, working with networks on policy issues and coordinating at national and global levels, building Industry knowledge constant innovation, increased transparency building physical and information Infrastructure overall it needs to address the critical issue of deepening poverty outreach. Microfinance needs a clear and coherent strategy the returns in terms of securing social justice and ensuring economic growth with equity far outweigh the costs.

## Conclusion

As a financial services delivery model, the Self Help Group approach is unique; it has emerged as a clearly superior model compared to the Grameen bank or MFI models. By emphasising savings before credit it takes care of both the legs of basic financial services. People's participation is fully ensured with autonomy for the groups of poor in credit decisions. Linkage to bank branches enables groups to access loans as also keep their savings safely. The groups have been able to build a corpus through their financial intermediation (arising from the margins between costs of resources and lending rates). The members while paying high interest rates (still lower than money lenders' rates) do not lose the same, as it helps the corpus of funds to grow. Ultimate succeed lies in the extent to which groups are able to encourage access to formal generating financial financial services through setup sustainable income generally projects help have poverty and more poor people form the margin to the main stream.

# Bibliography

Anderson, Jock and Niraj Verma. 2003. "Informal Finance in Rural India."

Background paper prepared for the World Bank. Washington D.C.: World Bank.

APEC.2002. "Microbanking Development, Regulation and Supervision."

Chapter 2 of 2002 APEC Economic Outlook, Singapore: Asia Pacific Economic Cooperation Secretariat.

Barth, J., G. Caprio, and R. Levine 2001. The Regulation and Supervision of Banking Systems around the World, Washington D.C.: World Bank.

Basu, Priya. 2005. India's Financial Sector: Recent Reforms, Future Challenges.

Washington D.C.: World Bank and Macmillan.

Basu, Priya and Pradeep Srivastava. 2005. "Exploring Possibilities: Micro Finance and Rural Credit Access for the Poor in India." Economic and Political Weekly, Vol. XL, No. 17: 1747-56.

Besley, Timothy, 1994. "How do Market Failures Justify Interventions in Rural Credit Markets?" The World Bank Research Observer 9: 27-48.

Bond, Philip and Robert Twnsend. 1996. "Formal and Informal Financing in a Chicago Ethnic Neighbourhood." Economic Perspectives 20(4): 3-27.

CGAP. 2000. "Focus Note No. 18: Exploring Client Preferences in Microfinance: Some observations from Safe Save." Washington D.C.: World Bank.

Deshpande, Ramesh and Niraj Verma, 2003. "Review of Rural Finance Institutions in India." Background paper prepared for the Word Bank. Washington D.C.: World Bank.

Fernando, Nimal and Richard Meyer, 2002. "ASA_The Ford Motor Model of Microfinance." ADB Finance for the Poor 3(2). Manila: Asian Development Bank.

Fisher, Thomas and M.S. Sriram. 2002. "Beyond Micro-Credit: Putting Development Back into Micro-Finance." New Delhi: Vistar.

Friedman, Milton. 1957. "The Permanent Income Hypothesis: Comment" American Economic Review 48: 990-1.

Galindo, A. 2001. " Creditor Rights and the Credit Market: Where Do We Stand?" Working Paper No. 448, Inter-American Development Bank, Washington D.C.

Government of India, Ministry of Finance. 2001. "Report of the Joint Committee on Revitalisation Support to Co-operative Credit Structure" (Patil Committee). New Delhi: Government of India.

Hashemi, Syed, Sidney Ruth Schuler, and Ann P. Riley. 1996. "Rural Credit Programs and Women's Empowerment in Bangladesh." World Development 24 (4): 635-53.

Hallberg, Kristin. 2001. "A Market-Oriented Strategy for Small and Medium-Scale Enterprises." IFC Discussion Paper No. 40. International Finance Corporation, Washington D.C.

Hess, Ulrich and Leora F. Klapper: 2003. "The Use of New Products, Processes and Technology for the Delivery of Rural and Microfinance Loans in India." Background paper prepared for the World Bank. Washington D.C.: World Bank.

Hickson, Robert. 1999. "Reaching Extreme Poverty: Financial Services for the very Poor." Nairobi: Micro Save-Africa.

Insurance Regulatory and Development Authority, 2002. Annual Report 2001-02.

Mahajan, Vijay and Bharti Ramola Gupta. 2003. "Microfinance in India: Banyan Tree and Bonsai." Background paper prepared for the World Bank. Washington D.C.: World Bank.

Mayer, Thomas 1972. Permanent Income, Wealth and Consumption: A Critique of Permanent Income Theory, Life-Cycle Hypothesis and Related Theories. Berkeley: University of California Press.

Meyer, Richard. 2002. "Microfinance, Poverty Alleviation and Improving Food Security: Implications for India." Chapter in Rattan Lal, ed., Food Security and Environmental Quality. Boca Raton, Florida: CRC Press.

Microcredit Ratings International Limited (M_CRIL) Review 2004, New Delhi. ———. 2003. "The Outreach Viability Conundrum: Can India's Regional Rural Banks Really Serve Low Income Clients?" New Delhi.

Morduch, Jonathan. 1999a. "Between the Market and State: Can Informal Insurance Patch the Safety Net?" World Bank Research Observer 14(2). August: 187-207.

——————.1999b. "The Microfinance Promise." Journal of Economic Literature 37: 1569-14.

—————— and Stuart Rutherford. 2003. "Microfinance: Analytical Issues for India" Background paper prepared for the World Bank. Washington D.C.: World Bank.

Mutesasira, Leonard. 1999. "Savings and Needs: An Infinite Variety." Kampala: MicroSave-Africa.

NSSO (National Sample Survey Organization). 1991. All India Debt and Investment Survey, Mumbai.

Patole, M. and O.Ruthven, "Metro Moneylenders: Debtors and Creditors in a West Delhi Squatter Settlement", IDPM Working Paper 28, Institute for Development Policy and Management, Manchester: IDPM 2001.

Puhazendi, V and K.J.S. Satyasi, "Microfinance and Rural People: An Impact Study", Mumbai: Department of Economic Analysis and Research, NABARD, 2000.

Patten, Richaard and Jay Rosengaard.1991. Progress with Profits: The Development of Rural Banking in Indonesia. San Francisco, CA: International Center for Economic Growth/HIID.

Rajan, Raghuram and Luigi Zingales. 2003. Saving Capitalism from the Capitalists. New York: Crown Business, 2003.

Micro Credity for Macro Impact on Poverty by Indira Misra.

RBI (Reserve Bank of India) 1954. All India Credit Survey. Bombay: RBI.

——————, 2002, Basic Statistical Returns, Mumbai.

——————,2002, Branch Banking Statistics, Mumbai.

——————, 2003, Handbook of Statistics, Mumbai.

———————— .2000. "Report of the Task Force to Study the Cooperative Credit System and Suggest Measures for its Strengthening." (Capoor Committee). Mumbai: RBI.

————————.2004. "Report of the Advisory Committee on Flow of Credit to Agriculture and Related Activities from the Banking System." (Vyas Committee). Mumbai: RBI.

————————. Various years. Report on Trend and Progress of Banking in India. Mumbai. Robinson, Marguerite. 2001. The Microfinance Revolution. Washington D.C.: The World Bank.

Romer David. 1996. Advanced Macroeconomics. New York:McGraw-Hill. Rutherford, Stuart. 1996. ASA, the Biography of an NGO. Dhaka: ASA.

————————.2000. The Poor and their Money. Delhi: Oxford University Press.

————————.2002. "Money Talks: Conversations with Poor Households in Bangladesh about Managing Money". University of Manchester Institute for Development Policy and Management, Finance and Development Research Programme Paper 32.

Ruthven, Orlanda and Sushil Kumar (2002). "Fine-grain Finance: Financial Choice and Strategy Among the Poor in Rural North India." University of Manchester Institute for Development Policy and Management, Finance and Development Research Programme Paper 57.

Srivastava, Pradeep. 2004. "Rural Credit and Finance in Uttar Pradesh: A Case study of Three Villages." Background paper prepared for the World Bank.Washington D.C.: World Bank.

————————and Rajesh Shukla. 2004. "Rural Financial Access Survey: Summary Findings." Background paper prepared for the World Bank. Washington DC.: World Bank.

Siebel, Hans Dieter. 2001. "SHG Banking: A Financial Technology for Reaching Marginal Areas and very poor." Cologne: University of Cologne.

Sinha, Sanjay and Meenal Patole. 2002. "Microfinance and the Poverty of Financial Services: How the Poor in India could be Better Served." University of Manchester Institute for Development Policy and Management, Finance and Development Research Programme Paper 56.

Stiglitz, Joseph E., and Andrew Weiss. 1981. "Credit Rationing in Markets with Imperfect Information." American Economic Review 71(3).

Thomas, Susan. 2004. "Agriculture Commodity Markets in India: Policy Issues for Growth." Background paper prepared for the World Bank. Washington D.C.: World Bank.

Todd, Helen, 1996. Women at the Center: Grameen Bank Borrowers After One Decade. Dhaka: University Press Ltd.

————————.2005 (forthcoming). "Aligning India's Financial Sector Regulatory and Supervisory Architecture to Country Needs," Washington D.C.: World Bank.

Williamson, Stephen D. 1986. "Costly Monitoring, Financial Intermediation, and Equilibrium Credit Rationing." Journal of Monetory Economics 18.

World Bank. 2002. "India: The Reform of India Post: Transforming a Postal Infrastructure to Deliver Modern Information and Financial Services" Washington D.C.: World Bank.

————————. World Bank. 2003. "Microfinance in India: Issues, Challenges and Policy Options." Washington D.C. World Bank.

————————.2003a. Improving Access to Finance in Brazil. Washington D.C.: World Bank.

————————2003b. "India: Development Policy Review: Sustaining Reform, Reducing Poverty". Washington D.C.: World Bank.

————————2004. "Migrant Labour Remittances in South Asia: Development Impact and Future Prospects." Washington D.C.: World Bank.

Wright, Graham. 2000. Microfinance Systems: Designing Quality Financial Services for the Poor. London: Zed Press; Dhaka: University Press Ltd.

Yunus, Mohammad.2002. Grameen Bank II. Designed to Open New Possibilities. Dhaka: Grameen Bank. (Available at www.grameen-info.org/bank/bank2.html.)

Ghate, Prabhu, 'State Assault on Micro-Finance, Economic Times' (May 18), New Delhi, 2006.

Datta, Shankar, 'Basics of Costs in Microfinance Operations' Sa-Dhan, Newsletter, Vol. 5, Issue 1 (Special Issue), New Delhi, March, 2004.

EDA Rural Systems, 2006. Self Help Groups in India: A study of the lights and shades, EDA Rural Systems and Andhra Pradesh Mahila Abhivruddhi Society (APMAS), 2006.

Pathak, N, 'Operating Expenses in Micro Finance' Sa-Dhan, Newsletter, Vol. 5, Issue 1 (Special Issue), New Delhi, March, 2004.

Prasad, V, 'Taking Interests at Large', Sa-Dhan, and News letter, Vol. 5, Issue 1 (Special Issue), New Delhi, March, 2004.

Mahajan, Vijay, 'The Microfinance and Poverty Alleviation', (mimio), New Delh, 2006.

Sinha, Sanjay et al, The Outreach/viability Conundrum 'Can India's Regional Rural Banks really serve low income clients' pp. 42-46 M-CRIL, Gurgaon, 2003.

M-CRIL, Microfinance Review 2005 (forthcoming).

Ghate, Prabhu, 'Microfinance in India – A state of the Sector Report, 2006'

Adams, D and von Pischke, J D (1992) 'Microenterprise credit programs: 'deja vu', World Development 20, 1463-1470.

Ardener, S and Burman, S (1995) Money-go-Rounds: the Importance of Rotating Savings and Credit Associations for Women, Oxford: Berg.

Barnes, Carolyn (1996) Assets and the Impact of Microenterprise Finance Programs, Washington DC: Management Systems International.

Beuningen, Coen van (1997) 'Outline for Impact Assessment in the Credit Line', mimeo, Consultative Group to Assist the Poorest (CGAP), Washington DC.

Bouman, F J A and Hospes, O (eds). (1994) Financial Landscapes Reconstructed, Boulder: Westview.

Buckley, G (1997) 'Microfinance in Africa: is it either the problem or the solution?', World Development 25(7), 1081-1094.

Casely, D and Lury, D A (1982) Monitoring and Evaluation of Agricultural and Rural Development Projects, Baltimore: Johns Hopkins University Press.

Chambers, R (1997) Whose Reality Counts? Putting the First Last, London: IT Publications.

Chao-Beroff, Renee (1997) 'Impact Assessment Seen From an NGO Practitioners'.

Scope', mimeo, Consultative Group to Assist the Poorest (CGAP), Washington DC.

Chen, M A and Dunn, E (1996) Household Economic Portfolios, Washington DC: Management Systems International.

Devereux, S and Hoddinott, M (1993) Field Research in Developing Countries, London: Harvester Wheatsheaf.

Dunn, Elizabeth (1996) Households, Microenterprises and Debt, Washington DC: Management Systems International.

Dunn, E, Kalaitzandonakes, N and Valdivia, C (1996) Risk and the Impacts of Microenterprise Services, Washington DC: Management Systems International.

Feinstein, Osvaldo (1997) 'A Transaction Costs Approach for Microfinance Project Assessment', mimeo, Consultative Group to Assist the Poorest (CGAP), Washington DC.

Fuglesang, A and Chandler, D (1986) Participation as Process: What We Can Learn From the Grameen Bank, Oslo: NORAD.

Gaile, G L (1997) Highlights and Recommendations from the Microenterprise Impact Virtual Meeting, Washington DC: Management Systems International.

Gaile, G L and Foster, J (1996) Review of Methodological Approaches to the Study of the Impact of Microenterprise Credit Programs, Washington DC: Management Systems International.

Goetz, A M and Sen Gupta, R (1996) 'Who Takes the Credit? Gender, Power and Control Over Loan Use in Rural Credit Programs in Bangladesh', World Development 24(1), 45-64.

Hashemi, S M, Schuler, S R and Riley, A P (1996) 'Rural Credit Programs and Women's Empowerment in Bangladesh', World Development 24(4), 635-654.

Hulme, D and Mosley, P (1996) Finance Against Poverty, Vol. 1 and 2, London: Routledge.

Holcombe, S (1995) Managing to Empower: the Gramean Bank's Experience of Poverty Alleviation, London: Zed Press.

Hossain, M (1988) Credit for Alleviation of Rural Poverty: the Grameen Bank in Bangladesh, Washington DC: IFPRI.

Hyman E and Dearden K (1998) 'Comprehensive Impact Assessment systems for NGO microenterprise development programs', World Development 26(2), 261-276.

Hyman, E and Dearden, K (1996) A Review of Impact Information Systems of NGO Microenterprise Programs, Washington DC: Management Systems International.

Inserra, Anne (1996) A Review of Approaches for Measurement of Microenterprise and Household Income, Washington DC: Management Systems International.

Khandker, S R (1996) Fighting Poverty with Microcredit: Experience of the Grameen Bank and Other Programmes in Bangladesh, Washington DC: World Bank.

Little, Peter (1997), 'Assessing the Impact of Microfinance Programs on Incomes and Assets', mimeo, Consultative Group to Assist the Poorest (CGAP), Washington DC.

Long, N and Long A (1992) Battlefields of Knowledge, London: Routledge.

Martyn-Johns, E (1996) Participatory Impact Assessment: Putting Theory into Practice, MA Dissertation, IDPM, University of Manchester.

Mayoux, Linda (1997) 'Impact Assessment and Women's Empowerment in Micro-Finance Programmes: Issues for a Participatory Action and Learning Approach', mimeo, Consultative Group to Assist the Poorest (CGAP), Washington DC.

Montgomery, R (1996) 'Disciplining or protecting the poor? Avoiding the social costs of peer pressure in micro-credit schemes', Journal of International Development 8(2), 289-305.

Montgomery, R, Davies, R, Saxena, N C and Ashley, S (1996) Guidance Materials for Improved Project Monitoring and Impact Review Systems in India, Swansea: Centre for Development Studies, University College Swansea.

Moris, J and Copestake, J (1993), Qualitative Enquiry for Rural Development: a Review, London: IT Publications.

Moser, C A and Kalton, G (1972) Survey Methods in Social Investigation, London: Heinemann.

Mosely, P and Hulme, D (1998) 'Microenterprise Finance: Is There a Conflict Between Growth and Poverty Alleviation?', World Development, 26(5) 783-790.

Mosley, Paul (1997), 'The Use of Control Groups in Impact Assessment for Microfinance', mimeo, Consultative Group to Assist the Poorest (CGAP), Washington DC.

Mosse, D (1994) 'Authority, gender and knowledge: theoretical reflections on the practice of Participatory Rural Appraisal', Development and Change 25(3), 497-525.

Mustafa, S et al (1996) Beacon of Hope: an Impact Assessment Study of BRAC's Rural Development Programme, Dhaka: BRAC.

New Economics Foundation (1996) A Social Audit Manual for Small Organizations, London, New Economics Foundation.

Otero, M and Rhyne, E, eds. (1994) The New World of Microenterprise Finance, London: IT Publications.

Peace, G and Hulme, D (1994) 'Microenterprise and Children: What are the Intra-household Impacts of Income-generating Programmes', Small Enterprise Development 5 (1), 21-29.

Pulley, R (1989) 'Making the Poor Creditworthy: a Case Study of the Integrated Rural Development Program in India', World Bank Discussion Paper 58, Washington DC: World Bank.

Remenyi, J (1991) Where Credit is Due, London: IT Publications.

Rogaly, B (1996) 'Micro-finance evangelism, 'destitute women', and the hard selling of a new anti-poverty formula', Development in Practice 6(2), 100-112.

Rutherford, S (1993) 'Learning to lend: Informal Savings and Credit Schemes in Bangladesh' SCF Working Paper No. 5, London: Save the Children Fund.

Schuler, S R and Hashemi, S M and Riley, A P (1997) 'The influence of women's changing roles and status in Bangladesh's fertility transition: evidence from a study of credit programs and contraceptive use', World Development 25(4), 563-576.

Schuler, S R and Hashemi, S M (1996) 'Credit Programs, Women's Empowerment and Contraceptive Use in Rural Bangladesh', Studies in Family Planning 25(2), 65-76.

Sebstad, J and Chen, G (1996) Overview of Studies on the Impact of Microenterprise Credit, Washington DC: Management Systems International.

Sebstad, J, Neill, C, Barnes, C and Chen, G (1995) Assessing the Impacts of Microenterprise Interventions: A Framework for Analysis, Washington DC: USAID.

Snodgrass, D (1996) The Economic Policy and Regulatory Environment, Washington DC: Management Systems International.

Wiig, Arne (1997) 'Credit Expansion in Microcredit Programmes: Dilemmas and Feasible Methods for Studying Them', mimeo, Consultative Group to Assist the Poorest (CGAP), Washington DC.

Wood, G and Sharrif S (1997) Credit Where Credit is Due, Dhaka and London: UPL and Zed Press.

YV Reddy Address at ISB Hyderabad August 2005.

Yaron, J, Benjamin, M and Piprek, G (1997) Rural Finance: Issues, Design and Best Practices, Washington DC: Agriculture and Natural Resources Department, World Bank.

Zadek, S and Gatward, M (1996) 'Transforming the Transnational NGOs: Social Auditing or Bust?', in M. Edwards and D. Hulme, Beyond the Magic Bullet: NGO Performance and Accountability in the Post-War.

Strategic Issues in Microfinance edited by Mwangi S Kimenyi Robert C Wieland and JD Von Pischke.

Combining social and financial intermediation to reach the poor the necessity and dangers Lynn Bennett.

Field level study reports submitted by select offices of the Rural Planning Credit Department RPCD.

Deepali Pant Joshi "Poverty & Sustainable Development" printed by M/s Gyan Publishing House, New Delhi.

Deepali Pant Joshi-Social Banking Promise Performance and Potential Foundation Cambridge Books 2006.

Deepali Pant Joshi Employment and Poverty Alleviation Programs in India in KK Bagchi edited.

RBI Trend and Progress of Banking in India 2007-08 Reserve Bank of India.

Source: Gauri Singh, Mission Director, Rajiv Gandhi Watershed MP Human Developemt Report.

# Index

**N**

**T**



**U**